Other Kaplan Books on Law School Admissions:

Law School Admissions Adviser
The Insider's Book of Law School Lists
Two Real LSATs Explained

LSAT*

1999–2000

By the Staff of Kaplan Educational Centers

Simon & Schuster

*LSAT is a registered trademark of Law School Admission Council, which is not affiliated with this product.

Kaplan Books
Published by Kaplan Educational Centers and Simon & Schuster
1230 Avenue of the Americas
New York, NY 10020

Contributing Editor: Trent Anderson
Project Editor: Julie Schmidt
Production Editor: Maude Spekes
Interior Design: Krista Pfeiffer
Managing Editor: David Chipps
Desktop Publishing Manager: Michael Shevlin
Executive Editor: Del Franz

Special thanks to: Doreen Beauregard, Alison May, Kiernan McGuire, Ben Paris, and David Rodman

Manufactured in the United States of America
Published simultaneously in Canada

March 1999
10 9 8 7 6 5 4 3 2 1

ISSN: 1090-9079
ISBN 0–684–85669–7

CONTENTS

DISCLAIMERS

This book was designed for self-study only and is not authorized for classroom use. For information on Kaplan courses, which expand on the techniques offered here and are taught only by highly trained Kaplan instructors, please call 1-800-KAP-TEST (within the U.S.A.) or 1-212-590-2842 (outside the U.S.A.).

The information in this book is up-to-date at the time of publication. The Law School Admission Council and Law School Data Assembly Service may have instituted changes after this book was published. Please read all material you receive from these organizations regarding the LSAT test and law school admissions carefully.

ABOUT THE AUTHORS

Trent Anderson is the executive director of Graduate Programs at Kaplan Educational Centers. He has worked extensively with LSAT and admissions consulting (for business school, law school, and graduate school). He has been teaching LSAT, developing innovative and effective pedagogy, and creating LSAT material since 1989. He has scored in the ninety-ninth percentile every time he has taken the LSAT and has helped tens of thousands of people get into law school. He received his B.A. from the University of California, Los Angeles and his J.D. and M.B.A. from the University of Southern California. He is a member of the California Bar, the Federal Districts Courts for the Central District of California, and the Ninth Circuit Court of Appeals.

Eric Goodman has been teaching the Kaplan LSAT course for nine years and works for Kaplan Educational Centers as a product consultant. When not teaching or writing for Kaplan, Eric works as a composer and musician in New York City.

Pat Harris, a 1993 graduate of the University of Michigan Law School in Ann Arbor, is currently employed as an assistant public defender in Nashville, Tennessee. When not in court, he travels the country, teaching seminars on law school admissions and interviewing law school admissions officers.

Benjamin Paris is a curriculum director responsible for the LSAT at Kaplan Educational Centers. He received his B.A. from Bowdoin College, completed the general course at the London School of Economics, and received his J.D. from New York University. He has taught thousands of students how to succeed on standardized tests, and develops content and pedagogy for Kaplan's LSAT course.

Bob Verini is currently director of academic development for the western U.S. and a national training associate for Kaplan Educational Centers. Since 1980, Bob has taught thousands of students how to ace the LSAT. He also trains new Kaplan instructors nationally, works in course development, and serves as an academic counselor in Kaplan's one-on-one Admissions Consulting program. He holds a B.A. from SUNY/Albany and an M.F.A. from Indiana University. When he takes a break from the LSAT, Bob is a writer, actor, and director, with several films and extensive stage experience to his credit. Bob is also one of the biggest money winners in the history of the game show *Jeopardy!*™ and was the winner of the 1987 Tournament of Champions.

PREFACE

Once upon a time, not so many years ago, a law degree was a sure-fire ticket to prosperity. With a J.D. or L.L.B. in hand, a person entering the job market could be virtually certain of finding a solid, well-paying position in the legal profession. Entry-level jobs were plentiful, and if you were a particularly hot prospect, you might even find yourself wooed by several big-name law firms, weighing their lucrative job offers over a late supper (on the firm's expense account, of course) at the best restaurants in town.

Well, in case you haven't heard, those glory days are over. In the job market of the 1990s, some law-school graduates are forced to drive cabs and wait tables for a living. Others have to labor away for years in marginal positions that used to be filled by summer interns or first-year grads. Still others have to use their law degrees in nontraditional legal jobs, doing work they never pictured themselves doing when they first decided to go to law school.

Why the big change? Well, there are many reasons, but the main one is probably the age-old law of supply and demand. Nowadays, there are just too many newly minted lawyers every year and not enough starting positions in law. Yes, the top graduates can still command impressive salaries and prestigious positions, and job prospects have improved recently. But the great jobs are still few and far between, and there are more people than ever vying for each one.

As a prospective law school student facing this kind of competitive atmosphere, you really have only two choices. Either you can give up your dream of becoming a lawyer, or else you can make yourself a plan—a plan whose first step is getting into the very best law school you possibly can.

We respectfully suggest that you make the latter choice.

And that's where Kaplan comes in. We at Kaplan have had decades of experience getting people into great law schools, and one thing we've learned is that *you have to have a comprehensive strategy*. You can't approach law school admission in a casual, piecemeal way. If you want to maximize your likelihood of success, you have to take advantage of every opportunity at your disposal to strengthen your application. You can't afford to waste a single opportunity!

That's the philosophy behind this Kaplan guide. First, in our LSAT section, we'll tackle what's probably the single most important element in your application—your LSAT score. We'll give you a quick course in the legendary Kaplan LSAT strategies and techniques, and give you tips on how to relax and stay in top form as the day of the test approaches. Then, we'll give you the Kaplan Practice Test to prepare for the real thing, complete with full strategic explanations for every question.

Getting the highest possible LSAT score is only part of the battle; all other elements of your application have to be maximized as well. In our section on getting into law school, Kaplan's expert in law school admissions will take you step-by-step through the application process, with an eye to making yourself unrejectable. While every element of your application is an opportunity to present yourself in a favorable light, it's also an opportunity to screw up big time. But if you're in control, you won't make foolish mistakes. We'll show you how to avoid the common pitfalls and make your application stand out from the crowd.

This book will help you ace the LSAT and gain admission to the school of your choice. But did you know that with Kaplan's *Think About Law* program, we can also help you shape your career path? *Think About Law* is a series of free forums held throughout the country for college students and professionals considering a career in the law. Our select panel of attorneys, representing both the public and private sectors as well as traditional and nontraditional areas of practice, will share their experiences with you and help you make smart career choices. *Think About Law* will take place throughout the month of April. Call us at 1-800-KAP-TEST or check our Web site for locations and times.

It's harder these days than it used to be to achieve the kind of law career to which you aspire. But keep in mind that tough times should be regarded as a challenge—an opportunity rather than an obstacle. It may be an academic jungle out there, but even in the harshest jungle, the smart and the savvy will thrive.

HOW TO USE THIS BOOK

Here's how to use the various components of this book:

STEP ONE: Read the "Mastering the LSAT" Section

Kaplan's live LSAT course has set the industry standard for decades. In this section, we've distilled the main techniques and approaches from our course in a clear, easy-to-grasp format. We'll introduce you to the mysteries of the LSAT and show you how to take control of the test-taking experience on all levels:

Level One: Test Content
Specific methods, strategies, and practice problems for every kind of LSAT question you're likely to see.

Level Two: Test Expertise
Item-specific techniques, as well as advice on how to pace yourself over the entire section, and how to choose which questions to answer and which to guess on. The peculiarities of a standardized test can sometimes be used to your advantage. We can teach you how.

Level Three: Test Mentality
The proper test attitude for executing all you've learned.

You'll also find the most important points in easy-to-read sidebars in the outer margins.

STEP TWO: Take Kaplan's LSAT Practice Test

Having trained in the Kaplan methods, you should then use the Practice Test—a timed, simulated LSAT—as a test run for the real thing.

STEP THREE: Use the Strategic Explanations

These explanations for every test question will enable you to understand your mistakes, so that you don't make them again on the test. Try not to confine yourself to the explanations of the questions you've answered incorrectly. Instead, read all of the explanations—to reinforce good habits and to sharpen your skills so that you can get the right answer even faster and more reliably next time.

STEP FOUR: Review to Shore up Weak Points

Go back to the LSAT section and review the topics in which your performance was weak. Read the Tips for the Final Week and Kaplan Advantage™ Stress Management section to make sure you're in top shape for the test.

Follow these four steps, and you can be confident that your application to law school will be as strong as it can be.

Special Bonus: Getting Into Law School Section

Sure, your LSAT performance is a very important criterion in your application, so the bulk of this book is devoted to test prep. But law schools base their admissions decisions on far more than just the LSAT. In fact, a host of other parts of your application can make or break your candidacy. So, to give you the very best odds, we provide expert advice to lead you through the parts of the application process before and beyond the LSAT. We'll give you an overview of the application process, drawing from our years of helping law school candidates, and outline a plan to make your application as strong as it can be. We've also included checklists and schedules to keep you on track.

A SPECIAL NOTE FOR INTERNATIONAL STUDENTS

In recent years, U.S. law schools have experienced an increase in inquiries from non-U.S. citizens, some of whom are already practicing lawyers in their own countries. This surge of interest in the U.S. legal system has been attributed to the spread of the global economy. When business people from outside the United States do business with Americans, they often find themselves doing business under the American legal system. Gaining insight into how the American legal system works is of great interest around the world.

This new international interest in the U.S. legal system is having an effect on law schools. Many schools have even developed special programs to accommodate the needs of this special population of lawyers and students from outside the United States.

If you are not from the United States, but are interested in learning more about the American legal system, or if you are considering attending a U.S. law school, Kaplan can help you explore your options.

Getting into a U.S. law school can be especially challenging for students from other countries. If you're not a U.S. citizen and you plan to attend a U.S. law school, or a special U.S. law program, here's what you'll need to get started.

- If English is not your first language, you'll probably need to take the TOEFL (Test of English as a Foreign Language) or provide some other evidence that you are proficient in English. Most law schools require a minimum TOEFL score of 600 or better.
- Depending on the program to which you are applying, you may also need to take the LSAT (Law School Admissions Test). All law schools in the United States require the LSAT for their J.D. programs. L.L.M. programs usually do not require the LSAT.
- Since admission to law school is quite competitive, you may also want to select three or four programs and complete applications for each school.
- You should begin the process of applying to law schools or special legal studies programs at least eighteen months before the fall of the year you plan to start your studies. Most programs will have only September start dates.
- Finally, you will need to obtain an I-20 Certificate of Eligibility in order to obtain an F-1 Student Visa to study in the United States.

For an overview of the law school admissions process, see the "Getting into Law School" section of this book. For more help with applying to law school, including details about the admissions requirements, program offerings, and other vital information on the 178 law schools accredited by the American Bar Association (ABA), see Kaplan's guide to U.S. law schools, *Law School Admissions Adviser.*

As a non-native speaker of English, you may feel the need to perfect your knowledge of legal English. Kaplan and Simon & Schuster have published a worthwhile resource for you: *Success with Legal Words,* a book of English-language exercises centered around legal vocabulary.

If you need more help with the complex process of law school admissions, information about the variety of programs available, and to improve your English in general, you may also be interested in Kaplan's Access America® program.

Access America English Language Programs

Kaplan created Access America to assist international students and professionals who want to enter the United States university system. The program was designed for students who have received the bulk of their primary and secondary education outside the United States in a language other than English. Access America also has programs for obtaining professional certification in the United States. A brief description of some of the help available follows.

The Access America Certificate Program in English for University Admission

The Access America Certificate Program in English for University Admission is a comprehensive English language training program that prepares serious students for admission to an accredited American university. Using a content-based approach to studying English, this course trains students in three main areas:

- Academic English for university admissions
- TOEFL test-taking skills and strategies
- University admissions counseling and placement

This course is designed for international students at the high-intermediate, advanced, and super-advanced levels of English proficiency who have as their end goal admission into a university degree program. Some American universities will accept Kaplan's Certificate of High Achievement in English for University Admissions in lieu of a TOEFL score. This means that they trust the Kaplan Certificate as a reliable evaluation of a student's readiness for university work. A list of schools providing TOEFL waivers for Kaplan's certificate will be provided upon request.

In this course, students use actual material written for native speakers of English and work on improving the following critical skills:

(1) Listening and lecture notetaking skills
(2) Extended and rapid textbook reading skills

(3) Vocabulary enhancement for developing nativelike intuition about words

(4) Understanding and applying English grammar in a real context

(5) Effective use of a monolingual dictionary

(6) Time management skills for academic study

(7) Computer literacy and computer keyboarding skills

(8) Successfully taking the TOEFL (on paper and on computer) and other standardized test skills

(9) Functional conversation performance skills

(10) Learning strategies

Graduate School/GRE (Graduate Record Exam) Preparation

If your goal is to enter a master's or Ph.D. program in the United States, Kaplan will help you achieve a high GRE score, while helping you understand how to choose a graduate degree program in your field.

Law School Admissions Test (LSAT) Preparation

If you plan to enter a law school in the United States, Kaplan will help you determine whether you need to take the LSAT, while helping you to choose an appropriate law program. If you must take the LSAT, Kaplan will help you prepare for it.

Business Accounting/CPA (Certified Public Accounting)

If you are an accountant who would like to be certified to do business in the United States, Kaplan will help you achieve a passing score on the CPA Exam, and will assist you in understanding accounting procedures in the United States.

Applying to Access America

To get more information, or to apply for admission to any of Kaplan's programs for international students or professionals, you can write to us at:

Kaplan Educational Centers
International Admissions Department
888 Seventh Avenue
New York, NY 10106

You can call us at 1-800-527-8378 from within the United States, or at 1-212-262-4980 outside the United States. Our fax number is 1-212-957-1654. Our e-mail address is world@kaplan.com. You can also get more information or even apply through the Internet at http://www.kaplan.com/intl.

MASTERING THE LSAT

By Eric Goodman

CHAPTER 1

AN INTRODUCTION TO THE LSAT

The LSAT is unlike any other test you've ever taken in your academic career. Most of the tests you've encountered in high school and college have probably been knowledge-based tests, that is, tests requiring you to recall and be conversant with a certain body of facts, formulas, theorems, or other acquired knowledge. The LSAT, on the other hand, is a skills-based test. It doesn't ask you to spit back memorized facts. It doesn't ask you to apply learned formulas to specific problems. In fact, all you'll be asked to do on the LSAT is think—thoroughly, quickly, and strategically. There's literally no content to study!

Sound too good to be true? Well, before you get the idea that you can waltz into the most important test of your life stone cold, let's clarify the very important distinction between study and preparation.

If you were taking the National Medical Boards, you would need to study things like anatomy beforehand, to make sure you were up-to-date on all of the required knowledge in that area. But the LSAT isn't designed to evaluate your grasp of this kind of field-specific knowledge. Instead, it's designed to test only the critical reading and analytical thinking skills that have been deemed necessary (by the governing body of law schools themselves) for success in the first year of law school. These are skills that you already possess to some extent; you've acquired them gradually over the decade-and-a-half (or more) of your education. But what you probably haven't yet acquired is the know-how to use these skills to best advantage in the rarified atmosphere of a standardized skills-based test.

And that's where test preparation—and this section of this book—comes in. In this section, we'll teach you to tailor your existing skills to the very specific and idiosyncratic tasks required by the LSAT. For example, you already know how to read; but we'll show you how to take your critical reading skills and use them most effectively to unlock the dense but highly structured arguments and passages on the LSAT. Similarly, while you've probably developed plenty of sound, logical ways of analyzing problems in everyday life, we'll teach you how to apply those natural deductive and analytical skills to the unusual demands of the Logic Games and Logical Reasoning sections of the LSAT.

So, while you can't technically study for a standardized skills-based test like the LSAT, you can and must prepare for it. And in the section that follows, we'll show you just how to do that.

Before launching into strategies, though, you need to know exactly what you're dealing with in the LSAT.

What Is the LSAT?

Let's start with the basics. The LSAT is, among other things, an endurance test. It consists of 175 minutes of multiple-choice testing, plus a thirty-minute writing sample. Add in the administrative details at both ends of the testing experience, plus a break of ten to fifteen minutes midway through, and you can count on being in the test room for at least four-and-a-half to five hours.

It's a grueling experience, to say the least. And if you can't approach it with confidence and rigor, you'll quickly lose your composure. That's why it's so important that you take control of the test, just as you've been taking control of the rest of your application process.

The LSAT consists of five multiple-choice sections—two Logical Reasoning sections (LR), one Logic Games section (LG), one Reading Comprehension section (RC), and one so-called "Experimental" section, which will almost certainly look exactly like one of the other multiple-choice sections. In addition to these five sections, there will be a Writing Sample section in which you'll have to write a short essay.

TAKE CONTROL

The LSAT should be viewed just like any other part of your application—as an opportunity to show the law schools who you are and what you can do. If you can take control of your LSAT experience, you can take the fullest advantage of that opportunity.

AN ESSENTIAL RESOURCE

If you plan to take the LSAT, you will need to obtain a copy of the *LSAT/LSDAS Registration & Information Book*. This book will provide you with the most up-to-date information on how to register for and take the LSAT and how to subscribe to the Law School Data Assembly Service. Call (215) 968-1001 or write to Law School Admission Council, Box 2000, Newtown, PA 18940-0998 for a copy.

Here's how the sections break down:

Section	Number of Questions	Minutes
Logical Reasoning	24–26	35
Logical Reasoning	24–26	35
Logic Games	23–24	35
Reading Comprehension	26–28	35
"Experimental"	24–28	35
Writing Sample	n/a	30

Some important things to note:

- The five multiple-choice sections can appear in any order, but the Writing Sample invariably comes last.
- The ten- to fifteen-minute break will come between the third and fourth sections of the test.
- The so-called "Experimental" section will look just like any other multiple-choice section, but it won't contribute to your score. (No, the test makers don't throw in the experimental section just to make you crazy; they do it to test out questions for use on future tests.)

We'll talk more about each of these question types in later chapters. But the big thing to take note of right now is this: You'll be answering roughly 125 questions (excluding the Writing Sample) over the course of three intensive hours. That's just a little over a minute per question, not counting the time required to read passages and set up games. Clearly, you're going to have to move fast. But you can't let yourself get careless. Taking control of the LSAT means increasing the speed of your work without sacrificing accuracy!

How Is the LSAT Scored?

You'll receive one and only one score for the LSAT (no separate scores for LR, LG, and RC, in other words). That one score will fall in a range of 120 to 180. Here's how they'll calculate it.

TIME IS OF THE ESSENCE

Many people could probably ace the LSAT if they had unlimited time. But they don't. To succeed on the LSAT, you've got to think smart and fast.

There are roughly 101 scored multiple-choice questions on each exam:

- About fifty from the two Logical Reasoning sections
- About twenty-four from the Logic Games section
- About twenty-seven from the Reading Comprehension section

(Remember, the Writing Sample doesn't receive a numerical score, while the Experimental section, no matter what question type it contains, doesn't count.)

The number of these 101 questions that you answer correctly is your "raw score." Your raw score will then be multiplied by a complicated scoring formula (which is different for each test, to accommodate differences in difficulty level) to yield the "scaled score"—the one that will fall somewhere in that 120–180 range. This scaled score is what is reported to the schools as your LSAT score.

Since the test is graded on a largely preset curve, the scaled score will always correspond to a certain percentile, which will also be given on your score report. A score of 160, for instance, corresponds roughly to the eightieth percentile, meaning that 80 percent of test takers scored at or below your level. The percentile figure is important because it allows law schools to get a sense quickly of where you fall in the pool of applicants.

All questions (except, again, those on the Experimental section) are worth the same amount—one raw point—and there's no penalty for guessing. That means that you should always fill in an answer for every question, whether you get to that question or not! Never let time run out on any section without filling in an answer for every question!

What's a "Good" LSAT Score?

Of course, what you consider a "good" LSAT score depends on your own expectations and goals, but here are a few interesting statistics:

If you got about half of all of the scored questions right (a raw score of roughly fifty), you would earn a scaled score of roughly 147, putting you in about the thirtieth percentile—not a great performance. But on the LSAT, a little improvement goes a long way. In fact, getting only one additional question right every ten minutes would give you a raw score of about sixty-four, pushing you into the sixtieth percentile—a huge improvement. That's why it's important to maximize your performance on every question. Just a few questions one way or the other can make a big difference in your score.

By the same token, however, you don't have to be perfect to do well. On most LSATs, you can get as many as twenty-eight wrong and still remain in the eightieth percentile—or as many as twenty-one wrong and still remain in the ninetieth percentile. Even students who receive perfect scaled scores of 180 usually get a handful of questions wrong.

SOME SAMPLE PERCENTILES

Percentile	Approx. Scaled Score (Range 120–180)	Approx. Raw Score
99th percentile	172	~91 correct out of 101
95th percentile	167	~84 correct out of 101
90th percentile	164	~80 correct out of 101
80th percentile	160	~73 correct out of 101
75th percentile	158	~69 correct out of 101
50th percentile	152	~59 correct out of 101

Note: Exact percentile-to-scaled-score relationships vary from test to test.

Although many factors play a role in admissions decisions, the LSAT score is usually one of the most important. And—generally speaking—being average just won't cut it. While the median LSAT score is somewhere around 152, you need a score of at least 163 to be considered competitive by most law schools. And if you're aiming for the top, you've got to do even better. According to the latest Kaplan/*Newsweek* edition of *How to Choose a Career & Graduate School,* the median LSAT scores of the best law schools in the country, such as Yale, Stanford, and Columbia, range from the high 160s to the low 170s. That translates to a percentile figure of ninety-five and up.

What Kinds of Questions Are on the LSAT?

Now let's take a quick look at each question type you'll encounter on the test. We'll get into strategies and techniques later. For now, just familiarize yourself with the kinds of questions asked on each section.

Logical Reasoning

What It Is
Each of the two scored Logical Reasoning sections consists of twenty-four to twenty-six questions based on short passages we call "stimuli." Each stimulus takes the form of an argument—i.e., a conclusion based on evidence. You need to understand the stimulus argument to answer the one or two questions based on it. Although you don't need to know the technical terms of formal logic, you do need the critical reasoning skills that enable you to analyze an argument and make judgments accordingly.

Why It's on the Test
The law schools want to see whether you can understand, analyze, evaluate, and manipulate arguments, and draw reliable conclusions—as every law student and attorney must. It's important to note that this question type makes up half of your LSAT score, so you know that the law schools value these skills.

What It's Like
Here are the directions to the section, along with a sample question:

Directions: This test is composed of questions that ask you to analyze the logic of statements or short paragraphs. You are to choose as the answer to each question the one choice you consider best on the basis of your common-sense evaluation of the statement and its assumptions. Although a question may seem to have more than one acceptable answer, there is only one best answer, and it is the one that does not entail making any illogical, extraneous, or conflicting assumptions about the question.

1. A study of twenty overweight men revealed that each man experienced significant weight loss after adding SlimDown, an artificial food supplement, to his daily diet. For three months, each man consumed one

SlimDown portion every morning after exercising, and then followed his normal diet for the rest of the day. Clearly, anyone who consumes one portion of SlimDown every day for at least three months will lose weight and will look and feel his or her best.

Which one of the following is an assumption on which the argument depends?

(A) The men in the study will gain back the weight they lost if they discontinue the SlimDown program.
(B) No other dietary supplement will have the same effect on overweight men.
(C) The daily exercise regimen was not responsible for the effects noted in the study.
(D) Women will not experience similar weight reductions if they adhere to the SlimDown program for three months.
(E) Overweight men will achieve only partial weight loss if they do not remain on the SlimDown program for a full three months.

Choice (C) is correct. We'll show you how to approach Logical Reasoning questions like this in a later chapter.

Logic Games

What It Is
There are twenty-three to twenty-four questions in the Logic Games (a.k.a. Analytical Reasoning) section, and these are almost always based on four games, with five to seven questions each. They require an ability to reason clearly and deductively from a given set of rules or restrictions, all under strictly timed conditions.

Why It's on the Test
The section exists to test your command of detail, your formal deductive abilities, your understanding of how rules limit and order behavior (which is the very definition of law itself), and your ability to cope with many pieces of data simultaneously in the course of solving problems.

LOGIC GAMES AT A GLANCE

- Thirty-five minutes long
- Accounts for just under 25 percent of your score
- Twenty-three to twenty-four questions
- Usually four games (common types: sequencing, grouping, matching)
- Tests how rules create systems of order and limit possible outcomes
- Attention to detail is key, as is the ability to maintain awareness of multiple facts simultaneously
- Basic logic is important: *if* versus *only if*; the logical meaning of *or*; the contrapositive
- Often the most intimidating section initially
- Often shows rapid improvement with practice

What It's Like

What follows are directions to the Logic Games section as well as a shortened sample game and questions:

Directions: Each group of questions is based on a set of conditions. You may wish to draw a rough sketch to help you answer some of the questions. Choose the <u>best</u> answer for each question and fill in the corresponding space on your answer sheet.

Questions 1–2

Five workers—Mona, Patrick, Renatta, Saffie, and Will—are scheduled to clean apartments on five days of a single week, Monday to Friday. There are three cleaning shifts available each day—a morning shift, an afternoon shift, and an evening shift. No more than one worker cleans on any given shift. Each worker works exactly two cleaning shifts during the week, but no one works more than one cleaning shift in a single day.

Exactly two workers clean on each day of the week.
Mona and Will clean on the same days of the week.
Patrick does not clean on any afternoon or evening shifts during the week.
Will does not clean on any morning or afternoon shifts during the week.
Mona cleans on two consecutive days of the week.
Saffie's second cleaning shift of the week occurs on an earlier day of the week than Mona's first cleaning shift

1. Which one of the following must be true?

   (A) Saffie cleans on Tuesday afternoon.
   (B) Patrick cleans on Monday morning.
   (C) Will cleans on Thursday evening.
   (D) Renatta cleans on Friday afternoon.
   (E) Mona cleans on Tuesday morning.

2. If Will does not clean on Friday, which one of the following could be false?

    (A) Renatta cleans on Friday.
    (B) Saffie cleans on Tuesday.
    (C) Mona cleans on Wednesday.
    (D) Saffie cleans on Monday.
    (E) Patrick cleans on Tuesday.

(Note that there are only two questions accompanying this game; a typical logic game will have five to seven questions.)

For Question 1, the answer is (C); for 2 it's (E). Games are highly amenable to systematic technique and the proper use of scratchwork, which we'll discuss in detail later.

Reading Comprehension

What It Is
The Reading Comprehension section consists of four passages, each about 450 words long, with five to eight questions. These long excerpts of scholarly passages are reminiscent of the kind of prose found in law texts. The topics are chosen from the areas of social sciences, humanities, natural sciences, and law.

Why It's on the Test
The purpose of the section is to see whether you can quickly get the gist of long, difficult prose—just as you'll have to do in law school.

What It's Like
Here are the directions and a sample passage. Note that the passage below is just an excerpt from a full-length passage; standard passages are generally longer.

Directions: Each selection in this test is followed by several questions. After reading the selection, choose the best response to each question and mark it on your answer sheet. Your replies are to be based on what is <u>stated</u> or <u>implied</u> in the selection.

It has been suggested that post–World War II concepts of environmental liability, as they pertain to hazardous waste, grew out of issues

---

READING COMPREHENSION AT A GLANCE

- Thirty-five minutes long
- Accounts for just over 25 percent of your score
- Usually consists of twenty-seven questions (common types: main idea, detail, inference, logic, extrapolation)
- Usually consists of four passages (natural sciences, social sciences, humanities, law)
- Tests ability to read dense, scholarly material and ascertain the structure, purpose, and logic—just as you will do in law school
- Key skill is identifying main idea of a passage, "the gist" of the argument. This is not the way you're taught to read in school!
- Does not require outside knowledge
- Is very different from SAT Reading Comp: denser, more difficult prose, more difficult inferences
- Is not a test of memorizing details
- Requires learning a new reading "mindset": reading with different goals and employing different techniques

regarding municipal refuse collection and disposal and industrial waste disposal in the period 1880–1940. To a great degree, the remedies available to Americans for dealing with the burgeoning hazardous waste problem were characteristic of the judicial, legislative, and regulatory tools used to confront a whole range of problems in the industrial age. At the same time, these remedies were operating in an era in which the problem of hazardous waste had yet to be recognized. It is understandable that an assessment of liability was narrowly drawn and most often restricted to a clearly identified violator in a specific act of infringement of the property rights of someone else. Legislation, for the most part, focused narrowly on clear threats to the public health and dealt with problems of industrial pollution meekly if at all.

1. According to the passage, judicial assessments of liability in waste disposal disputes prior to World War II were usually based on

   (A) excessively broad definitions of legal responsibility
   (B) the presence of a clear threat to the public health
   (C) precedents derived from well-known cases of large-scale industrial polluters
   (D) restricted interpretations of property rights infringements
   (E) trivial issues such as littering, eyesores, and other public nuisances

The answer: (D). We'll show you how to approach the Reading Comp questions later.

The Experimental Section

The experimental (unscored) section allows Law Services to test questions for use on future tests. This section will probably look just like one of the others—either LR, LG, or RC—so don't try to figure out which section is experimental and then just cruise through that section. That's an extremely risky proposition. Just do as well as you can on every section, and you're covered.

DON'T TRY TO GUESS THE EXPERIMENTAL

The LSAT battlefield is littered with the bodies of those who've tried to outsmart the test by guessing (incorrectly) which section is experimental and then using that time to rest. Don't take the chance! Perform your best on every section.

The Writing Sample

What It Is
The Writing Sample comes at the end of your LSAT day. You'll be given a scenario followed by two possible courses of action, and you'll have thirty minutes to make a written case that one is superior.

Why It's on the Test
The writing sample shows the law schools whether you can argue for a position while breaking down the argument of an opponent. This essay is ungraded, but is sent to law schools along with your LSAT score.

What It's Like
Here's a sample topic for a Writing Sample:

The *Daily Tribune*, a metropolitan newspaper, is considering two candidates for promotion to business editor. Write an argument for one candidate over the other with the following considerations in mind:

- The editor must train new writers and assign stories.
- The editor must be able to edit and rewrite stories under daily deadline pressure.

Laura received a B.A. in English from a large university. She was managing editor of her college newspaper and served as a summer intern at her hometown daily paper. Laura started working at the *Tribune* right out of college and spent three years at the city desk covering the city economy. Eight years ago the paper formed its business section and Laura became part of the new department. After several years covering state business, Laura began writing on the national economy. Three years ago, Laura was named senior business and finance editor on the national business staff; she is also responsible for supervising seven writers.

Palmer attended an elite private college where he earned both a B.S. in business administration and an M.A. in journalism. After receiving his journalism degree, Palmer worked for three years on a monthly business magazine. He won a prestigious national award for a series of articles on the impact of monetary policy on multinational corporations. Palmer came to the *Tribune* three years ago to fill the newly created position of

THE WRITING SAMPLE AT A GLANCE

- Is thirty minutes long
- Is unscored
- Consists of one essay
- Task is to choose between two alternatives and make a sound argument for your choice. The alternatives are intentionally chosen to be equally valid, such that the decision to take one side or the other will not give any advantage
- Tests ability to write a clear, persuasive argument
- Does not require outside knowledge
- Is photocopied and sent to schools along with your score report
- Is read and used to evaluate applications more frequently than is commonly thought
- Helps schools choose between relatively equal candidates, decide on borderline candidates

international business writer. He was the only member of the international staff for two years and wrote on almost a daily basis. He now supervises a staff of four writers. Last year, Palmer developed a bi-monthly business supplement for the *Tribune* that has proved highly popular and has helped increase the paper's circulation.

Obviously, there can be no right or wrong "answer" to the Writing Sample topic, but there are good and bad responses. We'll show you one possible response to this topic later, in the Writing Sample chapter.

How Do You Take Control of the LSAT?

Now that you have an idea of what the LSAT is and how it's set up, let's talk a little about how to approach the test in a general way. As we'll see, knowing the specific strategies for each type of question is only part of your task. To really do your best on the LSAT, you have to approach the entire test in the proper spirit. That spirit—and the proactive, take-control kind of thinking it inspires—is something we call the LSAT Mindset.

The LSAT Mindset
The LSAT Mindset is what you want to bring to every question, passage, game, and section you encounter. Being in the LSAT Mindset means reshaping the test-taking experience so that you are in the driver's seat. It means:

THE LSAT
MINDSET

Knowing strategies for each question type is only the beginning. You also have to approach the test with the proper attitude— a proactive, take-control kind of thinking we call the LSAT Mindset.

- Answering questions *if* you want to (by guessing on the most difficult questions rather than wasting time on them).
- Answering questions *when* you want to (by saving tough but doable games, passages, and questions for later, coming back to them after racking up points on the easy ones).
- Answering questions *how* you want to (by using our shortcuts and strategies to get points quickly and confidently, even if those methods aren't exactly what the test makers had in mind).

The following are some overriding principles of the LSAT Mindset that will be covered in depth in the chapters to come:

- Read actively and critically.
- Translate prose into your own words.
- Prephrase answer choices so you know what to look for.

KAPLAN

- Save the toughest questions, passages, and games for last.
- Know the test and each of its components inside and out.
- Allow your confidence to build on itself.
- Take full-length practice tests the week before the test to break down the mystique of the real experience.
- Learn from your mistakes—it's not how much you practice, it's how much you get out of the practice.
- Look at the LSAT as a challenge, the first step in your legal career, rather than as an arbitrary obstacle to it.

And that's what the LSAT Mindset boils down to: taking control. Being proactive. Being on top of the test experience so that you can get as many points as you can as quickly and as easily as possible.

To take control in this way, though, you have to be in command on all levels of the test. You may be great at individual Logical Reasoning questions, for instance, but that expertise won't do you much good unless you also have a plan for the entire LR section, so that you get a chance to use your expertise on as many LR questions in a section as possible. That's why we've developed a plan for integrating strategies and techniques on all levels of the test—from the microlevel of individual question strategies, to the midlevel of handling the mechanics of a whole section, to the macrolevel of bringing the right kind of thinking to the entire test as a whole. We call this plan (cleverly enough) "the Kaplan Three-Level Master Plan for the LSAT," and it should be your key to taking control.

The Kaplan Three-Level Master Plan

Level One: Test Content

Here we'll talk about managing individual questions, games, and reading passages. For success on the LSAT, you'll need to understand how to work through the specifics of each section. What's the difference between assumption and inference questions? What are the best ways of handling each? What's a matching game and how do I approach it? How should I read a Reading Comp passage and what should I focus on? What essay formats are best for the Writing Sample? Our instruction on Level One will provide you with all of the information, strategies, and techniques you'll need along these lines, and will help to lay the groundwork for your LSAT success.

YOU'VE GOT TO HAVE A PLAN

The three levels of the Kaplan master plan are:

- Test content
- Test expertise
- Test mentality

Level Two: Test Expertise

Next, we'll move up the ladder from individual questions, passages, and games to discussing how to manage full sections within the specified time limit. We'll show you how to handle the test mechanics so that you have a framework in which to use the Level One strategies—and the time to use them.

Level Three: Test Mentality

This is the level where you pull it all together, marshalling the strategies and expertise with the right mindset, so that you're in control of the entire test. With good test mentality, you can have everything at your fingertips—from the contrapositive to gridding techniques, from sequencing game strategies to pacing methods. We'll outline all of the subtle attitudinal factors, often overlooked, that are nonetheless integral to tying together all of the disparate elements of your training, so that you can perform your absolute best on the test.

Understanding the three levels, and how they interrelate, is the first step in taking control of the LSAT. In the next chapter, we'll start with Level One, Test Content.

LSAT CHECKLIST

Before the Test

❑ **Get the LSAT/LSDAS Registration and Information Book.**
It's available at most colleges and law schools, and at all Kaplan Centers; you can also order it by phone from LSDAS (Law School Data Assembly Service). Keep in mind that the information in this book is up-to-date at the time of publication, but LSDAS may have instituted changes after this book was published.

❑ **Choose a test date.**
June is best, October second best.

❑ **Complete and send LSAT/LSDAS Registration Form.**
Parts A, B, and D apply to the LSAT.
Make sure you list a first- and second-choice test center.
Don't forget to sign the form and include payment!

❑ **Receive your LSAT admission ticket.**
Check it for accuracy.
Check out your test center.

❑ **Create a test-prep calendar to ensure that you're ready by the day of the test.**

The Day of the Test

❑ **Make sure you have your LSAT admission ticket.**

❑ **Make sure you have one form of acceptable ID.**

❑ **Make sure you have the "LSAT Survival Kit" described in the Last-Minute Tips section of this book.**

CHAPTER 2

LSAT TEST CONTENT

In this chapter, we'll give you the nuts and bolts of LSAT preparation—the strategies and techniques for every individual question type on the test. For each of the multiple choice sections—Logical Reasoning, Logic Games, and Reading Comprehension—we'll present you with the following:

- **Basic Principles**
  The general rules-of-thumb that you need to follow to succeed on this section.

- **Crucial Question Types**
  Certain types of questions appear again and again on each section. We'll show you what these question types are and how best to deal with each one.

- **The Kaplan Method**
  A step-by-step way of organizing your work on every question in the section. The Kaplan Method will allow you to orchestrate all of the individual strategies and techniques into a flexible, powerful *modus operandi*.

We'll also give you a look at the best way to approach the unscored section of the LSAT—the Writing Sample.

But, let's begin now with the most important section of the LSAT, making up about half of your score: Logical Reasoning.

LOGICAL REASONING

The fact that Logical Reasoning comprises half of your LSAT score is actually good news, because you already have most of the Logical Reasoning skills you need for the test. In fact, we all do. But as we pointed out earlier, the LSAT tests your ability to use those skills thoroughly, quickly, and strategically in the context of a strictly timed, multiple-choice test.

On the LSAT, in law school, and in your law career, you'll need the ability to see and understand complex reasoning. It's not enough to sense whether an argument is strong or weak; you'll need to analyze precisely why it is so. This involves an even more fundamental skill, one that's called on by nearly every Logical Reasoning question—the ability to isolate and identify the various components of any given argument. And that brings us to the basic principles of Logical Reasoning.

The Seven Basic Principles of Logical Reasoning

Here are the basic things you must do to succeed on the LR sections.

Understand the Structure of Arguments

Success in Logical Reasoning depends on knowing the structure of arguments so that you can break an argument down into its core components.

First of all, let's clarify what's meant by the word *argument*. We don't mean a conversation in which two or more people are shouting at one another. No, the word *argument* in Logical Reasoning means any piece of text where an author puts forth a set of ideas and/or a point of view, and attempts to support it.

Every LSAT Logical Reasoning stimulus—that is, every argument—is made up of two basic parts:

- The conclusion (the point that the author is trying to make)
- The evidence (the support that the author offers for the conclusion)

Success on this section hinges on your ability to identify these parts of the argument. There is no general rule about where conclusion and evidence appear in the argument—the conclusion could be the first sentence, followed by the evidence, or else it could be the last sentence, with the evidence preceding it, or any sentence in between. Consider the following short stimulus.

> The Brookdale Public Library will require extensive physical rehabilitation to meet the new building codes passed by the town council. For one thing, the electrical system is inadequate, causing the lights to flicker sporadically. Furthermore, there are too few emergency exits, and even those are poorly marked and sometimes locked.

Let's suppose that the author of the argument above was only allowed one sentence to convey her meaning. Do you think that she would waste her lone opportunity on the statement: "The electrical system at the Brookdale Public Library is inadequate, causing the lights to flicker sporadically"? Would she walk away satisfied that she got her main point across? Probably not. Given a single opportunity, she would have to state the first sentence: "The Brookdale Public Library will require extensive physical rehabilitation. . . ." This is her conclusion. If you pressed her for her *reasons* for making this statement, she would then cite the electrical and structural problems with the building. This is the evidence for her conclusion.

But does that mean that an evidence-statement such as, "The electrical system at the Brookdale Public Library is inadequate" can't be a conclusion? No; we're saying that it's not the conclusion for this particular argument. Every idea, every new statement, must be evaluated in the context of the stimulus it appears in. Let's, for the sake of argument (no pun intended), see what a stimulus would look like in which the statement above serves as the conclusion:

> The electrical wiring at the Brookdale Public Library was installed over forty years ago, and appears to be corroded in some places *(evidence)*. An electrician, upon inspection of the system, found a few frayed wires as well as some blown fuses *(evidence)*. Clearly, the electrical system at the Brookdale Public Library is inadequate *(conclusion)*.

To succeed in Logical Reasoning, you have to be able to determine the precise function of every sentence in the stimulus. Use structural signals, or keywords, when attempting to isolate evidence and conclusion. Words in the stimulus such as *because, for,* and *since* usually indicate evidence is

STRUCTURAL SIGNALS

Certain clue words and phrases can help you isolate the conclusion and the evidence in a stimulus.

Clues that signal evidence include *because, since, for, as a result of,* and *due to.*

Clues that signal the conclusion include *consequently, hence, therefore, thus, clearly, so,* and *accordingly.*

about to follow, while words such as *therefore, hence, thus,* and *consequently* usually signal a conclusion.

The explanations of the Practice Test in the back of this book discuss the structure of all fifty LR arguments on the test, so read these carefully to shore up your understanding of this crucial aspect of Logical Reasoning.

Preview the Question Stem

Looking over the question stem before reading the stimulus tells you in advance what to focus on in your initial reading of the stimulus. In effect, it gives you a jump on the question. For example, let's say the question attached to the original library argument above asked the following:

> The author supports her point about the need for rehabilitation at the Brookdale Library by citing which of the following?

If you were to preview this question stem before reading the stimulus, you would know what to look for in advance—namely, evidence, the "support" provided for the conclusion. Similarly, if the question asked you to find an assumption that the author is relying on, this would tell you in advance that there was a crucial piece of the argument missing, and you could begin to think about it right off the bat.

Previewing the stem allows you to set the tone of your attack on each particular question, and thus will help you save time in the long run. As you'll soon see, this technique will come in especially handy when we discuss approaches to the various question types.

Paraphrase the Author's Point

After you read the stimulus, you'll want to paraphrase the author's main argument, i.e., restate the author's ideas in your own words. Frequently, the authors in Logical Reasoning (and in Reading Comprehension, as we'll see) say pretty simple things in complex ways. But if you mentally translate the verbiage into a simpler form, you'll find the whole thing more manageable.

In the library argument, for instance, you probably don't want to deal with the full complexity of the author's stated conclusion:

> The Brookdale Public Library will require extensive physical rehabilitation to meet the new building codes just passed by the town council.

Instead, you probably want to carry a much simpler form of the point in your mind, something like:

>   The library will need fixing up to meet new codes.

Often, by the time you begin reading through answer choices, you run the risk of losing sight of the gist of the stimulus. After all, you can only concentrate on a certain amount of information at one time. Restating the argument in your own words will not only help you get the author's point in the first place, but it'll also help you hold on to it until you've found the correct answer.

Judge the Argument's Persuasiveness

You must read actively, not passively, on the LSAT. An active reader is always thinking critically, forming reactions as he goes along. He constantly questions whether the author's argument seems valid or dubious. On a section where many of the questions deal with finding flaws in the author's reasoning, it's imperative to read with a very critical eye.

For instance, how persuasive is the argument in the library stimulus? Well, it's pretty strong, since the evidence certainly seems to indicate that certain aspects of the library's structure need repair. But without more evidence about what the new building codes are like, we can't say for sure that the conclusion of this argument is valid. So this is a strong argument, but not an airtight one.

Remember, part of what you're called on to do in this section is to evaluate arguments, so don't allow yourself to fall into the bad habits of the passive reader—reading solely for the purpose of getting through the stimulus. Those who read this way are clueless when it comes to answering the questions, and invariably find themselves having to read the stimuli twice or even three times. Then they wonder why they run out time on the section. Read the stimuli right the first time—with a critical eye and an active mind.

Make Sure You Answer the Question Being Asked

It's disheartening when you fully understand the author's argument, and then blow the point by supplying an answer to a question that wasn't asked. For example, when you're asked for an inference supported by the argument, it does you no good to jump on the choice that paraphrases the author's conclusion. Likewise, if you're asked for an assumption, don't be fooled into selecting a choice that looks vaguely like a piece of the author's evidence.

IN YOUR OWN WORDS

It's much easier to understand and remember an argument if you restate it simply, in your own words.

DON'T ANSWER A DIFFERENT QUESTION

You read the argument. You see a major weakness in it. You find an answer choice that points out this weakness. You choose that answer. And you miss the point. Why? Because the question stem was asking for a statement that strengthened the argument, not one that weakened it. Don't let this happen to you. Always double-check the question stem.

When asked why they chose a particular wrong choice, students sometimes respond by saying such things as, "Well, it's true, isn't it?" and "Look, it says so right there," pointing to the stimulus. Well, that's simply not good enough. The question stem doesn't ask, "Which one of the following looks vaguely familiar to you?" It asks for something very specific. It's your job to follow the test makers' line of reasoning to the credited response.

Also, be on the lookout for "reversers"—words such as *not* and *except*. These little words are easy to miss, but they change entirely what kind of statement you're looking for among the choices.

Try to Prephrase an Answer

This principle, which is really an extension of the last one, is crucial. You must try to approach the answer choices with at least a faint idea of what the answer should look like. This is not to say that you should ponder the question for minutes until you're able to write out your own answer—it's still a multiple-choice test, so the right answer is there on the page. Just try to get in the habit of instinctively framing an answer to each question in your own mind.

If you can come up with a hint of a possible answer, scan the choices. Sure, the correct answer will be worded correctly, will be grammatically correct, and will be more fleshed out than your little seed of an idea. But if it matches your thought, you'll know it in a second. And you'll find that there's no more satisfying feeling in Logical Reasoning than prephrasing correctly, allowing you to choose the correct answer quickly and confidently.

For instance, let's say a question for the library argument went like this:

> The author's argument depends on which of the following assumptions about the new building codes?

Having thought about the stimulus argument, an answer to this question may have sprung immediately to mind—namely, the assumption that the new codes apply to existing buildings as well as to new buildings under construction. After all, the library will have to be rehabilitated to meet the new codes, according to the author. Clearly, the assumption is that the codes apply to existing buildings. And that's the kind of statement you would look for among the choices.

By the way, don't be discouraged if not all questions are good candidates for prephrasing answers. Some questions just won't have an answer that jumps out at you. But if used correctly, prephrasing can work on many, many questions. It will really boost your confidence and increase your speed on the section when you can come up with a glimmer of what the right answer should look like, and then have it jump right off the page at you.

Keep the Scope of the Argument in Mind

One of the most important Logical Reasoning skills, particularly when you're at the point of actually selecting one of the five choices, is the ability to focus in on the scope of the argument. The majority of wrong choices on this section are wrong because they are "outside the scope." In everyday language, that simply means that these choices contain elements that don't match the author's ideas, or that simply go beyond the context of the stimulus.

Some common examples of scope problems are choices that are too narrow, or too broad, or literally have nothing to do with the author's points. Also, watch for and eliminate choices that are too extreme to match the argument's scope; they're usually signaled by words such as *all*, *always*, *never*, *none*, and so on. Choices that are more qualified are often correct for arguments that are moderate in tone, and contain words such as *usually*, *sometimes*, *probably*, etcetera.

To illustrate the scope principle, let's look again at the question mentioned above:

> The author's argument depends on which of the following assumptions about the new building codes?

Let's say one of the choices reads as follows:

> (A) The new building codes are far too stringent.

Knowing the scope of the argument would help you to eliminate this choice very quickly. You know that this argument is just a claim about what the new codes will require—that the library be rehabilitated. It's not an argument about whether the requirements of the new codes are good, or justifiable, or ridiculously strict. That kind of value judgment is outside the scope of this argument.

Recognizing scope problems is a great way of eliminating dozens of wrong answers quickly. Make sure to pay special attention to the scope issues discussed in the Practice Test explanations.

Scope It Out

A remarkable number of wrong answers in LR have scope problems. Always be on the lookout for choices that are too extreme, that contain value judgments that are not relevant to the argument, or that don't match the stimulus in tone or subject matter.

Some arguments lack an important bridge between their evidence and their conclusion. That bridge is the necessary assumption—a key part of many arguments that remains unspoken.

The Nine Crucial LR Question Types

Now that you're familiar with the basic principles of Logical Reasoning, let's look at the most common types of questions you'll be asked. As we said earlier, certain question types crop up again and again on the LSAT, and it pays to be familiar with them. Of the types discussed below, the first three predominate on most LR sections, but try to become familiar with the others as well.

Assumption Questions

An assumption bridges the gap between an argument's evidence and conclusion. It's a piece of support that isn't explicitly stated, but that is required for the conclusion to remain valid. When a question asks you to find an author's assumption, it's asking you to find the statement without which the argument falls apart.

In order to test whether a statement is necessarily assumed by an author, therefore, we can employ the Denial Test. Here's how it works: simply deny or negate the statement and see if the argument falls apart. If it does, that choice is the correct assumption. If, on the other hand, the argument is unaffected, the choice is wrong. Consider, as an example, this simple stimulus:

> Allyson plays volleyball for Central High School. Therefore, Allyson must be more than 6 feet tall.

You should recognize the second sentence as the conclusion, and the first sentence as the evidence for it. But is the argument complete? Obviously not. The piece that's missing—the unstated link between the evidence and conclusion—is the assumption, and you could probably prephrase this one pretty easily:

> All volleyball players for Central High School are more than 6 feet tall.

To test whether this really is an assumption necessary to the argument, let's apply the Denial Test, by negating it. What if it's *not true* that all volleyball players for Central High School are more than 6 feet tall? Can we still logically conclude that Allyson *must be* taller than 6 feet? No, we can't. Sure, it's possible that she is, but just as possible that she's not. By denying the statement, then, the argument falls to pieces; it's simply no longer

- They are one of the most popular LR question types.
- They are unstated in the stimulus.
- They bridge the gap between evidence and conclusion.
- They must be true in order for the conclusion to remain valid.
- They can be checked by applying the Denial Test.

valid. And that's our conclusive proof that the statement above is a necessary assumption of this argument.

As we've just seen, you can often prephrase the answer to an assumption question. By previewing the question stem, you'll know what to look for. And stimuli for assumption questions just "feel" like they're missing something. Often, the answer will jump right out at you, as in this case. In more difficult assumption questions, the answers may not be as obvious. But in either case, you can use the Denial Test to check quickly whichever choice seems correct.

Sample Stems
Here are some of the ways in which assumption questions are worded:

- Which one of the following is assumed by the author?
- Upon which one of the following assumptions does the author rely?
- The argument depends on the assumption that . . .
- Which one of the following, if added to the passage, will make the conclusion logical?
- The validity of the argument depends on which one of the following?
- The argument presupposes which one of the following?

The following is a list of assumption questions that you'll find on the Practice Test at the end of this book:

- Section 1: Questions 1, 6, 25
- Section 4: Questions 7, 14, 17

Strengthen and Weaken Questions

Determining an argument's necessary assumption, as we've just seen, is required to answer assumption questions. But it also is required for another common question type—strengthen-the-argument and weaken-the-argument questions.

One way to weaken an argument is to break down a central piece of evidence. Another way is to attack the validity of any assumptions the author may be making. The answer to many weaken-the-argument questions is the one that reveals an author's assumption to be unreasonable; conversely, the answer to many strengthen-the-argument questions provides additional support by affirming the truth of an assumption or by presenting more persuasive evidence.

STRENGTHEN/ WEAKEN QUESTIONS AT A GLANCE

- Weaken questions are very popular; strengthen questions are less so.
- They are related to assumption; strengtheners often shore up the central assumption, while weakeners often show the central assumption to be unreasonable.
- You must evaluate each choice as to the effect it would have on the argument if true.
- Correct choices don't prove or disprove argument, but simply tip the scale the most in the desired direction.

Let's take the same stimulus we used before, but look at it in the context of these other question types:

> Allyson plays volleyball for Central High School. Therefore, Allyson must be more than 6 feet tall.

Remember the assumption holding this argument together? It was that all volleyball players for Central High School are more than 6 feet tall. That's the assumption that makes or breaks the argument. So, if the question asked you to weaken the argument, you'd want to attack that assumption:

> Which one of the following, if true, would most weaken the argument?

> *Answer:* Not all volleyball players at Central High School are more than 6 feet tall.

We've called into doubt the author's basic assumption, thus damaging the argument.

But what about strengthening the argument? Again, the key is the necessary assumption:

> Which one of the following, if true, would most strengthen the argument?

> *Answer:* All volleyball players at Central High School are more than 6 feet tall.

Here, by making explicit the author's central assumption, we've in effect bolstered the argument.

Extra Tips

Weaken questions tend to be more common on the LSAT than strengthen questions. But here are a few concepts that apply to both question types:

- Weakening an argument is not the same thing as disproving it, while strengthening is not the same as proving the conclusion to be true. A strengthener tips the scale toward believing in the validity of the conclusion, while a weakener tips the scale in the other direction, toward doubting the conclusion.

- The wording of these question types always takes the form "Which one of the following, if true, would most [weaken or strengthen] the argument?" The *if true* part means that you have to accept the truth of the choice right off the bat, no matter how unlikely it may sound to you.
- Don't be careless. Wrong answer choices in these questions often have exactly the opposite of the desired effect. That is, if you're asked to strengthen a stimulus argument, it's quite likely that one or more of the wrong choices will contain information that actually *weakens* the argument. By the same token, weaken questions may contain a choice that *strengthens* the argument. So once again, pay close attention to what the question stem asks.

Sample Stems

The stems associated with these two question types are usually self-explanatory. Here's a list of what you can expect to see on the test:

Weaken:
- Which one of the following, if true, would most weaken the argument above?
- Which one of the following, if true, would most seriously damage the argument above?
- Which one of the following, if true, casts the most doubt on the argument above?
- Which one of the following, if true, is the most serious criticism of the argument above?

Strengthen:
- Which one of the following, if true, would most strengthen the argument?
- Which one of the following, if true, would provide the most support for the conclusion in the argument above?
- The argument above would be more persuasive if which one of the following were found to be true?

The following is a list of strengthen- and weaken-the-argument questions that you'll find on the Practice Test at the end of this book:

- Strengthen: Section 1, Question 15; Section 4, Question 1
- Weaken: Section 1, Questions 11, 14, 19; Section 4, Questions 6, 10, 15, 16, 23

THE OLD BAIT AND SWITCH

A common LR trap is to have a statement that nicely weakens the argument hiding among the choices for a strengthen question (or the reverse— a great strengthener statement in the choices for a weaken question). Don't fall for this classic trap!

- They are one of the most popular LR question types.
- The answer must be true if statements in the stimulus are true.
- They often stick close to the author's main point.
- The question stems vary considerably in appearance.
- They can be checked by applying the Denial Test.

Inference Questions

Another of the most common question types you'll encounter on the LR section is the inference question. The process of inferring is a matter of considering one or more statements as evidence, and then drawing a conclusion from them.

Sometimes the inference is very close to the author's overall main point. Other times, it deals with a less central point. A valid inference is something that must be true if the statements in the passage are true—an extension of the argument rather than a necessary part of it.

For instance, let's take a somewhat expanded version of the volleyball team argument:

> Allyson plays volleyball for Central High School, despite the team's rule against participation by nonstudents. Therefore, Allyson must be over 6 feet tall.

> *Inference:* Allyson is not a student at Central High School.

Clearly, if Allyson plays volleyball *despite* the team's rule against participation by nonstudents, she must not be a student. Otherwise, she wouldn't be playing *despite* the rule; she'd be playing in accordance with the rule. But note that this inference is not an essential assumption of the argument, since the conclusion about Allyson's height doesn't depend on it.

So be careful; unlike an assumption, an inference need not have anything to do with the author's conclusion—it may simply be a piece of information derived from one or more pieces of evidence. However, the Denial Test works for inferences as well as for assumptions: a valid inference always makes more sense than its opposite. If you deny or negate an answer choice, and it has little or no effect on the argument, chances are that choice is not inferable from the passage.

Sample Stems

Inference questions probably have the most varied wording of all the Logical Reasoning question stems. Some question stems denote inference fairly obviously. Others are more subtle, and still others may even look like other question types entirely. Here's a quick rundown of the various forms that inference questions are likely to take on your test:

- Which one of the following is inferable from the argument above?
- Which one of the following is implied by the argument above?

- The author suggests that . . .
- If all the statements above are true, which one of the following must also be true on the basis of them?
- The author of the passage would most likely agree with which one of the following?
- The passage provides the most support for which one of the following?
- Which one of the following is probably the conclusion toward which the author is moving?

The following is a list of inference questions that you'll find on the Practice Test:

- Section 1: Questions 2, 13, 20, 22
- Section 4: Questions 4, 5, 13, 20, 22

Flaw Questions

This question type—known also by the moniker of Critique the Logic—asks you to recognize what's wrong with an argument. There are two basic types.

In the general type, the correct choice will critique the reasoning by pointing out that it contains a classic fallacy (e.g., "The argument attacks the source of an opinion, rather than the opinion itself."). In this case, the flaw falls into a general, well-defined category.

In the specific type of flaw question, the correct choice won't refer to a classic fallacy, but rather will attack a specific piece of the argument's reasoning. An example of this would be: "It cannot be concluded that the number of male turtles has increased simply because the percentage of turtles that are male has increased."

Notice that the subject of the above statement isn't turtles; it's the author's faulty reasoning *about turtles*. Similar to many other question types, the required skill is the ability to identify the structure of the author's argument—specifically, where the argument goes wrong.

The following is the flaw question that you'll find on the Practice Test at the end of this book:

- Section 1: Question 7

Method of Argument Questions

Method-of-argument questions bear a similarity to flaw questions. Once again, you'll be asked to demonstrate an understanding of how an

STAY IN LINE!

A good inference:

- Stays in line with the gist of the passage
- Stays in line with the author's tone
- Stays in line with the author's point of view
- Stays within the scope of the argument or the main idea
- Is neither denied by, nor irrelevant to, the argument or discussion
- Always makes more sense than its opposite

FLAW QUESTIONS AT A GLANCE

- They ask: "What's wrong with this argument?"
- Some correspond to well-defined categories.
- Some are specific to individual arguments.
- Understanding structure of arguments is the key.

- They may or may not involve faulty logic.
- They are similar to Reading Comp questions that ask about author's intentions and passage structure.
- Understanding the structure of arguments is the key.

PARALLEL-
REASONING
QUESTIONS
AT A GLANCE

- They must mimic structure or form, not content, of stimulus.
- They are sometimes amenable to algebraic symbolization.
- The key is to summarize argument's overall form and match it to that of the correct choice.

author's argument is put together. However, unlike flaw questions, method-of-argument questions don't always involve faulty logic. You're simply asked to pick the choice that describes how the author goes about presenting his or her case. The key skill—once again—involves being able to analyze the structure of an argument. If you can't identify the evidence and conclusion, you'll have difficulty describing how an argument works.

Also like flaw questions, there are two distinct types of method-of-argument questions—one general, one specific. The first deals with classic arguments. These are the classic argumentative structures, such as, "arguing from a small sample to a larger group," or "inferring a causal relationship from a correlation." The other type of method-of-argument question gives you a description of the argument in much more specific terms. An example of this might read, "The author presents the case of his mother in order to show that not all astronauts are men."

Focus on the following: "What is the evidence? What is the conclusion? How does the author link the evidence and conclusion together?" These are the questions you have to ask yourself in order to determine the author's method of argument.

The following is a list of method-of-argument questions that you'll find on the Practice Test at the end of this book:

- Section 1: Questions 10, 16
- Section 4: Questions 2, 25

Parallel-Reasoning Questions

Parallel-reasoning questions require you to identify the answer choice that contains the argument most similar, or parallel, to that in the stimulus in terms of the reasoning employed. To do this kind of question, you need to grasp the distinction between an argument's form and its content. "A causal relationship concluded from a correlation" is a form—a type—of reasoning. Any argument with this form can contain virtually any content. Your task is to abstract the stimulus argument's form, with as little content as possible, and then locate the answer choice that has the form most similar to that of the stimulus. Don't let yourself be drawn to a choice based on its subject matter. A stimulus about music may have an answer choice that also involves music, but that doesn't mean that the *reasoning* in the two arguments is similar.

A good approach to these questions is to see first if the argument can be symbolized algebraically, using Xs and Ys. Take the following example:

> All cows eat grass. This animal eats grass. Therefore, it must be a cow.

This (flawed) argument can be symbolized in the following way:

> All X do Y. This does Y. Therefore, this must be an X.

If the stimulus can be symbolized this way, your job will be to search for the choice that can be symbolized in the same way. Your answer might look something like this:

> Every politician *(all X)* tells lies *(does Y)*. Stegner is lying *(this does Y)*. So he must be a politician *(therefore, this must be an X)*.

Notice how the exact wording doesn't have to match ("all X" means "every X"), and notice that the subject matter doesn't have to match in the least. What's important is the parallel structure.

Sometimes, though, an argument's reasoning isn't amenable to symbolization. In such a case, see if you can put a label on the type of argument being used, such as "Arguing from a Part to a Whole," or "Circular Reasoning (evidence and conclusion are identical)." Naming the argument will often help eliminate two or three choices that don't even come close to this general form.

But whatever way you choose, as long as you can summarize the argument's form without including content, you're well on your way to finding the parallel argument among the choices.

Extra Tips
Here are a few more tips on parallel reasoning:

- *All* elements of the original argument must be present in its parallel. For example, if the original argument made a generalization to a specific case, a second argument, no matter how similar in structure otherwise, cannot be parallel unless it makes a comparable generalization.
- Stay away from answer choices written about the same subject matter as the original. This is an old trick of the test makers, intended to

THE OLD SIMILAR-CONTENT TRAP

On some parallel-reasoning questions, one of the wrong choices will be an unparallel argument that nonetheless has similar content to the original argument. Don't fall for the trap. The question is interested in structure, not content.

catch those who mistakenly try to mimic the content rather than the structure of the stimulus.

- Statements that are logically parallel don't have to have all logical elements in the same sequence. Provided all elements of the first argument exist in the second, even in a different order, the two arguments are parallel.

The following is a list of parallel-reasoning questions that you'll find on the Practice Test at the end of this book:

- Section 1: Questions 18, 24
- Section 4: Questions 3, 11

Paradox Questions

A paradox exists when an argument contains two or more seemingly inconsistent statements. You'll know you're dealing with a paradoxical situation if the argument ends with what seems to be a bizarre contradiction. Another sure sign of a paradox is when the argument builds to a certain point, and then the exact opposite of what you would expect to happen happens.

In a typical paradox question, you'll be asked either to find the choice that "explains the paradoxical result" or "resolves the apparent discrepancy." Basically, this will be the choice that reconciles the seemingly inconsistent statements that make up the argument while allowing them all to still be true.

Take the following question:

> Fifty-seven percent of the registered voters in this district claimed to support the Democratic candidate, and yet the Republican candidate won the election with 55 percent of the vote.

Which of the following would resolve the apparent discrepancy above?

The stimulus seems paradoxical since the Republican won the election, even though more registered voters preferred the Democrat. But do all registered voters vote? No. So a correct answer for this question might read something like this:

> Because of an intensive get-out-the-vote effort in traditionally Republican neighborhoods, a disproportionate number of registered Republicans actually voted in the election.

PARADOX QUESTIONS AT A GLANCE

- The correct choice will resolve apparent discrepancy or contradiction.
- The correct choice should have an intuitive "click."
- The correct choice will often involve realizing that two groups presented as identical are actually not.

This statement reconciles the seemingly contradictory elements of the argument by showing that the group of registered voters is not identical to the group of people who actually voted in the election.

Extra Tips
Here are a few tips for handling this question type:

- Before attempting to resolve a paradox, make sure you have a good grasp of what the paradox is. If it doesn't hit you right off the bat, look hard for an unexpected result, or what seems to be a blatant contradiction between the author's evidence and conclusion.
- Resolving paradoxes is often a matter of recognizing that two things that are being compared aren't really the same thing. Read critically to note these subtle distinctions.
- In paradox questions, avoid choices that merely amplify points already raised in the argument.

The following is a list of paradox questions that you'll find on the Practice Test at the end of this book:

- Section 1: Questions 3, 21
- Section 4: Questions 12, 21

Principle Questions
Principle questions involve fitting a specific situation into a global generality (or, occasionally, vice versa). Usually, you'll be given an argument, and then asked to find the principle that seems to justify the author's reasoning. For example, suppose that an author's evidence leads to this conclusion in the final sentence of the stimulus:

Therefore, Marvin should provide a home for his ailing grandmother until she gets back on her feet.

The question stem might read: "The author's position most closely conforms to which one of the following principles?" In other words, what principle best accounts for or justifies the author's position? The answer could sound like this:

If a close relative is in need, one should always do his or her best to help that person, regardless of personal inconvenience.

PRINCIPLE QUESTIONS AT A GLANCE

- They're a relatively new question type.
- They are the closest question type to the actual workings of the law.
- The correct choices usually express author's key concepts and terms.

On the other hand, the question stem might read: "Which one of the following principles would justify Marvin's refusal to follow the author's recommendation?" In this case, the answer may sound something like this:

> No person should be obligated to provide support for another person, even if that other person is a close relative.

Notice the general nature of both principles. While they don't specifically mention Marvin or his grandmother, or the exact conditions of the stimulus *per se,* the general situation (helping a relative in need) is addressed in both.

The correct answer to principle questions is usually the one that expresses the key concepts and contains the key terms that the other choices leave out. Be extremely wary of choices that are outside the scope of the argument. Most of the wrong choices contain principles that sound very formal and look good on the page by themselves, but that don't address the author's main concern.

The following is a list of principle questions that you'll find on the Practice Test at the end of this book:

- Section 1: Questions 5, 9
- Section 4: Questions 9, 19

Formal Logic Questions

The manner in which formal logic is tested on the LSAT has evolved over the last few years. Gone (at least for now) are the days when the test makers would line up formal if/then and all/some/none statements and ask you what can, must, or cannot be true on the basis of them. Nowadays, the test makers bury formal statements in the context of a casual argument, asking for an inference that can be drawn from the passage. You may not easily recognize formal logic when you see it, and questions of this nature are fewer in number than in the past. But formal logic skills are tested in Logic Games as well, so it's best to get a solid handle on it now.

Let's look at an example:

> Ian will go to the movies only when his wife is out of town. He'll go to a matinee alone, but will see a movie at night only if accompanied by Ezra and Mabel.

This simple stimulus looks like any other casual argument in Logical Reasoning, but in fact, it's made up of a couple of formal logic statements, each fraught with its own implications. Formal logic statements resemble rules in Logic Games. Be on the lookout for Logical Reasoning stimuli that contain sentences that can be boiled down to such hard and fast rules. When you come across examples of these, you can apply the following principles of formal logic to help you arrive at the correct answer.

The Contrapositive

For any if/then statement—or a statement that can be translated into if/then form—the contrapositive of the statement will result in an equally valid second statement. This is a nice shortcut to employ when faced with formal logic on the test.

The contrapositive can be formed by reversing and negating the terms of any if/then statement. The general model goes like this:

If X, then Y.

The contrapositive of this statement is:

If *not* Y, then *not* X.

The contrapositive of a valid if/then statement will always be valid itself.

Let's illustrate this with a simple example. Consider the following strict formal statement:

If the building has vacancies, then the sales office will be open.

To form the contrapositive, reverse and negate the terms, like so:

If the sales office is NOT open, then the building does NOT have vacancies.

This would be a valid inference based on the original statement. The contrapositive, while quite a fancy term, is nothing more than everyday common sense.

Now let's apply the contrapositive to the first sentence of the earlier example. Here's the original:

Ian will go to the movies only when his wife is out of town.

- They have a direct bearing on Logic Games as well as Logical Reasoning.
- They are usually tested in the context of a casual argument.
- The formal statements can be boiled down to hard and fast rules.
- The contrapositive can be applied to any if/then statement.

THE CONTRAPOSITIVE

The contrapositive is probably the most important rule of logic you need for LSAT success. It's essential that you learn what it is and how to use it.

This is a little trickier, because it's not stated in the form of a true if/then statement. But we can translate this statement into an if/then statement without changing its original meaning:

If Ian goes to the movies, *then* his wife must be out of town.

If the statement above is true, which one of the following must be true on the basis of it? Why, the contrapositive of it, of course:

If Ian's wife is *not* out of town, then Ian does *not* go to the movies.

Simple enough, right? One caveat: wrong answers often result from either forgetting to switch around the terms before negating them, or negating only one of the terms. For example, from the above example, if Ian doesn't go to the movies, we can't infer anything about whether his wife is in or out of town. Similarly, if Ian's wife IS out of town, we can't tell for sure whether Ian goes to the movies or not.

If one part of the formal logic statement contains a compound phrase, then both parts of the phrase must be taken into account. For example, let's take the other part of the stimulus above:

Ian will see a movie at night only if accompanied by Ezra *and* Mabel.

Translation: If Ian sees a movie at night, then he's accompanied by Ezra *and* Mabel.

Contrapositive: If Ian is *not* with Ezra *and* Mabel, then he does *not* see a movie at night.

Correct Interpretation: If either Ezra or Mabel is missing, then Ian's out of luck. If he's with only one of them, or neither of them, then he can't go to a night movie.

Finally, if one part of a formal statement is already in the negative, the same rules that apply to math apply to forming the contrapositive: negating a negative yields a positive.

If the sun is shining, then Samantha does not wear green.

Contrapositive: If Samantha *is* wearing green (if she's *not not* wearing green), then the sun is *not* shining.

Necessary Versus Sufficient Conditions

For success in formal logic, it's crucial that you distinguish clearly between necessary and sufficient conditions. Here are examples of each:

> *Sufficient:* If I yell loudly at my cat Adrian, he will run away.
> *Necessary:* The TV will work only if it is plugged in.

My yelling loudly is a sufficient condition for Adrian to run away. It's all I need to do to get the cat to run; it's sufficient. But it's not necessary. My cat will run if I throw water at him, even if I don't yell loudly.

The TV's being plugged in, on the other hand, is a necessary condition of its working. My TV won't work without it, so it's necessary. But it's not sufficient. Other conditions must apply for the TV to work (for example, the electricity to the house must be on).

You must be clear on what kinds of deductions you can and can't make from statements of necessary and sufficient conditions. For instance, sufficient conditions are usually signaled by an if/then statement, which means that the contrapositive can be used.

> If I yell loudly at my cat Adrian, he will run away.

Given that the above statement is true, which one of the following statements must also be true?

> **Not Valid:** If I don't yell loudly at my cat Adrian, he will not run away.
> **Not Valid:** If my cat Adrian has run away, then I yelled loudly at him.
> **Valid:** If my cat Adrian has not run away, then I did not yell loudly at him.

The third statement is the contrapositive, and is the only one of the three statements that's inferable from the original. My yelling loudly is sufficient to make Adrian run away, but it's not necessary; that is, it'll do the trick, but it's not the *only* possible thing that will make him head for the hills. If I squirt him with a water gun, he'll also run away. This is why the first two statements are not inferable from the original statement.

NECESSITY VERSUS SUFFICIENCY

It's necessary that you learn the difference between necessary and sufficient requirements, but knowing that is not sufficient in and of itself to get a great score.

Necessary conditions, on the other hand, are usually signaled by the word *only:*

The TV will work only if it is plugged in.

Given that the above statement is true, which one of the following statements must also be true?

Not Valid: If my TV is plugged in, it will work.
Not Valid: If my TV is not working, then it must not be plugged in.
Valid: If my TV is working, then it must be plugged in.
Valid: If my TV is not plugged in, then it won't work.

Plugging the TV in is necessary for the TV to work. To work, the TV needs to be plugged in. However, plugging in the TV is not sufficient to make the TV work. True, the TV won't work without plugging it in, but plugging it in is not a *guarantee* that the TV will work. What if other conditions interfere? Maybe the picture tube is broken. Maybe my electricity is out due to a hurricane. So the first two statements above are not inferable from the original statement, while the last two are.

The following is a list of questions containing elements of formal logic that you'll find on the Practice Test at the end of this book. (Keep in mind, though, that these principles of formal logic are just as important in Logic Games.)

- Section 1: Question 2
- Section 4: Question 20

The Kaplan Four-Step Method for Logical Reasoning

Now that you've learned the basic LR principles and have been exposed to the full range of question types, it's time to learn how to orchestrate all of that knowledge into a systematic approach to Logical Reasoning. We've developed a four-step approach that you can use to attack each and every question on the section.

Here are the four steps:

1. Preview the question stem.
2. Read the stimulus.
3. Try to prephrase an answer.
4. Choose an answer.

1. Preview the Question Stem

As we mentioned in the discussion of basic principles, previewing the stem is a great way to focus your reading of the stimulus, so that you know exactly what you're looking for.

2. Read the Stimulus

With the question stem in mind, read the stimulus, paraphrasing as you go. Remember to read actively and critically, pinpointing evidence and conclusion. Also get a sense for how strong or weak the argument is.

3. Try to Prephrase an Answer

Sometimes, if you've read the stimulus critically enough, you'll know the answer without even looking at the choices. It will be much easier to find it if you have a sense of what you're looking for among the choices.

4. Choose an Answer

If you were able to prephrase an answer, skim the choices looking for something that sounds like what you have in mind. If you couldn't think of anything, read and evaluate each choice, throwing out the ones that are outside the scope of the argument. After settling on an answer, you may wish to briefly double-check the question stem to make sure that you're indeed answering the question that was asked.

Using the Kaplan Four-Step Method for Logical Reasoning

Now let's try this approach on a genuine Logical Reasoning item:

A study of twenty overweight men revealed that each man experienced significant weight loss after adding SlimDown, an artificial food supplement, to his daily diet. For three months, each man consumed one SlimDown portion every morning after exercising, and

STEP BY STEP

The Kaplan Four-Step Method is designed to give structure to your work on the LR section. But be flexible in using it. These are guidelines, not commandments.

then followed his normal diet for the rest of the day. Clearly, anyone who consumes one portion of SlimDown every day for at least three months will lose weight and will look and feel his or her best.

Which one of the following is an assumption on which the argument depends?

(A) The men in the study will gain back the weight they lost if they discontinue the SlimDown program.
(B) No other dietary supplement will have the same effect on overweight men.
(C) The daily exercise regimen was not responsible for the effects noted in the study.
(D) Women will not experience similar weight reductions if they adhere to the SlimDown program for three months.
(E) Overweight men will achieve only partial weight loss if they do not remain on the SlimDown program for a full three months.

1. Preview the Question Stem

We see, quite clearly, that we're dealing with an assumption question. Good—immediately we can adopt an "assumption mindset," which basically means that, before even reading the first word of the stimulus, we know that the conclusion will be lacking an important piece of supporting evidence. We now turn to the stimulus, already on the lookout for this missing link.

2. Read the Stimulus

The first sentence introduces a study of twenty men using a food supplement product, resulting in weight loss for all twenty. The second sentence describes how they used it: once a day, for three months, after morning exercise. So far so good; it feels as if we're building up to something. The structural signal word *clearly* usually indicates that some sort of conclusion follows, and in fact it does: the author concludes in the third sentence that anyone who has one portion of the product daily for three months will lose weight, too.

You must read critically! Notice that the conclusion doesn't say that anyone who follows the *same routine* as the twenty men will have the same results; it says that anyone who simply *consumes the product* in the same way will have the same results. You should have begun to sense the inevitable lack of crucial information at this point. The evidence in the second sentence describes a routine that includes taking the supplement after daily exercise, whereas the conclusion focuses primarily on the supplement and entirely ignores the part about the exercise. The conclusion, therefore, doesn't stem logically from the evidence in the first two sentences. This blends seamlessly into Step 3.

3. Prephrase an Answer

As expected, the argument is beginning to look as if it has a serious short-coming. Of course, we expected this because we previewed the question stem before reading the stimulus.

In really simplistic terms, the argument proceeds like so: "A bunch of guys did A and B for three months, and had X result. If anyone does A for three months, that person will experience X result, too." Sound a little fishy? You bet. The author must be assuming that A (the product), not B (exercise), must be the crucial thing that leads to the result. If not (the Denial Test), the conclusion makes no sense.

So, you might prephrase the answer like this: "Something about the exercise thing needs to be cleared up." That's it. Did you think your prephrasing had to be something fancy and glamorous? Well, it doesn't. All you need is an inkling of what the question is looking for, and in this case, it just seems that if we don't shore up the exercise issue, the argument will remain invalid and incomplete. So, with our vague idea of a possible assumption, we can turn to Step 4, which is . . .

4. Choose an Answer

Since we were able to prephrase something, it's best to skim the choices looking for it. And, lo and behold, there's our idea, stated in a very LSAT-like manner, in choice (C). (C) clears up the exercise issue. Yes, this author must assume (C) to make the conclusion that eating SlimDown alone will cause anyone to lose weight.

At this point, if you're stuck for time, you simply choose (C) and move on. If you have more time, you may as well quickly check the remaining choices, to find (we hope) that none of them fits the bill.

Of course, once you grasp the structure of the argument and have located the author's central assumption, you should be able to answer any question they throw at you. This one takes the form of an assumption question. But it could just as easily have been phrased as a weaken-the-argument question:

THE ART OF PREPHRASING

Your prephrasing of an answer need not be elaborate or terribly specific. Your goal is just to get an idea of what you're looking for, so the correct answer will jump out at you.

Which one of the following, if true, casts the most doubt on the argument above?

Answer: Daily exercise contributed significantly to the weight loss experienced by the men in the study.

And here's a flaw question that could have been based on the same stimulus:

The author's reasoning is flawed because it . . .

Answer: . . . overlooks the possibility that the results noted in the study were caused by daily exercise rather than by the consumption of SlimDown.

What's Next

So there you have it—a quick demonstration of how to use the strategies and techniques outlined in this chapter to work through the complete Logical Reasoning process. Try to apply these techniques as best you can on the following practice set and on the fifty Logical Reasoning examples in the Practice Test. Pay careful attention to all of the written explanations, even those for the ones you got right.

After the practice set, we'll move on to another major section of the test, Logic Games.

Logical Reasoning Practice Set

<u>Directions:</u> This test is composed of questions that ask you to analyze the logic of statements or short paragraphs. You are to choose as the answer to each question the one choice you consider correct on the basis of your common-sense evaluation of the statement and its assumptions. Although a question may seem to have more than one acceptable answer, there is only one answer, and it is the one that does not entail making any illogical, extraneous, or conflicting assumptions about the question. These questions do not presuppose any knowledge of formal logic on your part. (The answer and explanation can be found at the end of each question.)

Question 1

In his long and epochal career, Beethoven was both synthesizer and innovator, the supreme classicist who startled the musical world of his time by his bold surges forward toward the chromaticism to come. But because his later music made so much use of unprecedented dissonance, a few cynical critics have suggested that the composer's progressively worsening deafness must have weakened his ability to imagine and produce consistently harmonious music. In other words, he was writing what he misheard, according to these critics. I maintain that, on the contrary, if the deaf Beethoven had been trying to create in a medium he had known intimately but could no longer manipulate successfully, he would have been all the more likely to _____.

Which one of the following best completes the passage above?

(A) depend heavily upon the rules of conventional harmony to produce predictable sounds
(B) compose dissonances from his inability to hear what he had written

(C) rely upon his own judgment in deciding what type of music to compose
(D) avoid cynical criticism by composing only consistently harmonious music
(E) suspect that his ear had become so untrustworthy that he should end his career before full maturation

Ⓐ Ⓑ Ⓒ Ⓓ Ⓔ

Answer and Explanation

In Question 1, you have to fill in the blank. You'll want to get an idea of the direction in which the passage is going, so that you can extrapolate to the most likely ending.

The passage begins by labeling Beethoven as two things. He was both an innovator—meaning he brought music forward, moving toward what the passage says was "the chromaticism to come" (whatever that is)—and a synthesizer, presumably not the Mogue variety but someone who "put it all together," that is, who also worked with classical forms. *But*— structural signal of contrast here—some critics have said that Beethoven's innovations (his work with dissonance) were *not* some kind of wonderful experimentation, but merely a manifestation of his increasing deafness—hence, they represent an unharmonious flaw in his later music.

The author doesn't hold with this interpretation. She does, after all, label them "cynical critics." And she says, "I maintain that, on the contrary. . . ," which is another signal of contrast announcing that the author is about to take issue. Her belief is that if Beethoven's deafness was (as is alleged) impairing his ability to handle his musical medium, then he would have been all the more likely to do. . . what? Well, she wants to finish with a statement of a contrary effect. Her argument is: If the cause the cynics describe were, in fact, the case (if deafness made Beethoven less competent), then there would be an opposite effect, an effect something like choice (A). A less competent

Beethoven would have played it safe by producing conventional, traditional music.

Choice (B) directly echoes or parallels the opinion of the cynical critics—it doesn't stand in contrast to it—so it's not an opinion that would be cited to bolster the author's own feelings about Beethoven. Jumping to choice (E)—by seeming to agree that Beethoven was losing his abilities towards the end of his career—you can see that choice (E), too, is more in line with the view of the cynical critics.

Choice (C)'s sentiment is somewhat in line with that of the author; it makes a bit of sense in that it suggests that Beethoven composed what he wanted to compose. But it doesn't act as a clear contrast to the notion that Beethoven composed dissonant music because his hearing was impaired and didn't know what sounds he was making, so it doesn't act in a satisfactory way to fill in the blank.

Finally, choice (D) brings up the issue of "harmonious music," which you want. But by assigning a motive to Beethoven—that he was trying to defuse critical response—choice (D) goes far afield. No such reference to motive has a place in the argument as written. Choice (A) best completes the paragraph in Question 1.

Question 2

Many factors affect the home-building industry, but the number of single-family homes under construction generally rises as interest rates decline. Contractors are able to plan their hiring schedules and order essential building materials in response to reliable predictors of the movement of prevailing interest rates.

It can be inferred from the passage above that

(A) the price of building materials rises when interest rates decline
(B) no factor affecting home building is as reliable a predictor as interest rates
(C) assessments of growth in the housing industry are sometimes based upon expected fluctuations of interest rates
(D) a contractor does not order building materials until a hiring schedule is set up
(E) most housing being built today is single-family housing

Ⓐ Ⓑ Ⓒ Ⓓ Ⓔ

Answer and Explanation

Question 2's stimulus isn't much of an argument, is it? It's little more than a series of flat statements on a topic. And that topic is interest rates, one of the major factors affecting the housing industry. Interest rates are cited as having an inverse relationship with the building of single-family dwellings: as rates go down, construction goes up, literally. In line with that (says the second sentence), contractors order building materials based on predictions of which way interest rates will go. This should make sense. If the contractors believed that rates were about to decrease, they would be likely to order more supplies in expectation of a greater demand for single-family homes. Conversely, an expected rise in interest rates would prompt a cutback in supply orders, in expectation of less demand.

All of this is in line with choice (C). And remember, when you're asked what can be inferred from the passage, you really want something that must be true—something in line with the scope and point of view. Choice (C) is just a broader rephrasing of the relationship cited in the stimulus and is thus the best answer. (Note that the choice is rendered even more reasonable by its use of the qualifier *sometimes*. Because it's not an extreme statement with no exceptions possible, it's easy to sign on to (C) as a reflection of the author's equally moderate views.)

Choice (A) brings up the cost of building materials, but since the passage says nothing at all about the costs of home building—there isn't a single reference

KAPLAN

to costs—it goes beyond the scope and must therefore be rejected quickly. You can't infer that those who sell building materials raise their prices in response to the greater demand they expect from the lower interest rates.

Choice (B) distorts the paragraph. Interests rates are cited as *a* good predictor. But are they the best? Who knows? And anyway, they're cited only in terms of one type of home—the single-family dwelling. Choice (B) evokes the entire industry—again, going beyond the scope.

As for choice (D), just because the author mentions hiring schedules before mentioning orders for new materials does not mean that one of those things must come first on the builder's agenda.

And (E) is an unwarranted inference since the author's only concern is one type of dwelling, the single-family home. You cannot fairly extrapolate from this paragraph to any statement about the home-building industry in general.

Again, it was choice (C) for Question 2.

Question 3

Critics of current commercial TV programming expect that Federal Communications Commission (FCC) rules restricting such popular items as children's adventure cartoons and sexually explicit motion pictures would result in more responsible programming, such as public affairs panel discussions, medical self-help series, and live productions of classic drama. But would they so fervently advocate government intrusion into broadcasting if they knew a little more about the real workings of the marketplace? Actually, enforced restrictions on programming would result in milder but still mindless offerings: more situation comedies about bewildered housewives, more coverage of obscure sporting events in minor cities, and more talk shows devoted to the private lives of forgettable "instant celebrities."

The author of the above passage assumes that

(A) current commercial TV programming is not irresponsible
(B) FCC restrictions of commercial TV programming will not necessarily be easy to enforce
(C) those who wish to restrict certain popular TV programs will dislike their popular replacements
(D) the FCC should have no control over the broadcast industry, which is likely to serve the public better if it is not regulated
(E) the marketplace is the true test of whether or not a new program idea is worthwhile

Ⓐ Ⓑ Ⓒ Ⓓ Ⓔ

Answer and Explanation

The speaker in Question 3 doubts that stricter FCC regulations will result in better quality television. Some expect that greater restrictions on kid's shows and dirty movies will prompt TV programmers to give us more, shall we say, elevating fare. But the speaker feels that stronger FCC rules will do no such thing—that the networks will be able to conform to the rules while continuing to provide the same vapid programming choices that have always been popular (that's the reference to the marketplace). The networks (it is predicted) will simply switch from controversial themes—that is, from sex and violence—to milder but still mindless shows. In other words, the networks won't attempt (as the proregulators predict) to put on more educational shows. They will just shift to whatever dopey (yet popular) fare is not restricted by the FCC.

You're to find an assumption, and the credited choice—the thing the speaker must be taking for granted as true—is (C). The speaker is taking for granted that the people who dislike TV as it is now will also dislike the shows that will be broadcast after the rules are instituted. After all, the speaker is essentially saying to the proregulators, "You're wrong in wanting to institute those rules because you'll get no better programming than before." But the speaker ignores the possibility that those in favor of the FCC rules will gladly greet the new dumb sitcoms and sports shows as a welcome change from the sex and violence that the rules are designed to reduce.

Choice (A) says that current TV is not irresponsible. But the speaker doesn't argue that the proposed rules are superfluous because current TV programming is responsible. Rather, the speaker argues that the rules won't make TV any better. In fact, the whole passage indicates that the author believes the opposite of (A): that much programming is irresponsibly mindless.

Choice (B) is not a necessary assumption either, since the speaker is not concerned with the ease or difficulty of enforcement but rather with how effective or ineffective the rules would be when enforced.

Choice (D) isn't assumed because the author doesn't argue that unregulated TV will be better, but rather that regulated TV will not be any better. The thrust here is that, because of the marketplace, TV will always be a vast wasteland.

Finally, choice (E) suggests that the true test of programming worth is the marketplace. Well, the speaker does believe that it's the marketplace that determines what we see on TV. But what the public sees is, to the speaker, execrable: sexy, violent, dopey, and worthless. Choice (E)'s rather democratic sentiment is completely at odds with the author's argument, and so it's not something that is assumed or built into that argument. Again, choice (C) is correct for Question 3.

Question 4

The federal government currently interferes blatantly in the relationship between parent and child. The Internal Revenue Service provides a child-care or dependent's deduction on the annual income tax return. In effect, the government, by rewarding some providers of support, determines which taxpayers are to be considered worthy enough to care for dependents.

Which one of the following, if true, weakens the argument above?

(A) A taxpayer need only attach the appropriate schedule to the tax form to apply for the deduction.
(B) The deduction is likely to offer a proportionately greater benefit to the lower income taxpayer.
(C) A child must be living at home with the provider of support in order to qualify as a dependent.
(D) The deduction actually affects a fairly small percentage of taxpayers.
(E) The deduction is available to anyone who supplies the principal support of a dependent.

Ⓐ Ⓑ Ⓒ Ⓓ Ⓔ

Answer and Explanation

Always watch for tone words! The charge in Question 4's stimulus that the government interferes "blatantly," wrongly using its bureaucratic power, alerts you immediately to the author's opinion.

It seems that the IRS gives a child-care deduction to certain people who provide support to a dependent. The complaint is that the government exercises unfair control in its choice of which people receive this deduction and which do not. The author believes that the government can have no justifiable basis on which to make this decision, and is in effect deciding which people are worthy of caring for dependents and which are not.

The choice that most weakens this argument is (E). If the tax deduction is, as choice (E) says, available to anyone who is the principal supporter of a dependent, then that answers the implicit charge that the government has arbitrarily set itself up as an authority, with the right to decide people's personal worth. If the IRS, in other words, is using an appropriate criterion that is applied equitably to all, then the charge that the deduction is being selectively used to decide people's worth is rendered groundless. If you provide someone's principal support, then you get the deduction. If not, you don't. So (E) really damages the reasoning.

Choice (A) might have fooled you, because it seems to be saying that anyone who wants the deduction can have it. But it really says that anyone who attaches the appropriate schedule may apply for the deduction; they won't necessarily get it. The fact that the IRS will consider anyone doesn't mean that it isn't (as the author alleges) making the final decision on inappropriate criteria, choosing people arbitrarily on the basis of what it deems to be their personal worth. So choice (A) is incorrect.

Choice (B) mentions the deduction but is otherwise beyond the argument's scope, going off on the interesting but irrelevant topic of the relative size of the deduction for lower-income taxpayers.

As for choice (C), even if it were true, the government might still be reaching its decision as to who gets the deduction based on improper criteria. All choice (C) gives us is one of those criteria—the requirement that a dependent be a coresident. But perhaps the other criteria are just as objectionable as the author seems to feel they are.

Finally, choice (D)'s implication that only a few people will get the deduction is another "error in scope," because choice (D) has nothing to do with the main issue, which is the government's methods or motives. The "weakener" you need has to somehow demonstrate that the government—contrary to what the author believes—is awarding the deduction based on proper criteria. Only choice (E) does that, and that's why it's correct for Question 4.

Question 5

Detective-adventure series and other action programming on prime-time television have been criticized for inciting some viewers, male adolescents in particular, to commit acts of violence. The most carefully engineered studies have not, however, supported this assumption. Rather, it seems likely that someone who is frustrated and resentful, and therefore prone to violence, is drawn to the kind of programming that shows characters who release their frustrations in acts of violence.

Which one of the following would provide the most logical concluding sentence for the paragraph above?

(A) In fact, action programming probably helps a frustrated viewer release his hostility without resorting to violence.

(B) Moreover, there are studies that indicate that male adolescents are more likely than other viewers to believe that the world shown in action programming is realistic.

(C) In other words, an unusual interest in action programming may be an indication of a violence-prone personality rather than an incitement to violence.

(D) Be that as it may, action programming continues to grow in popularity with the American TV audience.

(E) Therefore, the reasonable observer of the American scene will conclude that action programming should be banned from prime-time viewing hours.

Ⓐ Ⓑ Ⓒ Ⓓ Ⓔ

Answer and Explanation

In Question 5 the author counters the view that violent TV shows incite people to commit violent acts. Apparently a correlation has been noticed—and a correlation, of course, is an acknowledgment that two phenomena accompany each other, whether or not they're causally related. A correlation has been noted between watching TV violence and committing violent acts. Apparently it's true that people who watch violent shows are more likely to commit violent crimes than those who don't watch those shows. And this finding might well suggest that the TV shows are causing the viewers to commit the crimes. But the author believes that the correlation is better explained in another way—that violence-prone people tend to watch violent shows because they feel an affinity to the violence-prone characters of the shows. So to the author, the critics cited in the first sentence are guilty of confusing cause and effect. The TV shows don't make the viewer violence prone; rather, it's frustration and resentment that make people violence prone and make these people watch violent TV programs.

The passage ends abruptly without a proper conclusion—for obvious reasons, since you're asked to come up with that yourself. The best answer is (C), which takes the author's argument to its logical conclusion: A person's addiction to action TV shows may reveal something about that person's tendency towards violence, but it doesn't indicate an inducement to commit violence.

Choice (A) goes too far. It states that the effect of action shows is salutary, by helping the violence-prone viewer vent his hostility in a nonthreatening way. But that doesn't at all follow from the argument, which merely contends that the crime-and-TV-show correlation can be explained in an alternative way. To say, as choice (A) does, that TV violence can act as a corrective goes far afield.

Choice (B) raises the issue of who finds the action programs realistic. This issue comes from left field. You're looking for a summation of the given argument. (B) introduces a new point, and you really can't say what effect this new point has on the passage. It's certainly not a good conclusion.

Choice (D) is irrelevant—you would never expect a paragraph about whether action TV leads to violence to end with a quick reference to action shows' general popularity.

And it's more likely that the author would disagree with choice (E) than end her discussion with it. In a way her views are a defense of action programming against the charge of aiding and abetting violent crime. Therefore, choice (E)'s call for a ban on action shows is just plain uncalled for. In any case, the idea of

a ban comes from left field, and cannot provide a logical concluding sentence. Once again, it was choice (C) for Question 5.

Questions 6–7: Although the legislative process in our democratic government is based on the proposition that Congress must represent the interests of the majority of its constituents, this principle that the majority rules is frequently contradicted by the efforts of lobbyists. Minority interests with the wherewithal to finance hard-sell lobbying campaigns can distort an elected official's sense of public opinion, thereby exercising a destructive influence over political decisions.

Question 6

The argument above depends upon the truth of which one of the following assumptions?

(A) The democratic process is a reflection of our capitalist economic system.
(B) The democratic process requires that minority interests be protected by Constitutional amendment.
(C) Minority interests cannot be protected without spending large sums of money on lobbying activities.
(D) The democratic process cannot function properly unless the activities of big business are restrained.
(E) The democratic process depends on the ability of all members of society to have equal influence on the legislative process.

Ⓐ Ⓑ Ⓒ Ⓓ Ⓔ

Answer and Explanation

In the stimulus for Questions 6 and 7, the conclusion is expressed in the main clause of the first sentence: lobbyists have a negative effect on the principle of "the majority rules" as practiced in Congress. The reason for that conclusion—the evidence or support—comes in the second sentence: Wealthy minority interests can afford to finance lobbyists, who pressure elected officials. These lobbyists make the officials believe that the opinions of the lobby are held by the people at large. So, the argument goes, some people (namely the rich interest groups) have a greater influence on decision making than do others. And this, it's alleged, thwarts majority rule.

Thinking about a key assumption connecting this evidence to that conclusion—and that's what Question 6 is asking for—you should note that the author jumps from the idea that lobbyists distort Congress's sense of public opinion, to the conclusion that lobbyists undermine the majority-rule concept. And in order to make this leap, the author must be assuming that all members of society have to have equal influence on legislation, in order for majority-rule to work. All the evidence says is that lobbyists distort Congress's sense of public opinion—it doesn't claim that the opinion of the majority is completely silenced. The majority-rule principle (according to this passage) implies that Congress should represent the interests of the majority of its constituents. So, by asserting that the lobbyists muck things up, the author must be taking for granted that all members of society have to be heard from, have to have equal influence, in order for the concept of majority-rule to work. That's what choice (E) is saying and why choice (E) is correct for Question 6.

Of the incorrect choices, (A)'s reference to capitalism takes it way, way beyond the scope of the argument. The only connection between money and the argument's content is a more or less tangential one—the idea that money helps the lobbyists distort Congress's sense of public opinion. Choice (A) blows that out of proportion. Choice (B), meanwhile, is too specific. To say that minority interests have to be protected by Constitutional amendment is to propose a specific solution to a problem floating around the argument, but the author need not be assuming or signing on to that solution as he reasons. Choice (C)

is off the point because the argument is concerned with protecting majority interests—the concept of majority-rule is what's allegedly in danger here. (This could be brought up as an objection to choice (B), as well.) Finally, choice (D) plays off your possible assumption that the minority interests in the passage are big-business fat cats, but as far as the passage goes it may be the case that other minority interests, ones not connected with big business at all, engage in lobbying, too. Once again, choice (E) is correct for Question 6.

Question 7

Which one of the following, if true, would most weaken the argument above?

(A) The majority opinion on many political issues is ill-informed and unconsidered.
(B) Elected officials are rarely influenced by pressures of lobbying campaigns.
(C) Interests groups can accumulate large sums of money through fund-raising activities.
(D) All groups and interests are entitled to hire professional lobbyists to represent their cause.
(E) There is no clear-cut majority position on many political issue facing Congress.

Ⓐ Ⓑ Ⓒ Ⓓ Ⓔ

Answer and Explanation

Now there's another major assumption at work here—it's not among the answer choices for Question 6, but it's the key to Question 7. The author is assuming that Congress, bullied and influenced by the lobbyists, goes about the act of legislating under that influence. He's assuming (in short) that lobbyists' efforts are, by and large, successful. But if, as choice (B) says, it's a rare day when an elected official is at all moved by a lobbying campaign, then the lobbyists are not successful. If (B) is true, if Congress gives these minority interests a deaf ear, then that denies the allegation (in the last sentence) that the lobbyists have destructive influence over decisions. That in turn categorically defuses the author's concerns about the danger to majority-rule. Thus choice (B) is an excellent weakener and the correct answer for Question 7.

Choice (A) is no good because the argument isn't about the quality of the majority opinion; the author is only concerned with whether the majority's opinion is being sufficiently represented, and doesn't care if that opinion is rather ignorant or foolish. Choice (C) supports the argument: If interest groups can (as it says) raise a lot of cash, they can then use the cash for lobbying purposes—the exact sort of situation that has the author all bent out of shape. So (C) lends fuel to the author's flame. As for choice (D), even if groups are entitled to employ lobbyists, it doesn't weaken the author's claim that the effect of lobbyists is dangerous. There are many things all of us are entitled or permitted to do that may not be good for us or for society. Finally, choice (E): there need not be any clear-cut majority position on any one issue in order for the argument to make sense. The point again is that lobbies obscure the majority position such that Congress can't even tell whether it is clear-cut, or even what it is. Even if the majority position were not, as (E) says, one definite position but a mush of many, the author wants Congress to be able to have a clear view that that is the case. Despite choice (E), the lobbyists may still muddy Congress's view, as the author alleges. But if choice (B) is true, then the lobbyists do not muddy the view, and that's why the answer to Question 7 is choice (B).

Question 8

If we reduce the rate of income taxation, people will spend a larger portion of their gross incomes on consumer goods. This will stimulate economic growth and result in higher salaries and thus in higher government revenues, despite a lower rate of taxation.

Which one of the following arguments most closely resembles the reasoning in the statements above?

(A) If we reduce the amount of overtime our employees work, production costs will decline and our total income will thus increase.
(B) If we make it harder to participate in the school lunch program, people will have to pay for more of their food and the farm income will therefore increase.
(C) If a movie is classified as obscene, more people will want to see it and the morals of the general community will be corrupted more than they would be otherwise.
(D) If we give our employees more paid holidays, their efficiency while actually on the job will improve and our total productivity will thus increase.
(E) If we give our children more spending money, they will learn to manage their finances better and will thereby realize the virtue of thrift.

Ⓐ Ⓑ Ⓒ Ⓓ Ⓔ

Answer and Explanation

To look for an argument that "resembles" the stimulus is to find a parallel argument, one whose structure is as close as possible to that of the original. The stimulus says that if you lower taxes, people will buy more things. Doing so will stimulate economic growth, which in turn will raise salaries, which in turn will bring in more money for the government. Of course you're not concerned here with whether this is a sound program or a bogus one, but with how it's put together. And the bottom line is, what you have here is something of a paradox: begin by lowering taxes, which (you'd assume) would lower government revenues, and in the end, government revenues will increase. To abstract it further, it goes like so: engaging in a particular action will (in the end) give you a result that's the opposite of what you might have expected.

And that's what you get in correct choice (D). Though it would be reasonable to expect that more employee days off would reduce productivity (since they'd be spending less time on the job), in fact productivity will be greater, the exact opposite effect, because of the greater efficiency that (D) says will emerge. The chain of events described in the stimulus may be a little longer—it has more steps—than choice (D), but its overall shape is very similar.

Choice (A) presents no paradox at all. You would expect that reducing overtime would bring down costs and increase total income. Naturally it would. The course of action choice (A) outlines is predictable. But what you want in your answer is a surprising result from a course of action.

Choice (B) departs from the stimulus's pattern. The original gives you the government reducing income taxes and getting more money back because of it. (B) has the government changing the rules about the school lunch program and the farmers—a third party—reaping a benefit. This is a bit underhanded, but it's certainly not a paradox; more importantly, the benefit to a third party is not at all what happens in the stimulus.

Choice (C)'s plan certainly carries a bit of irony in its assertion that rating a movie "X" ends up corrupting the morals of the community. But as in choice (B)—and *unlike* correct choice (D)—the agent who performs the first action here (the censor) is not the one who reaps the ultimate benefit or, indeed, is directly affected by the action. Choice (E), meanwhile, may be even less of a paradox than choice (A). It is not at all surprising that a kid given more practice managing money ends up learning the value of thrift. It is surprising that a company's giving employees more days off should make them better workers and bring the business more revenue, and that's why choice (D) is correct for question eight.

Question 9

If a judge is appointed for life, she will make courtroom decisions that reflect the accumulated wisdom inherent in this country's judicial history, relying upon the law and reason rather than upon trends in political thinking. If, on the other hand, the judge is appointed or elected for short terms in office, her decisions will be heavily influenced by the prevailing political climate. In sum, the outcome of many court cases will be determined by the method by which the presiding judge has been installed in her post.

Which one of the following, if true, does not support the argument in the passage above?

(A) Surveys indicate that judges enjoy their work and want to remain in office as long as possible.

(B) Judges appointed for life are just as informed about political matters as are judges who must run for reelection.

(C) The rulings of judges who must run for reelection are generally approved of by the voters who live in their elective districts.

(D) Most judges appointed for life hand down identical rulings on similar cases throughout their long careers.

(E) Only judges who are selected for short terms of office employ pollsters to read the mood of the electorate.

Ⓐ Ⓑ Ⓒ Ⓓ Ⓔ

Answer and Explanation

Four of the five answer choices in Question 9 support the logic, so you'll be looking for a statement that either weakens the logic or has no effect on it. The conclusion is that the way a judge came into his or her job, and thus how much job security he or she has, often determines how a case will come out—that judges decide differently depending on whether they were elected or appointed for life or only for a short term. How so? Short-term judges (it goes on to say) think about their cases in light of which way the political winds are blowing, whereas appointed-for-life judges don't care about political trends and rely solely on a long tradition of judicial theory. In the end, then, the author evidently believes that the wiser judge is the life-term judge.

Since the author provides nothing concrete to back up his claim that short-term judges keep looking back over their shoulders to politics, while life-term judges don't, the answer choices have many opportunities to support the reasoning. Choice (A), for instance, supports the idea that the short-term judges are likely to be moved by the prevailing political climate. If, as (A) says, they really want to keep their jobs, they will be more likely to decide the way the voters want them to decide in order to improve their election chances. Likewise, choice (C) supports that connection between the approval of the voters (which is necessary for re-election, of course) and the voters' view of the judge's decisions, by showing that short-term judges "happen" to rule in a way the voters approve of. And if you jump ahead to choice (E), here you get perhaps the strongest support for the allegation that short-term judges have one eye on the scales of justice and the other on the mood of the voters—according to (E) they're the only judges who use pollsters, whose sole purpose is to track public opinion.

So choices (A), (C), and (E) lend greater credence to the allegations about short-term judges.

Meanwhile, Choice (D) lends support to the other part of the argument—the view of lifelong judges—in its comment that appointed judges show great consistency in their thinking over the years. Choice (D) implies that those judges, as alleged by the author, do turn a blind eye to the vicissitudes of politics and decide based on fundamental, lasting principles.

You're left with choice (B), which may in fact weaken the argument. If (B) is right in its claim that long-term judges keep their ear to the political ground as much as short-term judges do, then that damages the distinction between judges raised in the argument. And when that distinction is hurt, so is the conclusion based on it. Even if long-term judges don't act on their political knowledge, choice (B) is simply irrelevant. You might have seen this directly—you might have picked (B) right from the start. But it was useful to go through this process and demonstrate how you could have answered it by process of elimination. Either way may be helpful for you on a given question on the LSAT. Certainly, either way gets you to choice (B) for Question 9.

Question 10

These so-called pacifists are either the victims or the propagators of a false logic. They claim that weapons reductions would result in a so-called climate of peace, thereby diminishing the likelihood of conflicts leading to war. But what are the facts? In the past ten years, during which time we have seen increased spending for such defense requirements as state-of-the-art weapons systems and augmented combat personnel, there have been fewer military actions involving our forces than in any previous decade in the twentieth century. Our own installations have not been attacked and our allies have rarely found it necessary to ask for our armed support. In other words, defense readiness is, in the real world, the most efficient peace-making tool.

Which of the following is an assumption underlying the conclusion of the passage above?

(A) Military actions involving our forces can be instigated by any of a number of different factors.

(B) Our buildup of weapons systems and combat personnel has prevented our adversaries from increasing their own spending on defense.

(C) The increased defense spending of the past ten years has lessened the need for significant military expenditure in future decades.

(D) At the present time, state-of-the-art weapons systems and the augmentation of combat personnel are equally important to a nation's resources.

(E) The number of military actions involving our forces would have been greater in the past decade if we had not increased our defense spending.

Ⓐ Ⓑ Ⓒ Ⓓ Ⓔ

Answer and Explanation

The author in Question 10 is refuting some "so-called pacifists" (that's his phrase) who, you learn by inference, have been calling for weapons reductions to create a climate of peace. The author, however, believes quite the opposite, that a "climate of peace" has been created by increased military spending on things like new weapons systems and more personnel. How does the author support this claim that a climate of peace exists, and exists because of the greater military spending? He does so by pointing to the number of attacks on this country and its allies. Fewer attacks, it is said, have occurred since military spending began to rise, and thus the author sees a causal connection between the "defense readiness" maintained by greater spending, and the low number of attacks.

Now the assumption underlying this causal connection is your goal in Question 10, and you find it in choice (E). It has to be true that had defense spending not gone up, the number of attacks on this country and its allies would have increased. Otherwise there would be no causal connection between the two phenomena, as the author claims. Remember the assertion is that high defense spending has caused fewer military engagements (and, in turn, a "climate of peace"). That assertion is true only if choice (E) is true, and that's what you need in a major assumption.

Choice (A), in its reference to the possible causes of military actions, is irrelevant. The author doesn't refer to what causes them, but simply asserts that military readiness can prevent them irrespective of the cause. With regard to choice (B), the author doesn't tell you how and why more defense spending has prevented military actions, just that it has done so. The so-called "climate of peace," in the author's view, is based on the greater spending on defense this country has engaged in, and is not necessarily attributable to any trends in defense spending on the part of this country's adversaries (which is choice (B)'s thrust). And the author makes no claim about the future of peace or of military spending, choice (C). The thrust of the argument is toward the past, and what past spending has done to peace in the past. Whether all this readiness can permit future cuts is a matter upon which the author doesn't speculate. Finally, choice (D)'s equation of weapons and personnel is silly, specious, and irrelevant. Both are mentioned as key elements of the current peace climate, and both have benefited from having more money available. But while the author might have an opinion as to which (weapons or personnel) are more valuable, he's keeping it to himself if he does. So you cannot ascribe choice (D)'s view to him. You can be sure he subscribes to choice (E), which makes it the best answer for Question 10.

Question 11

It is possible for a panhandler to collect a considerable amount of money from passersby if she can convince them that she is destitute and that begging is the only way for her to help herself. If, on the other hand, passersby get the impression that they are being conned or that the panhandler is just being lazy, they will not give her anything at all.

Which one of the following statements can be most reliably concluded from the passage above?

(A) Most panhandlers are unwilling to work.
(B) If someone begs when she does not need to, people will not give her any money.
(C) Most passersby would give a panhandler money if they thought that she was not conning them.
(D) Passersby often base their decision of whether or not to give money to a panhandler on their impressions of her and her honesty.
(E) People who give money to panhandlers are not influenced by how much change they have in their pockets when they decide the amount of money they will give.

Ⓐ Ⓑ Ⓒ Ⓓ Ⓔ

Answer and Explanation

In Question 11, you're asked for a conclusion. The stimulus argument basically describes some conditions and factors that influence whether or not, and how much, passersby will give to panhandlers.

There are two conditions here. First, if passersby find a panhandler to be destitute and forced to beg, they may give her quite a bit of money. Second, and on the other hand, if passersby think they are being conned, or that the panhandler is merely lazy, they won't give her anything at all.

So basically the passage is showing you how the perceptions that people have of panhandlers affect their reactions to them. Thus, the most reliable conclusion is choice (D). People decide whether to give to a panhandler based on how they perceive her—as sincere, or lazy and dishonest. It's choice (D) for Question 11.

As soon as you realize that the passage is describing only how people's perceptions influence their reactions, you can eliminate a couple of wrong answers. The passage never tells you whether most panhandlers are lazy or not; it merely speaks of what happens if people perceive them as lazy. Thus, (A) is incorrect.

The same problem exists in (B). You don't know that some beggars can't fool passersby. The stimulus speaks of people's perceptions, not the reality underneath those perceptions.

As for (C), it's a misreading of the first condition. Appearing truly needy is necessary for getting money from passersby; yet it need not be sufficient. Furthermore, (C) speaks of most passersby, which needn't be true at all. Perhaps most people never give money to panhandlers.

And finally, (E) concludes that a completely new factor, the amount of change one has, doesn't influence the decision making of passersby. There are no grounds for concluding this. The stimulus presents some factors in the decision making, but it never says that these are the only factors. So (E) could well be false, and the correct answer for Question 11 remains choice (D).

LOGIC GAMES

Nothing inspires more fear in the hearts of LSAT test takers than Analytical Reasoning—affectionately known as Logic Games. Why? Partly, it's because the skills tested on the section seem so unfamiliar— you need to turn a game's information to your advantage by organizing your thinking and spotting key deductions, and that's not easy to do.

Games tend to give most trouble to students who don't have a clearly defined method of attack. And that's where Kaplan's basic principles, game-specific strategies and techniques, and Five-Step Method for Logic Games will help most, streamlining your work so you can rack up points quickly and confidently.

The following are the major analytical skills that the Logic Games section is intended to measure:

- **Organization**—the ability to efficiently assimilate, both in your head and on the page, the formidable amount of data associated with each game
- **Mental agility**—the ability to keep track of multiple pieces of information simultaneously, and still maintain enough flexibility to shuffle the pieces around in different ways for each question
- **Memory**—the ability to retain the work done in the setup stage while focusing on the new information in each question stem
- **Concentration**—the ability to keep focused on the task at hand and not let your mind wander

Let's now take a look at the major principles that should guide your work on this section.

The Four Basic Principles of Logic Games

The rallying cry of the Logic Games–impaired is: "If only I had more time, I could do these!" Well, this is no consolation on the day of the test, when you simply won't have any extra time. You can spend as much time on a game as you like when you're sitting in your own living room, but when your proctor says, "You have thirty-five minutes . . . begin," he or she is not kidding around. Remember, the test makers aren't testing just to see who can answer the twenty-three to twenty-four LG questions correctly, but also who can do so in thirty-five minutes.

DON'T BE A GAMEOPHOBE!

Many LSAT takers live in fear of the Logic Games section. But Logic Games are definitely manageable —if you take control of the test as we recommend.

Logic Games is perhaps the most speed-sensitive section of the test. The test makers know that if you (not to mention an intelligent ten-year-old) could spend hours methodically trying out every choice in every question, you'd probably get everything right. But what does that prove? Nothing. Who's going to get the sought-after legal position or win the important client—the person who can write the legal brief and prepare the court case in four days, or the person who can do the same job in four hours? It's all about efficiency, both on the test and in your future career.

And that brings us to the first, and somewhat paradoxical-sounding, Logic Games principle:

First Principle: To Go Faster, Slow Down

To gain time in Logic Games, you must spend a lot of time thinking through and analyzing the setup and the rules. This is not only the most important principle for logic games success, it's also the one that's most often ignored, probably because it just doesn't seem right intuitively; people having timing difficulties tend to speed up, not slow down. But by spending a little extra time up front thinking through the stimulus, the "action" of the game, and the rules, you'll be able to recognize the game's key issues and make important deductions that will actually save you time in the long run.

Games are structured so that, in order to answer the questions quickly and correctly, you need to search out relevant pieces of information that combine to form valid new statements, called deductions. Now, you can either do this once, up front, and then utilize the same deductions throughout the game, *or* you can choose to piece together the same basic deductions—essentially repeating the same work—for every single question.

For instance, let's say that two of the rules for a Logic Game go as follows:

If Bob is chosen for the team, then Eric is also chosen.
If Eric is chosen for the team, then Pat will not be chosen.

You can, as you read through the rules of the game, just treat those rules as two separate pieces of independent information. But there's a deduction to be made from them. Do you see it? If Bob is chosen, Eric is, too. If Eric is chosen, Pat is not. That means that, if Bob is chosen, Pat is not chosen. That's an important deduction—one that will undoubtedly be required from question to question. If you don't take the time to make it up front, when you're first considering the game, you'll have to make it over and

TAKE TIME TO MAKE TIME

We know it sounds paradoxical, but you really do save time in the long run by taking the time to think about a logic game's scenario before jumping into its questions.

over again, every time it's necessary to answer a question. But if you *do* take the time to make this deduction up front, and build it into your entire conception of the game, you'll save that time later. You won't be doing the same work several times.

The choice is yours; we just find that the rush-to-the-questions method is inefficient, time-consuming, and stress-inducing.

So, always try to take the game scenario and the rules as far as you can before moving on to the questions. Look for common elements among the rules (like Eric in the rules above)—this will help you combine them and pull out major deductions. The stimulus creates a situation, and the rules place restrictions on what can and cannot happen within that situation. If you investigate the possible scenarios, and look for and find major deductions up front, you'll then be able to rack up points quickly and confidently.

Second Principle: Understand What a Rule Means, Not Just What It Says

If you're interested in demonstrating how well you can read a statement and then spit it back verbatim, you'd be better off training to be a legal secretary instead of a legal practitioner or scholar. That's why you'll never see this on the LSAT:

> RULE: Arlene is not fifth in line.
> QUESTION: Which one of the following people is not fifth in line?
> ANSWER: Arlene.

True, some LG questions are easy—but not that easy. The LSAT, after all, measures critical thinking, and virtually every sentence in Logic Games has to be filtered through some sort of analytical process before it will be of any use. You may have to use the information about Arlene to help you eliminate a choice or lead you to the right answer, but even in the simplest of cases, this will involve the application, as opposed to the mere parroting, of the rule.

So, getting back to the principle, it's not enough just to copy a rule off the page (or shorthand it, as we'll discuss momentarily); it's imperative that you think through its exact meaning, including any implications it might have. And don't limit this behavior to the indented rules; statements in the games' introductions are very often rules in and of themselves, and warrant the same meticulous consideration.

NO PARROTS, PLEASE

To fully grasp a rule in Logic Games, you must know more than just what it says. You've got to know what the rule means in the context of the game and in combination with other rules.

ACCENTUATE THE POSITIVE

Always try to turn negative rules—"Box 2 does not contain any gumdrops"—into a positive statement—"Box 2 must contain chocolates and mints."

GAME WISDOM

You must know the rules of a Logic Game cold—what they mean, how they impact on other rules, and what implications they have in the context of the game scenario.

For instance, let's say a game's introduction sets up a scenario in which you have three boxes, each containing at least two of the following three types of candy—chocolates, gumdrops, and mints. Then you get the following rule:

Box 2 does not contain any gumdrops.

What does that rule say? That there aren't any gumdrops in Box 2. But what does that rule *mean*, when you think about it in the context of the game? That Box 2 *does* contain chocolates and mints. Each box contains at least two of three things, remember. Once you eliminate one of the three things for any particular box, therefore, you know that the other two things *must* be in that box.

Part of understanding what a rule means, moreover, is grasping what the rule *doesn't* mean. For example, take the rule we mentioned earlier:

RULE: If Bob is chosen for the team, then Eric is also chosen.
MEANS: Whenever Bob is chosen, Eric is, too.
DOESN'T MEAN: Whenever Eric is chosen, Bob is, too.

Remember the discussion of formal logic in the Logical Reasoning chapter? If I yell loudly at my cat Adrian, he will run away. That does mean that whenever I yell at him loudly, he runs away. But it *doesn't* mean that whenever he runs away, I've yelled at him.

Third Principle: Use Scratchwork and Shorthand

The proper use of scratchwork can help you do your best on Logic Games. As you may recall, the directions state: "You may wish to draw a rough sketch to help answer some of the questions." Notice that they use the wording *rough sketch*, not *masterpiece*, *work of art*, or *classic picture for the ages*. The LSAT is not a drawing contest; you get no points for creating beautiful diagrams on the page.

However, although some games aren't amenable to scratchwork, for most games you'll find that it is helpful to create a master sketch, one that encapsulates all of the game's information in one easy-to-reference picture. Doing so will not only give your eye a place to gravitate toward when you need information, but it will also help to solidify in your mind the action of the game, the rules, and whatever deductions you come up with up front.

Remember to keep your scratchwork simple—the less time you spend drawing, the more time you'll have for thinking and answering questions.

Pay careful attention to the scratchwork suggestions in the explanations to the four games on the Practice Test in the back of this book.

Part of your scratchwork should involve jotting down on your page a quick and shortened form of most rules. Shorthand is a visual representation of a mental thought process, and is useful only if it reminds you at a glance of the rule's meaning. Whether you shorthand a rule or commit it to memory, you should never have to look back at the game itself once you get to the questions.

The goal of the entire scratchwork process is to condense a lot of information into manageable, user-friendly visual cues. It's much easier to remember rules written like so:

B → E
No G in 2

than ones written like so:

If Bob is chosen for the team, then Eric is also chosen.
Box 2 does not contain any gumdrops.

This is helpful as long as you know, for instance, what the arrow from B to E means, and you're consistent in using it. If you can develop a personal shorthand that's instantly understandable to you, you'll have a decided advantage on the day of the test.

Fourth Principle: Try to Set off Chains of Deduction

When hypothetical information is offered in a question stem, try to use it to set off a chain of deductions. Consider the following question. (Since this question is excerpted without the accompanying introduction and rules, ignore the specific logic of the discussion; it's just presented to make a point.)

If the speedboat is yellow, which one of the following must be true?

(A) The car is green.
(B) The airplane is red.
(C) The train is black.
(D) The car is yellow.
(E) The train is red.

The question stem contains a *hypothetical*, which is an if-clause offering information pertaining only to that particular question. The wrong approach is to acknowledge that the speedboat is yellow, and then proceed to test out all of the choices. The muddled mental thought process accompanying this tragic approach might sound something like this:

> "All right, the speedboat's yellow, does the car have to be green? Well, let's see, if the speedboat's yellow, and the car is green, then the train would have to be yellow, but I can't tell what color the airplane is, and I guess this is okay, I don't know, I better try the next choice. Let's see what happens if the speedboat's yellow and the airplane is red. . . ."

Don't do this kind of dithering! Notice that the question doesn't ask: "What happens if, in addition to this, the car is green?" or "What happens if this is true and the airplane is red?" So why is the confused test taker above intent on answering all of these irrelevant questions? Never begin a question by trying out answer choices; that's going about it backwards. Only if you're entirely stuck, or are faced with a question stem that leaves you no choice, should you resort to trial and error.

Most Logic Games questions are amenable to a more efficient and systematic methodology. The correct approach is to incorporate the new piece of information into your view of the game, creating one quick sketch if you wish. How do you do this? Simple—apply the rules and any previous deductions to the new information in order to set off a new chain of deductions. Then follow through until you've taken the new information as far as it can go. Just as you must take the game and rules as far as you can before moving on to the questions, you must carry the information in a question stem out as far as you can before moving on to the choices.

So make sure to stay out of answer-choice land until you have sufficiently mined the hypothetical. If the question-stem contains a hypothetical, then your job is to get as much out of that piece of information as you can before even looking at the choices. This way, *you* dictate to the test, and not the other way around. You'll then be able to determine the answer and simply pick it off the page.

You'll have a chance to see these major Logic Games principles in action when you review the explanations to the four games in the Practice Test in the back of this book.

A LAST RESORT

Trial and error with the answer choices should be your last resort, not your first. It's much quicker to follow a chain of deduction until it leads you to the answer. In some cases, trial and error is necessary, but don't turn to it unless you have to.

The Three Crucial LG Skills

Although the Logic Games section can contain a wide variety of situations and scenarios, certain skills are required again and again. These are the most common:

Sequencing

Logic Games that require sequencing skills have long been a favorite of the test makers. No matter what the scenario in games of this type, the common denominator is that in some way, shape, or form, they all involve putting entities in order. In a typical sequencing game, you may be asked to arrange the cast of characters numerically from left to right, from top to bottom, in days of the week, in a circle, and so on. The sequence may be a sequence of degree—say, ranking the eight smartest test takers from one to eight. On the other hand, the sequence may be based on time, such as one that involves the order of shows broadcast on a radio station. In some cases, there are two or even three orderings to keep track of in a single game.

Fixed and Unfixed Sequences

There are generally two types of sequence games: the fixed, or standard sequence, and the unfixed, or "free floating" sequence. In a fixed sequence game, the placement of entities is very strictly defined. We may be told, for example, that "A is third," or that "X and Y are adjacent," and so on. These are definite, concrete pieces of information, and the game centers around placing as many people into definite spots as possible. In contrast to this, in an unfixed or "free floating" sequence game, our job is to rank the entities only in relation to one another. We're usually never asked to fully determine the ordering of the cast of characters. Instead, the relationships *between* the entities constitute the crux of the game.

Typical Issues

The following is a list of the key issues that underlie sequencing games. Each key issue is followed by a corresponding rule—in some cases, with several alternative ways of expressing the same rule. At the end, we'll use these rules to build a miniature Logic Game, so that you can see how rules work together to define and limit a game's "action." These rules all refer to a scenario in which eight events are to be sequenced from first to eighth:

- Which entities are concretely placed in the ordering?

    X is third.

- Which entities are forbidden from a specific position in the ordering?

    Y is not fourth.

- Which entities are next to, adjacent to, or are immediately preceding or following one another?

    X and Y are consecutive.
    X is next to Y.
    No event comes between X and Y.
    X and Y are consecutive in the ordering.

- Which entities *cannot be* next to, adjacent to, or immediately preceding or following one another?

    X does not immediately precede or follow Z.
    X is not immediately before or after Z.
    At least one event comes between X and Z.
    X and Z are not consecutive in the sequence.

- How far apart in the ordering are two particular entities?

    Exactly two events come between X and Q.

- What is the relative position of two entities in the ordering?

    Q comes before T in the sequence.
    T comes after Q in the sequence.

How a Sequence Game Works
Let's see how rules like those above might combine to create a simple Logic Game.

    Eight events—Q, R, S, T, W, X, Y, and Z—are being ordered from first to eighth.

X is third.
Y is not fourth.
X and Y are consecutive.
Exactly two events come between X and Q.
Q occurs before T in the sequence.

How would you approach this simplified game? Remember our third basic principle: use scratchwork and shorthand. With eight events to sequence from first to eighth, you'd probably want to draw eight dashes in the margin of your test booklet, maybe in two groups of four (so you can easily determine which dash is which). Then take the rules in order of concreteness, starting with the most concrete of all—Rule 1—which tells you that X is third. Fill that into your sketch:

$$\underline{}\ \underline{}\ \underline{X}\ \underline{}\quad \underline{}\ \underline{}\ \underline{}\ \underline{}$$

Jump to the next most concrete rule, Rule 4, which tells you that exactly two events come between X and Q. Well, since Q can't obey this rule coming before X, it must come after X—in the sixth space.

$$\underline{}\ \underline{}\ \underline{X}\ \underline{}\quad \underline{}\ \underline{Q}\ \underline{}\ \underline{}$$

Rule 5 says that Q comes before T. Since Q is sixth, T must be either seventh or eighth. To indicate this, under the sketch, write T with two arrows pointing to the seventh and eighth dashes.

Meanwhile, Rule 3 says that X and Y are consecutive. X is third, so Y will be either second or fourth. Rule 2 clears up that matter. Y can't be fourth, says Rule 2, so it will have to be second:

$$\underline{}\ \underline{Y}\ \underline{X}\ \underline{}\quad \underline{}\ \underline{Q}\ \underline{}\ \underline{}$$
$$\nwarrow T \nearrow$$

And this is how the rules work together to build a sequence game. The questions might then present hypothetical information that would set off the "chain of deduction" we mentioned in the basic principles section. You'll see how this works on the two sequencing games on the Practice Test—Games 2 and 4. Those are full-strength sequencing games, so make sure to pay careful attention to the written explanations.

GROUPING AT A GLANCE

- It's a very popular game type.
- It comes in two varieties—selection and distribution.
- The number element is often crucial (how many chosen, how many in each group, etcetera).
- Its action involves deciding if each entity is in or out; if it is in, you may then need to determine where (in distribution games).

Grouping

All games begin with a set of entities. What sets grouping apart is the "action" of the game, or specifically, what you're asked to do with the entities. In a pure grouping game, unlike sequencing, there's no call for putting the entities in order. Instead, you'll usually be required to "select" a smaller group from the initial group, or "distribute" the entities in some fashion into more than one subgroup. As a distinct skill, grouping differs from sequencing in that you're not really concerned with what order the entities are in, but rather how they're grouped—who's in, who's out, and who can and cannot be with whom in various subgroups.

Grouping Games of Selection and Distribution

In "selection" games, you'll be given the cast of characters and told to select from them a smaller group, based, of course, on a set of rules. For example, a game may include eight musical cassettes, from which you must choose four. Sometimes the test makers specify an exact number for the smaller group, and other times they don't. A small variation of this type occurs when the initial group of entities is itself broken up in groups to begin the game. An example would be a farmer choosing three animals from a group of three cows and five horses.

In "distribution" games, we're more concerned with who goes where than we are with who's chosen and who isn't—who's in and who's out, in other words. Sometimes, every entity will end up in a group—an example is placing or distributing eight marbles into two jars, four to a jar. On the other hand, it's perfectly viable for a game to mandate the placement of three marbles in each jar, leaving two marbles out in the cold.

It's important for you to be aware of the numbers that govern each particular grouping game, because although all grouping games rely on the same general skills, you have to adapt these skills to the specific situations of each. Still, all grouping games revolve around the same basic questions. Is this entity in? Is it out? If it's not in this group, is it in that one?

Like sequencing games, grouping games have a language all their own, and it's up to you to speak that language fluently when you come across games that require this particular skill on your test.

Typical Issues—Grouping Games of Selection

The following is a list of the key issues that underlie grouping games of selection. Each key issue is followed by a corresponding rule—in some cases, with several alternative ways of expressing the same rule. At the end, again, we'll use these rules to build a miniature Logic Game.

These rules all refer to a scenario in which you are to select a subgroup of four from a group of eight entities—Q, R, S, T, W, X, Y, and Z:

- Which entities are definitely chosen?

   Q is selected.

- Which entities rely on a different entity's selection in order to be chosen?

   If X is selected, then Y is selected.
   X will be selected only if Y is selected.
   X will not be selected unless Y is selected.

Note: A common misconception surrounds the rule, "If X is selected, then Y is selected." This works only in one direction; if X is chosen, Y must be, but if Y is chosen, X may or may not be. Remember the discussion of the second principle above—understand what a rule means, but also what it doesn't mean!

- Which entities must be chosen together, or not at all?

   If Y is selected, then Z is selected, and and if Z is selected, then Y is selected.
   Y will not be selected unless Z is selected, and vice versa.

- Which entities cannot both be chosen?

   If R is selected, then Z is not selected.
   If Z is selected, then R is not selected.
   R and Z won't both be selected.

How Grouping Games of Selection Work
We can combine these rules to create a rudimentary grouping game of selection:

   A professor must choose a group of four books for her next seminar. She must choose from a pool of eight books—Q, R, S, T, W, X, Y, and Z.

Q is selected.
If X is selected then Y is selected.
If Y is selected, Z is selected, and if Z is selected, then Y is selected.
If R is selected, Z is not selected.

One good way of dealing with this kind of game is to write out the eight letters—four on top, four on the bottom—and then circle the ones that are definitely selected while crossing out the ones that are definitely not selected. Thus, Rule 1 would allow you to circle the Q:

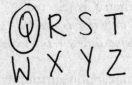

The other rules can't be built into the sketch just yet, since they describe eventualities (what happens if something else happens). Here's where you'd want to use shorthand:

- Rule 2 translates as, "If X, then Y" or "X ——> Y"
- Rule 3 might be rendered as, "YZ together" (as a reminder to choose them together, if at all).
- Rule 4 could be shorthanded as, "Never RZ" (since R and Z are mutually exclusive).

The rules would then be poised to take effect whenever a question would add new hypothetical information, setting off a chain of deduction. For instance, let's say a question reads like so:

If R is selected, which of the following must be true?

This new information would put the rules into motion. R's inclusion would set off Rule 4—"Never RZ"—so we'd have to circle R and cross out Z:

This would in turn set off Rule 3—"YZ together." Since Z is out, Y is out, because they must be chosen together or not at all:

Now Rule 2 comes into play. "X ——> Y" means that if Y is not chosen, X can't be either (since X's inclusion would require Y's). So we can take the chain of deduction one step further:

A correct answer to this question, then, might be "X is not selected." And that, in a nutshell, is how a (simplified) grouping game of selection works.

Typical Issues—Grouping Games of Distribution
Here are the issues involved in the other kind of grouping game—grouping games of distribution—along with the rules that govern them. These rules, by the way, refer to a scenario in which the members of our old favorite group of eight entities—Q, R, S, T, W, X, Y, Z—have to be distributed into three different classes:

- Which entities are concretely placed in a particular subgroup?

    X is placed in Class 3.

- Which entities are barred from a particular subgroup?

    Y is not placed in Class 2.

- Which entities must be placed in the same subgroup?

  X is placed in the same class as Z.
  Z is placed in the same class as X.
  X and Z are placed in the same class.

- Which entities cannot be placed in the same subgroup?

  X is not placed in the same class as Y.
  Y is not placed in the same class as X.
  X and Y are not placed in the same class.

- Which entity's placement depends on the placement of a different entity?

  If Y is placed in Class 1, then Q is placed in Class 2.

How Grouping Games of Distribution Work
The above rules, neatly enough, also can combine to form a miniature grouping game of distribution.

Eight students—Q, R, S, T, W, X, Y, and Z—must be subdivided into three different classes—Classes 1, 2, and 3.
  X is placed in Class 3.
  Y is not placed in Class 2.
  X is placed in the same class as Z.
  X is not placed in the same class as Y.
  If Y is placed in Class 1, then Q is placed in Class 2.

A good scratchwork scheme for games of this type would be to draw three circles in your booklet, one for each of the three classes. Then put the eight entities in the appropriate circles as that information becomes known.

Here again, start with the most concrete rule first, which is Rule 1, which definitively places X in Class 3. Rule 2 just as definitively precludes Y from Class 2, so build that into the scratchwork, too:

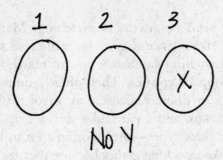

Rule 3 requires Z to join X in Class 3:

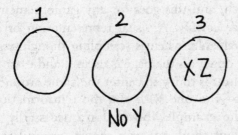

Rule 4, prohibiting Y from being in the same class as X, means that Y can't be in Class 3. But we already know that Y can't be in Class 2. We can deduce, therefore, that Y must go in Class 1. That in turn puts Rule 5 into play: if Y is in Class 1 (as it is here), Q is in Class 2:

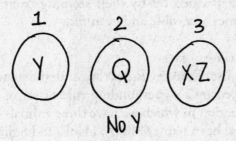

And that is the dynamic of most grouping games of distribution (though, again, in much simplified form). For a real, LSAT-strength distribution game, check out the first game on the Practice Test in the back of this book.

Matching

The third skill we need to discuss is matching. Matching games have haunted LSAT test takers since they came into favor some years ago. As the name implies, matching games ask you to match up various characteristics about a group of entities. They often require you to distribute many characteristics at once. A game may involve three animals, each assigned a name, a color, and a particular size. It's no wonder test takers get bogged down in these types—there's often a lot to keep track of.

Some people dislike matching games because they feel as if they're being bombarded with information, and they don't know where to start. Organization, as in any game, is crucial for matching games. A table or grid can be helpful, but for some games you need to rely on your instincts to organize the information efficiently based on the particulars of the game. If you do use a sketch, and this goes for any game, remember that *thinking must always precede writing*. A visual representation of a mental thought process can be invaluable, whereas scribbling thoughtlessly for the sake of getting something down on the page is useless, and even detrimental.

One matching hint is to try to center the game around the most important characteristic—the one with the most information attached to it. Going back to the example above, don't necessarily assume that you should organize your thinking, or a sketch, around the animals—there may be a better attribute, one that you know more about, that should take center stage. An efficient test taker spends less time panicking and being intimidated by all of the information in a matching game, and more time visualizing the action and creating a mental picture or a sketch on the page that places the elements into a logical order. If you think through the scenarios and don't get scared off by their seeming complexity, you should find matching games accessible and even fun.

Typical Matching Game Issues
The following is a list of the key issues that underlie matching games. Each key issue is followed by a corresponding rule or set of rules. All of these rules refer to a situation in which we have three animals—a dog, a cat, and a goat. Each animal has a name (Bimpy, Hank, and Sujin), a color (brown, black, or white), and a size (large or small):

- Which entities are matched up?

    The dog is brown.
    The black animal is small.

- Which entities are not matched up?

    Bimpy is not white.
    The goat is not large.

- Which entity's matchups depend on the matchups of other entities?

    If the cat is large, then Hank is brown.
    If the white animal is small, then Sujin is not the dog.

Notice that these last rules take the form of if/then statements, which, based on our discussion of Logical Reasoning in the previous chapter, means that the contrapositive can be employed. Whenever rules take this form, you should always work out the contrapositive and then add the result, as a valid deduction, to your view of the game. Remember, the contrapositive can be formed by reversing and negating the terms of an if/then statement. For the first, we get:

    If Hank is NOT brown, then the cat is NOT large.

Taking the contrapositive of the second rule results in this statement:

    If Sujin IS the dog, then the white animal is NOT small.

Both of these new pieces of information are just as powerful as any of the indented rules given in the game's introduction.

How Matching Games Work
You know the drill by now. Let's take some of the rules above and form them into a minilogic game:

    A rancher owns three animals—a dog, a cat, and a goat. The animals are named Bimpy, Hank, and Sujin, though not necessarily in that order. One of the animals is brown, one is black, and one is white. Two of the animals are large and one is small.

        The dog is brown.
        The black animal is small.
        Bimpy is not white.
        The goat is not large.
        If the cat is large, then Hank is brown.

THE CONTRAPOSITIVE REDUX

Use the contrapositive on all if/then rules in Logic Games. It will almost always yield an important deduction.

IT'S LIKE MATH

Like math questions, Logic Games questions have definite right and wrong answers. Once you find the answer that works, pick it and move on. There's no need to check out the other choices.

A good way to approach this game would be to set up a grid or chart to keep track of all of the attributes to be matched up:

(animal)	Dog	Cat	Goat
(name)			
BHS			
(size)			
LLS			
(color)			
br bl wh			

Notice that Rules 1 and 4—the most concrete rules—can be built into the sketch immediately.

(animal)	Dog	Cat	Goat
(name)			
BHS			
(size)			
LLS			not L
(color)			
br̶ bl wh	br		

But remember, think about what Rule 4 means, not just what it says. There are only two sizes here—small and large. If the goat is not large, it must be small, and since there are two large and only one small animal, we can deduce the size of the other two as well:

(animal)	Dog	Cat	Goat
(name) BHS			
(size) ~~LLS~~	L	L	S not L
(color) ~~br~~ bl wh			

Once we know that the cat is large, moreover, Rule 5 kicks in, telling us that Hank is brown. And since we've already deduced that the brown animal is the large dog, we know that Hank is the large brown dog.

And that's how a simple matching game works. The third game of the Logic Games section on the Practice Test is a typical matching game for you to work on. Pay careful attention to the way in which it's set up, as outlined in the written explanations.

More Logic Game Tips

Here are some other points to keep in mind on the LG section:

Hybrid Games

Many games are what you might call "hybrid games," requiring you to combine sequencing, grouping, and/or matching skills (we'll have a look at one later on when we talk about the five-step method). Keep in mind that while we try to recognize games as a particular type, it's not necessary to attach a strict name to every game you encounter. For example, it really doesn't matter if you categorize a game as a sequencing game with a grouping element or as a grouping game with a sequencing element, as long as you're comfortable with both sets of skills.

LOOK FOR THE COMMON ELEMENT

Rules that deal with one or more of the same entities can often be combined to make important deductions.

No "Best" Choice

Unlike the answer choices in Logical Reasoning and Reading Comprehension, in which the correct answer is the "best" choice, the answers in Logic Games are objectively correct or incorrect. Therefore, when you find an answer that's definitely right, have the confidence to circle it and move on, without wasting time to check the other choices. This is one way to improve your timing on the section.

Common Elements and Deductions

Rules that contain common elements are often the ones that lead to deductions. Consider the following three rules:

> If Sybil goes to the party, then Edna will go to the party.
> If Jacqui goes to the party, then Sherry will not go to the party.
> If Edna goes to the party, then Dale will go to the party.

Rules 1 and 2 have no entities in common, which is a sure sign that we can't deduce anything from combining them. The same goes for Rules 2 and 3. But since Rules 1 and 3 have Edna in common, a deduction is possible (although not guaranteed). In this case, combining Rules 1 and 3 would allow us to deduce another rule: if Sybil goes to the party, then Dale will go also.

Focus on the Important Rules

Not all rules are equal—some are inherently more important than others. Try to focus first on the concrete ones and the ones that have the greatest impact on the situation, specifically the ones that involve the greatest number of the entities. These are also the rules to turn to first whenever you're stuck on a question and don't know how to set off the chain of deduction.

Know the Forms of Question Stems

You must have a solid command of the various forms of Logic Games question stems. When you take a few seconds to think through what kind of statements would be the right and wrong answers to a particular question, your work becomes more time efficient. You're also less likely to slip up at the last minute and pick the wrong thing. The following should clear up any misconceptions you may have regarding what the choices should look like for each of the major types of questions:

- If the question reads: Which one of the following statements *could be true?*—the right answer will be a statement that could be true, and the four wrong choices will be statements that definitely cannot be true (that is, statements that must be false).

- If the question reads: Which one of the following statements *cannot be true?*—the right answer will be a statement that cannot be true, and the four wrong choices will be statements that either must be true or merely could be true.

- If the question reads: Which one of the following statements *must be true?*—the right answer will be a statement that must be true, and the four wrong choices will be statements that either cannot be true or merely could be true.

- If the question reads: All of the following statements *could be true EXCEPT . . . ,* the right answer will be a statement that cannot be true, and the four wrong choices will be statements that either could be true or even must be true.

- If the question reads: All of the following statements *must be true EXCEPT . . . ,* the right answer will be a statement that either cannot be true, or merely could be true, and the four wrong choices will be statements that must be true.

- If the question reads: Which one of the following statements *could be false?*—the right answer will be a statement that cannot be true or could be true or false, and the four wrong choices will be statements that must be true.

- If the question reads: Which one of the following statements *must be false?*—the right answer will be a statement that cannot be true, and the four wrong choices will be statements that either must be true or merely could be true.

IS NOTHING CLICKING?

If you find you can't make a single important deduction by combining rules, you're probably missing something. Check the game introduction and rules again to make sure you're not misinterpreting something.

The Kaplan Five-Step Method for Logic Games

Now that you have some Logic Games background, it's time to see how you can marshall that knowledge into a systematic approach to games. The five steps of the Kaplan Method are as follows.

1. Get an Overview
Read carefully the game's introduction and rules to establish the "cast of characters," the "action," and the number limits governing the game.

2. Visualize and Map out the Game
Make a mental picture of the situation, and let it guide you as you create a sketch, or some other kind of scratchwork, if need be to help you keep track of the rules and handle new information.

3. Consider the Rules Individually
As you think through the meaning and implications of each rule, you have three choices. You can:

- Build it directly into your sketch of the game situation
- Jot down the rule in shorthand form to help you remember it
- Underline or circle rules that don't lend themselves to the first two techniques

4. Combine the Rules
Look for common elements among the rules; that's what will lead you to make deductions. Treat these deductions as additional rules, good for the whole game.

5. Work on the Questions Systematically
Read the question stems carefully! Take special notice of words such as *must, could, cannot, not, impossible,* and *except.* As always, use the hypothetical information offered in *if*-clauses to set off a chain of deduction.

THE KAPLAN FIVE-STEP METHOD FOR LOGIC GAMES

1. Get an overview.
2. Visualize and map out the game.
3. Consider the rules individually.
4. Combine the rules.
5. Work on the question systematically.

Using the Kaplan Five-Step Method for Logic Games

Here's how the approach can work with an actual Logic Game:

Questions 1–2

Five workers—Mona, Patrick, Renatta, Saffie, and Will—are scheduled to clean apartments on five days of a single week, Monday to Friday. There are three cleaning shifts available each day—a morning shift, an afternoon shift, and an evening shift. No more than one worker cleans in any given shift. Each worker cleans exactly two shifts during the week, but no one works more than one cleaning shift in a single day.

Exactly two workers clean on each day of the week.
Mona and Will clean on the same days of the week.
Patrick doesn't clean on any afternoon or evening shifts during the week.
Will doesn't clean on any morning or afternoon shifts during the week.
Mona cleans on two consecutive days of the week.
Saffie's second cleaning shift of the week occurs on an earlier day of the week than Mona's first cleaning shift.

1. Which one of the following must be true?

    (A) Saffie cleans on Tuesday afternoon.
    (B) Patrick cleans on Monday morning.
    (C) Will cleans on Thursday evening.
    (D) Renatta cleans on Friday afternoon.
    (E) Mona cleans on Tuesday morning.

2. If Will does not clean on Friday, which one of the following could be false?

    (A) Renatta cleans on Friday.
    (B) Saffie cleans on Tuesday.
    (C) Mona cleans on Wednesday.
    (D) Saffie cleans on Monday.
    (E) Patrick cleans on Tuesday.

(Note that there are only two questions accompanying this game; a typical logic game will have five to seven questions.)

1. Get an Overview

We need to schedule five workers, abbreviated M, P, R, S, and W, in a particular order during a five-day calendar week, Monday to Friday. The ordering element tells us we're dealing with a sequencing task, though there is a slight grouping element involved in that a couple of the rules deal with grouping issues—namely, which people can or cannot clean on the same day of the week as each other. That makes this a "hybrid" game—but remember, it doesn't matter what you call it, as long as you can do it.

Be very careful about the numbers governing this game; they go a long way in defining how the game works. There are to be exactly two workers per day (never cleaning on the same shift). Each worker must clean exactly two shifts, and since workers are forbidden to take two shifts in the same day, this means that each worker will clean on exactly two days. So, in effect, ten out of the fifteen available shifts will be taken, and five will be left untouched.

2. Visualize and Map out the Game

Go with whatever you feel is the most efficient way to keep track of the situation. Most people would settle on a sketch of the five days, each broken up into three shifts, like so:

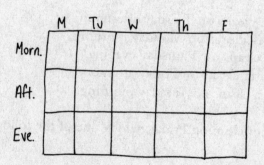

Into this sketch—one letter per box—each entity will have to go twice (each worker does two shifts, remember). So your pool of entities to place would be: MMPPRRSSWW. You might want to include five Xs (or Øs) for the five shifts that won't be taken by anyone.

3. Consider the Rules Individually

We've already dealt with some of the number-related rules hidden in the game's introduction. Now let's consider this statement from the intro:

> No more than one worker cleans in any given shift.

Make sure you interpret rules like this correctly. You may have to paraphrase, in your own words, its exact meaning. In this case: two workers per shift is no good, three is out of the question, etcetera. But it doesn't mean that any given shift *must* have a worker. If the test makers meant to imply that, they would have written, "Exactly one worker cleans on every given shift." Notice the difference in wording. It's subtle, but it has a huge impact on the game.

Let's consider the other rules:

1) We've already handled Rule 1. You may wish to jot down "2 a day," or something like that, to remind you of this important information.

2) Mona and Will clean on the same days, and that holds for both of the days they clean. Shorthand this any way that seems fitting (one suggestion is to draw MW with a circle around it on your page).

3) and 4) We can handle these two rules together because they're so similar. You can shorthand these rules as they are, but you'd be doing yourself a great disservice. Instead, first work out their implications, which is actually a pretty simple matter. If Patrick doesn't clean afternoons or evenings, he *must* clean mornings. If Will doesn't clean mornings or afternoons, he *must* clean evenings. Always take the rules as far as you can, and *then* jot down their implications on your page for reference.

5) This one is pretty self-explanatory; Mona's shifts must be on consecutive days, such as Thursday and Friday. MM might be a good way to shorthand this.

6) Here's another sequencing rule—you must place both Ss for Saffie on earlier days of the week than the two Ms, for Mona. That means that Saffie and Mona can't clean on the same day (although we already knew that from Rule 2), and that Mona's shifts can't come before Saffie's. Try shorthanding this as (S...S...MM).

4. Combine the Rules

This is the crucial stage for most games. Here, notice that Mona appears in three of the six indented rules; that's a good indication that combining these rules should lead somewhere useful. Combining Rule 2 and Rule 5 gives us two Mona/Will days in a row:

Will must be scheduled for evening shifts (remember, we turned Rule 4 into this positive statement). That means that Mona would take the morning or afternoon shift on these consecutive days.

Rule 6 concerns Mona as well: two Saffies before the two Monas. How is this possible? We need two Ss on different days to come before the two consecutive Ms. If Saffie's cleaning shifts are as early in the week as possible, she'll clean on Monday and Tuesday. That means that the earliest day that Mona can clean (and Will as well, thanks to Rule 2) is Wednesday. There's our first really key deduction:

> Mona and Will cannot clean on Monday and Tuesday; they must clean Wednesday, Thursday, or Friday.

Do we stop there? No, of course not. The difference between the Logic Games expert and the Logic Games novice is that the expert knows how to press on when further deductive possibilities exist. If you relate this deduction back to Rule 5, it becomes clear that Mona and Will must clean on Wednesday and Thursday, *or* on Thursday and Friday. This brings us to another big deduction:

> Either way, Mona and Will must clean on Thursday. Thanks to Rule 4, we can slot Will in for Thursday evening. Mona will then take Thursday morning *or* afternoon. The other Mona/Will day must be either Wednesday or Friday, to remain consecutive.

The following sketch shows what your completed sketch may look like, with as many of the rules built into it as possible.

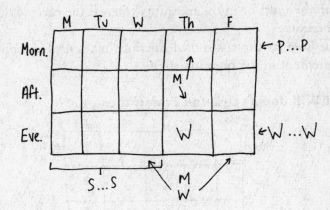

Now that we've combined the rules and have even uncovered a few big deductions, it's time to move on to the questions.

5. Work on the Questions Systematically

Now you'll see how all the work we did up front pays off. Question 1 offers no hypothetical information; it simply asks what must be true. And since we've already deduced a few things that must be true, we can scan the choices for one that matches any one of our newly discovered pieces of information. It doesn't take long to spot choice (C)—it's our big deduction staring us right in the face. You shouldn't even waste time checking the other choices. Instead, have the confidence that you've done the right work the right way, and circle (C) and move on. [Just for the record, for those of you who are curious, (A), (B), and (D) could be true, but need not be, while (E), as we discovered earlier, is an impossibility.]

Question 2 contains a hypothetical: no Will on Friday. One glance at our sketch tells us that the second Mona/Will cluster must therefore be placed on Wednesday, next to the Thursday Mona/Will group. Saffie must then clean on Monday and Tuesday, in order to satisfy Rule 6 (although we don't yet know the exact shifts she takes during those days).

That brings us to the two questions that test takers ask all too infrequently: "Who's left?" and more importantly, "Where can they go?" Two Ps and two Rs are left to place, with one spot on Monday, one spot on Tuesday, and two spots on Friday open to place them. How can this be done? Friday can't get both Ps or both Rs (from the last sentence in the introduction), so it will have to get one of each, with P in the morning and R in either the afternoon or evening. The other P and the other R will join S on Monday or Tuesday, in either order. Of course, whichever day P is on, he must be in the morning, whereas the exact shifts for R and S are ambiguous.

Look at how far the chain of deductions takes us, beginning with the simple statement in the question stem:

If Will doesn't clean on Friday, then . . .

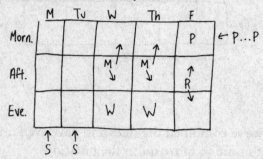

With all of this information at our disposal, there's not a question in the world we can't answer correctly. This one asks for a statement that could be false—which means that the four wrong choices will all be things that must be true. And in fact, choices (A) through (D) match the situation in this question perfectly, while (E) merely could be true: Patrick's first cleaning shift of the week *could be* on Tuesday, but it just as easily *could be* on Monday as well. (His second shift must be on Friday, of course.) (E) is therefore the only choice that could be false.

Conclusion

This concludes our general discussion of the Logic Games section. Try to use the Five-Step Method, and all of the techniques mentioned in this chapter, when you work through the following set of practice questions and the four games on the Practice Test. Game 2 in the Practice Test is a type of calendar hybrid similar to the one above, so you should have a head start on that one.

Logic Games Practice Set

Directions: Each group of questions is based on a passage or a set of conditions. You may wish to draw a diagram to answer some of the questions. Choose the best answer for each question. (The answer and explanation can be found at the end of each question.)

Questions 1–5: Six people—Matt, Ned, Qi Li, Stanley, Tonga, and Vladimir—are sitting around a rectangular table with six seats, one at the head of the table, one at the foot, and two on each long side of the table. The chairs are numbered 1 through 6 in a clockwise fashion, beginning with the chair at the head of the table, such that Chairs 1 and 4, 2 and 6, and 3 and 5 are directly across the table from each other.

Consecutively numbered chairs are considered adjacent. Chairs 1 and 6 are also considered adjacent.

Ned is sitting in chair 1 or chair 4.

Stanley and Tonga are sitting in adjacent chairs on one long side of the table.

Qi Li and Stanley are not sitting in adjacent chairs.

Question 1

Which one of the following could be the seating arrangement of the six people in Chairs 1 through 6, respectively?

(A) Ned, Vladimir, Tonga, Stanley, Matt, Qi Li
(B) Vladimir, Stanley, Tonga, Ned, Matt, Qi Li
(C) Qi Li, Matt, Ned, Stanley, Tonga, Vladimir
(D) Ned, Tonga, Qi Li, Vladimir, Stanley, Matt
(E) Qi Li, Vladimir, Matt, Ned, Tonga, Stanley

Answer and Explanation

This game involves placing people around a table, and it's pretty straightforward. The table is clearly described, maybe even too clearly. It's awfully wordy for all it has to say.

There is a rectangle in which Chair 1 and 4 are at opposite ends, the head and foot, with Chairs 2 and 3 adjacent to each other on one side, and Chairs 5 and 6 adjacent on the other. You go clockwise around the table, the rules tell you, and, although you might have figured it out for yourself, you're even told exactly which chairs are opposite which. So this all turns out to be pretty simple to sketch.

Rule 2 says Ned is in Chair 1 or 4. Of course, that means he is either at the head or foot of the table. You could have written a note to yourself at the top of the page: "N head or foot." And, as a result, each time you drew the table to answer a question, you would have seen that note and remembered right away to put Ned at the bottom or the top of the rectangular table.

Same thing for the other rules. You could have written in big letters "ST" at the top of the page to remind yourself that those two characters, Stanley and Tonga, have to be next to each other along one of the table's two long edges. Alternatively, you might have written "ST = 2 and 3 or 5 and 6." That's just another way of noting the relevant information. And there's no need to do much more with Rule 4 than write something like "Q not = S," a reminder always to separate Qi Li and Stanley.

Armed with all that information, you should be able to make short work of Question 1, which asks for the one and only one acceptable sequence. Ned has to be in Chair 1 or 4. That means that choice (C) is unacceptable since (C) puts him in Chair 3. Cross out (C); there's no point in ever looking at it again. Next, remember that Stanley and Tonga have to be adjacent, and that eliminates choice (D), which puts two people between S and T in either direction.

Moreover, they have to be adjacent along a long side of the table, that is, in Chairs 2 or 3 or 5 and 6. This eliminates choice (A), in which they are next to each other but Stanley is sitting in Chair 4, that is, at the foot of the table.

Nothing seems to have violated Rule 4 yet, but dollars to doughnuts, one choice will. And it turns out to be choice (E). You can't have Q in 1 and S in 6 because that, according to the first rule, counts as adjacency. You're left with choice (B), which must be okay since the other four choices violate rules. (B) is correct, although you needn't bother to check it at this point as long as you're sure the others are wrong. Just choose (B) and get out.

Question 2

If Vladimir is sitting in Chair 4, then which one of the following pairs must be sitting in adjacent seats?

(A) Matt and Ned
(B) Matt and Qi Li
(C) Ned and Qi Li
(D) Ned and Stanley
(E) Stanley and Vladimir

Ⓐ Ⓑ Ⓒ Ⓓ Ⓔ

Answer and Explanation

A quick sketch for Question 2 puts V in Chair 4, and should immediately put Ned in Chair 1. He has to be in one or the other, and since someone else is in 4, he has to be in Chair 1. On one side of the table, as always, you put Stanley and Tonga. You don't know which side right now. That leaves two people, Qi Li and Matt, and they, too, will be along one long side of the table. That's all that's left. So, when Question 2 asks who has to be next to each other, you should look

for Qi Li and Matt, and you'll find them in correct choice (B). All of the other pairs *could* be adjacent but needn't be. So it's choice (B), and you're done with that one almost as quickly as you started.

Question 3

If Qi Li is sitting in Chair 1, then which one of the following must be sitting adjacent to her?

(A) Ned
(B) Matt
(C) Stanley
(D) Tonga
(E) Vladimir

Ⓐ Ⓑ Ⓒ Ⓓ Ⓔ

Answer and Explanation

Question 3 can be done very quickly, too. Putting Qi Li in Chair 1, as you're told to do, means that Ned goes to Chair 4 this time. That leaves Stanley and Tonga, once again, along one of the long sides. But remember Rule 4: you have to separate Qi Li and Stanley. Therefore, Qi Li, who will have to sit next to either S or T, since she's at the head, will be next to Tonga for sure, choice (D). Ned, choice (A), is opposite Qi Li. Stanley, choice (C), can't be next to her. And, certainly, either Matt, choice (B), or Vladimir, choice (E), will have to be next to Qi Li, too, although you cannot choose between them. So it's Tonga, choice (D), for Question 3.

Question 4

If Stanley and Vladimir are sitting in adjacent chairs, then Matt could be sitting in any of the following EXCEPT:

(A) Chair 1
(B) Chair 2
(C) Chair 3
(D) Chair 5
(E) Chair 6

Answer and Explanation

Question 4 asks, "Where could Matt *not* be?" The rules tell you very little about Matt, so build on the concrete information you're given about the other characters and see where that leaves Matt at the end.

Stanley and Vladimir are next to each other, you're told to assume. Stanley and Tonga are likewise next to each other, right? So, both V and T will flank Stanley at the table. However, you specifically know that Stanley and Tonga take up one long side of the table. This means that Vladimir will have to end up at one end of the table or the other, either the head or the foot. Well, the other end, the head or the foot, is reserved for Ned. So if you look at the answer choices with the head and the foot going to Vladimir and Ned, there's no way that Matt or anyone else, besides those two, could occupy Chair 1 or Chair 4. The former has been chosen as the correct answer, choice (A). As for the others, Matt could take any of those. He and Qi Li will occupy 2 and 3 or 5 and 6, but more than that you don't know. So it's choice (A) for Question 4.

Question 5

If Stanley is sitting in Chair 3 and Matt is sitting in Chair 6, then which one of the following pairs CANNOT sit directly across the table from each other?

(A) Ned and Qi Li
(B) Ned and Vladimir
(C) Qi Li and Stanley
(D) Qi Li and Vladimir
(E) Stanley and Vladimir

Answer and Explanation

Question 5, in its exploration of who can or cannot sit across from whom, explicitly places two people in chairs and allows you to do likewise with a third. Specifically, if Stanley is in Chair 3, Tonga (who again has to be next to Stanley along a long side of the table) has to take the other chair along that side, Chair 2. Stanley in 3, Tonga in 2, and Matt in 6. Now, at this point, a lot depends on the placement of Ned. Both Chair 1, the head, and Chair 4, the foot, are available to him. If Ned is in Chair 1, the head, that is between Tonga on his left and Matt on his right, that leaves two chairs, 4 and 5, available to Qi Li and Vladimir. But Qi Li can't take Chair 4 while Stanley is in Chair 3. Rule 4 forbids it. So you would have to have Vladimir in 4 and Qi Li in 5. Under those circumstances, you would see choice (C), Qi Li and Stanley opposite each other in Chairs 5 and 3 respectively, and also choice (B), Ned and Vladimir opposite each other at the ends of the table.

But suppose Ned's in Chair 4 at the foot. With Matt in 6, Ned in 4, Stanley in 3, and Tonga in 2, the possibilities are slightly more numerous. Chairs 1 and 5 remain for Qi Li and Vladimir, with no restrictions as to which one is in which. Under those circumstances, you could certainly have Ned in 4 opposite Qi Li in 1, leaving Vladimir in 5 opposite Stanley in 3. And thus A and E must be rejected. Either is a possibility. But under no circumstances will you ever see Qi Li and Vladimir opposite each other (as it turns out, in none of these scenarios did you see that), and that makes choice (D) correct for Question 5.

Questions 6–11: A history teacher has administered two different tests—one on ancient history, one on modern history—to the five students in his honors class. The five students are Ken, Lea, Marc, Nell, and Otis. The ten exams were graded on the descending scale of A, B, C, D, and F, with A being the highest grade and F the lowest.

No student who received a B on the ancient history exam received lower than a C on the modern history exam.

Marc and exactly one other student each received an A on the modern history exam.

Exactly two students received Fs on the ancient history exam.

Ken and Otis each received a higher grade on the modern history exam than on the ancient history exam.

Lea received a B on her ancient history exam.

Question 6

If Nell and Marc each received an A on the ancient history exam, then which one of the following must be Ken's grade in the ancient history exam?

(A) A
(B) B
(C) C
(D) D
(E) F

Answer and Explanation

In this game, you have to wade through some manipulations of two parallel grading scales. This is a grouping game of distribution. Five students each take two tests and receive a grade of A, B, C, D, or F on each test. You have to distribute the grades, and you're given five indented rules to help you figure out who got what grade.

The first rule can be best understood as a simple if/then statement. If a student got a B in ancient history, then that student got no lower than a C in modern history. Put another way, if a student got a B in ancient history, then that student got an A, B, or C in modern history. You could very well have written it that way at the top of the page. That way every time in the course of the game you saw someone get a B in ancient history, you could have referred to the note to see what follows.

Next you get a rule about someone's specific grade. You can keep track of that data as well as everything else you've learned about people's specific grades in a very simple way. Draw two columns, one labeled *ancient history* and the other *modern history,* and label them with the names of the five students. You can enter Marc's A under the modern history column, and at the bottom of that column you can note *one more A,* or something like that. In the same way, at the

KAPLAN

bottom of the ancient history column, you can note two Fs, and thus incorporate the information provided by Rule 3. You can also, skipping ahead to Rule 5, note Lea's B in ancient history. The point of jotting all this down, remember, is so that you can easily refer to it and access it in the course of the questions.

The remaining rule, the fourth one, is a little tougher to jot down. You could write *better grade* in the modern history column next to Ken's name, and do the same thing next to Otis's name in the same column. If you were to note for Ken and Otis that the better grade would fall in the modern history column, you would probably be able to remember that their ancient history grades are lower, and proceed accordingly. But again, it doesn't matter how you deal with a rule, whether you jot it down or write it in shorthand on the page, provided that you get the rule right, and that you are able to remember it during the course of the game.

By the way, you might have stopped at some point to note that, since Ken and Otis did better on the modern exam than the ancient, neither of them could have gotten an F in modern history. Right? You can't do worse than an F. This may not seem very significant as a deduction, but it is deducible, and it does prove to be a key element in a question coming up, as you'll see in a few minutes.

Okay, there's at least one more major thing you should realize. Lea is affected by Rule 1. Based on that rule, you can jot down A, B, or C next to Lea in the modern history column, because Lea must have received one of those three grades on that exam. Can you deduce anything else here? Not really. Anyone— Ken, Lea, Nell, or Otis—could get the remaining A in modern history. Any two of Ken, Marc, Nell, and Otis could get the two Fs in ancient history. And you have no idea of how anything else falls out. So it's time to move on to the questions.

Question 6 starts out very concretely by telling you to assume that Nell and Marc got As on the ancient history test. This works out pretty simply. You know from Rule 3 that there were exactly 2 Fs on that test. And you know already that Lea didn't get an F because she got a B. With Nell and Marc also eliminated from contention for those Fs, it has to follow that the only two people who remain, Ken and Otis, got the Fs. So not only did Ken get an F, choice (E), but so did Otis.

This sort of process of elimination is very important in Logic Games. Here, you have to keep thinking of the fact that once you've identified the grades of one or more students, the restrictions given in the rules may allow you to figure out some more grades. And in this game there are only five students involved, which also has an impact. Anyway, (E) is correct for Question 6.

Question 7

Which one the following students could possibly have received an F on the modern history exam?

(A) Ken
(B) Lea
(C) Marc
(D) Nell
(E) Otis

Ⓐ Ⓑ Ⓒ Ⓓ Ⓔ

Answer and Explanation

Question 7 involves a little more thinking, but it's still pretty easy if you keep your cool. Who could have received an F in modern history? You should see immediately that it's impossible for Lea to get an F on a modern history exam, because she received a B on the ancient history exam, so, according to Rule 1, she must get at least a C on the modern history exam. Marc couldn't have received an F on the exam, either, because Rule 2 tells you that he got an A. So Marc is out. What about the remaining folks, Ken, Otis, and Nell? This was covered back in the discussion of Rule 4. Ken and Otis did worse on ancient history than on modern history, but if one of them had received an F on modern history, where could he go from there? If a student got an F in modern history there would be no room to do worse on ancient history, as the rule requires. Therefore, Ken and Otis did better than an F on modern history. This leaves you with Nell, choice (D), the correct answer to Question 7. Maybe no one got an F on that test, but only Nell *could* have done so.

Question 8

If exactly three of the students each received a D on the modern history exam, then all of the following must be true EXCEPT:

(A) Ken received an F on the ancient history exam.
(B) Lea received an A on the modern history exam.
(C) Marc received a B on the ancient history exam.
(D) Nell received a D on the modern history exam.
(E) Otis received an F on the ancient history exam.

Ⓐ Ⓑ Ⓒ Ⓓ Ⓔ

Answer and Explanation

Question 8 is one of those in which you're given four true statements and you have to find the one bad apple. The best way to approach this is to take the information you're given, plug it in, and see what happens. Do that first before you worry about eliminating all the answer choices. In this case, if three students got Ds on the modern history exam, then you have all the grades mapped out. Why? Because after those three Ds there are only two students unaccounted for, and you already know that Marc and one other student got As. Furthermore, you know that Lea must be the one who got the A with Marc because, having

received a B on the ancient history exam, she can't get less than a C on the modern exam. Therefore, Ken, Otis, and Nell must be the three students who, according to the stem, have received Ds on the modern exam. This means you've ruled out choices (B) and (D). You know that both of those choices must be true. What else can you conclude? Rule 4 comes in handy here. Ken's and Otis's Ds on the modern test mean that both of them got Fs on ancient history. Right? Their ancient history grade has to be lower than their modern history grade, and only F is lower than D. So choices (A) and (D) are also true. Ken and Otis must have received Fs. That leaves choice (C), which certainly may be true, but doesn't have to be. Marc might have received an ancient history B, but not necessarily, so it's choice (C) for Question 8.

Question 9

If Ken and Otis each received a C on the ancient history exam, and if Nell received an A on the modern history exam, then what is the maximum total number of Bs that could have been received by the five students?

(A) 3
(B) 4
(C) 5
(D) 6
(E) 7

Ⓐ Ⓑ Ⓒ Ⓓ Ⓔ

Answer and Explanation

Question 9 begins more concretely than any of the previous questions. You start by resketching your columns off to the side, a sketch that includes what you've learned from the rules and then puts in what you're told for this question: Ken's and Otis's ancient history Cs, and Nell's modern history A. The question: "What's the maximum number of Bs all around?"

Start with ancient history. You have to factor in the need for two Fs in the ancient history column, and with Ken, Lea, and Otis now variously getting Bs or Cs in ancient history, Marc and Nell have to bite the bullet and take those Fs. So only one B will come out of ancient history, the one bestowed on Lea by the original rule.

Look at the B grade in modern history. The As are set. According to this question and Rule 2, Marc and Nell get those As. Ken and Otis, according to Rule 4, have to improve on their ancient history Cs, and there are no As left. Therefore, Ken and Otis definitely get Bs here. Lea could get a modern history B, too. Rule 1 doesn't forbid it. So you have three definite Bs and one potential B for a total of four. There could be as many as four Bs here, so (B) is the correct choice for Question 9.

Question 10

Assume that each student was awarded 4 points for each A, 3 for each B, 2 for each C, 1 for each D, and no points for each F. If Otis received a total of 6 points for his two exams, then what is the maximum total number of points Ken could have received for his?

(A) 4
(B) 5
(C) 6
(D) 7
(E) 8

Ⓐ Ⓑ Ⓒ Ⓓ Ⓔ

Answer and Explanation

Question 10 tells you to understand and make use of a 0–4 grading point system, one that (happily enough) you are probably familiar with from everyday life. You're also told that Otis received a total of 6

points between his two exams. Given the system—4 points for an A, 3 for a B, 2 for a C, 1 for a D, and 0 for an F—without too much trouble you can figure out exactly what Otis's two grades were. Why? Because there's only one combination of grades that can give Otis 6 points while abiding by Rule 4. He must have received a C on the ancient history exam and an A on the modern—2 plus 4. Of course, 3 plus 3 is impossible, because one of the grades has to be better than the other. Now, the big impact of all this is determining that you're out of As to give in modern history. The only As go to Marc and someone else, and in this question you've just deduced that the other A belongs to Otis. Therefore, the best grade Ken can possibly get in modern history is a B for 3 points. And since his ancient history grade has to be inferior to his modern history grade, the best he can possibly do in ancient history is a C for 2 points. His points add up to 5, so that's the best possible point total Ken can get. And 5 points is correct—choice (B) for Question 10.

Question 11

Assume that each student was awarded 4 points for each A, 3 for each B, 2 for each C, 1 for each D, and no points for each F. If Lea and Marc received the same total number of points for the two exams, and if Nell received an A on both exams, then what is the maximum number of points Otis could have received for his two exams?

(A) 3
(B) 4
(C) 5
(D) 6
(E) 7

Ⓐ Ⓑ Ⓒ Ⓓ Ⓔ

Answer and Explanation

This same point system is in effect for Question 11. The length of Questions 10 and 11 might have seemed a little daunting at first until you realized that both of them make use of the same familiar, logical point system. Anyway, your goal is a decision about Otis's maximum score.

Nell gets two As. The net effect of that is, once again, all the available modern history As have been given. As noted several times, only Marc and one other person get As on the test. Here, that other person is Nell. You're to assume that Lea, with 3 points for her B in ancient history, and Marc with 4 points for his A in modern history, end up with the same point total. You should investigate what that total is or could be and remember, thanks to Rule 1, the only possibilities for Lea's modern history grade are A, B, and C.

But wait a minute. A grade of A is out—there are no modern history As left. So Lea's total is either 6 based on receiving two Bs or 5 points for a B in ancient history and a C in modern. Marc, too, will have a total of 5 or 6, and since he already has 4 points from modern history, it follows that in ancient history Marc got either a C for 2 points or a D for 1 point.

Now think a little more about ancient history. You need 2 Fs there. They don't belong to Lea, Marc, or Nell, so it's Ken and Otis who get Fs or 0 points. And that makes Otis's best possible total 3, choice (A). With an F in ancient history and no more As available in modern, the best Otis can hope for is a 3-point B in modern history, so it's choice (A) for Question 11.

KAPLAN

READING COMPREHENSION

Reading Comprehension is the only question type that appears on all major standardized tests, and the reason isn't too surprising: no matter what academic area you pursue, you have to make sense of dense, unfamiliar prose. Law, of course, is no exception. The topics for LSAT Reading Comp passages are taken from four areas:

- Social sciences
- Natural sciences
- Humanities
- Law

These passages tend to be long, densely worded, and difficult—not unlike at least some of the material you'll face in law school. So right now is a good time to start shoring up your reading skills, both for the test and for your future study and practice of law.

A Word About Outside Knowledge

On the LSAT, no outside knowledge on your part is presupposed, and that holds for the Reading Comp section, too. It's not necessary to know anything about the topics covered in the passages; everything you'll need to answer every question is included in the passages themselves. However, the passages are always logical, and always reflect ideas that you have heard about and can understand. Don't read in a vacuum—relate what you read to your world, and recognize the common sense of the text. One warning, though: the questions test your understanding of the author's points, not your previous understanding or personal point of view on the topic.

So use your own knowledge and experience to help you to comprehend the passages, but be careful not to let it infer with answering questions correctly.

THE PERILS OF OUTSIDE KNOWLEDGE

Certainly knowing a little about the topic discussed in a Reading Comp passage can be helpful. If you can relate the ideas in the passage to what you know of the world, you'll be more confident. But remember to answer the questions based on what's in the passage, not on what you may have learned elsewhere about the topic.

The Seven Basic Principles of Reading Comprehension

Improvement at Reading Comprehension requires practice and patience. You may not see dramatic improvement after taking only one section. But with ongoing practice, the principles below will help to increase your skill and confidence on this section by the day of the test.

1. Read the First Third of the Passage Carefully

The first third of any passage usually introduces the topic and scope, the author's main idea/primary purpose, the author's tone, and almost always hints at the structure that the passage will follow. Let's take a closer look at these crucial elements of a Reading Comp passage.

Topic, Scope, and Purpose

Topic and *scope* are both objective terms, meaning they include no specific reference to the author's point of view. The difference between them is that the topic is broader; the scope narrows the topic. Scope is particularly important because the (many) answer choices that depart from it will always be wrong. The broad topic of "The Battle of Gettysburg" would be a lot to cover in 450 words. We should ask, "What *aspect* of the battle does the author take up?"— and, because of length limitations, it's likely to be a pretty small chunk. Whatever that "chunk" is—the prebattle scouting, or how the battle was fought, or the effects of the battle on the U.S. political scene—that will be the passage's scope. Answer choices that deal with anything outside of this narrowly defined chunk will be wrong.

The topic/scope distinction ties into the all-important author's purpose. The author deliberately chooses to narrow the scope by including certain aspects of the broader topic and excluding others. Why the author makes those choices has to do with why the passage is being written in the first place. We can say that the topic is broadly stated and objective (for instance, a passage's topic might be "solving world hunger"). Scope is also objective, but narrower (a new technology for solving world hunger) and leads rather quickly to the author's subjective purpose (the author is writing in order to describe a new technology and its promising uses). And this is what turns into the author's main idea, which will be discussed at greater length in the next principle.

All this leads to a clear point of attack. Don't just "read" the passage; instead, try to do the following three things: identify the topic; narrow it

ZOOMING IN

Reading the first third of the passage is a zooming-in process. First, you get a sense of the general topic. Then you pin down the more specific scope of the passage. Finally, you glean the author's purpose in writing the passage—and the main idea that he or she is trying to get across about that particular subject.

down to the precise scope that the author includes; and make a hypothesis about why the author is writing and where he or she is going with it. A clear conception of these three things translates directly into points.

Structure and Tone

In a quest to master the content side of the passages—namely, *what* the author says—test takers are notorious for ignoring the less glamorous, but just as important, structural side—namely, *how* the author says it. One of the keys to success on this section is to understand not only the purpose, but also the structure of each passage. Why? Simply because the questions ask both what the author says, *and* how he or she says it. The following is a list of the classic LSAT passage structures:

- Passages based on a strong opinion
- Passages based on a serious problem or situation
- Passages based on differing opinions
- Passages based on significant new findings (often science passages)

Many LSAT passages have been based on one of these classic structures, or a variation thereof. You've most likely seen these structures at work in passages before, even if unconsciously. Your task is to seek them out actively as you begin to read a passage—usually, the structure is announced within the first third of the passage. Let these classic structures act as a "jump start" in your search for the passage's "big picture" and purpose.

As for "how" the author makes his or her point, try to note the author's position within these structures, usually indicated by the author's tone. For example, in the third structure, the author may simply relate the two sides of the story, or may at some point jump in and take a side, or even reject the conflicting opinions in favor of her own. In the first structure, the opinion could be the author's, in which case the author's tone may be opinionated, argumentative, heated, or passionate. On the other hand, the author could simply be describing the strongly held opinions of someone else. This author's writing style would be more descriptive, factual, and even-handed. His or her method may involve mere storytelling, or the simple relaying of information, which is altogether different from the former case.

Notice the difference in tone between the two types of authors. Correct answer choices for a primary purpose question in the former case would use terms like *argue for, propose,* and *demonstrate,* whereas correct

DON'T BE TONE DEAF

Some passages have a strong tone—i.e., the author has a definite viewpoint on the topic and is expressing it with emotion. Other passages have a more even tone—they report information without much emotion or a discernible angle. Distinguishing one from the other is an important skill in Reading Comprehension.

choices for the same type of question in the latter case would use terms like *describe* and *discuss*. Correct answers are always consistent with the author's tone, so noting the author's tone is a good way to score points.

2. Focus on the Main Idea

Almost every passage boils down to one big idea. We discussed above how topic leads to scope, and then in turn to the author's purpose in writing the passage. An author's primary purpose and main idea are forever intertwined. Take, for example, the hypothetical passage stated above, in which the author had the following purpose.

> The author is writing in order to describe a new technology and its promising uses.

The main idea is simply a restatement of this without the active verb structure:

> Biochemical engineering (or whatever new technology is discussed) can help solve world hunger.

Your job is to cut past the fancy wording and focus on this big idea.

Most often, the main idea will be presented in the first third of the passage. But occasionally the author will build up to it gradually, in which case you may not have a solidified conception of the author's purpose or big idea until the very end.

In any case, the main idea must appear somewhere in the passage, and when it does, you must take conscious note of it. For one thing, the purpose of everything else in the passage will be to support this idea. Furthermore, many of the questions—not only "main idea" or "primary purpose" questions, but all kinds of questions—are easier to handle when you have the main idea in the forefront of your mind. Always look for choices that sound consistent with the main idea. Wrong choices often sound inconsistent with it.

3. Get the Gist of Each Paragraph

The paragraph is the main structural unit of any passage. After you've read the first third of the passage carefully, you need only find the gist, or general purpose, of each succeeding paragraph, and then attempt to relate

WHAT'S THE BIG IDEA?

You should always keep the main idea in mind, even when answering questions that don't explicitly ask for it. Correct answers on even the detail questions tend to echo the main idea in one way or another.

each paragraph back to the passage as a whole. To find the gist of each paragraph, ask yourself:

- Why did the author include this paragraph?
- What shift did the author have in mind when moving on to this paragraph?
- What bearing does this paragraph have on the author's main idea?

This process allows you create a "mental roadmap" of the passage, which ties in strongly with the structure and main idea. When questions arise that require you to look back into the passage, having a roadmap will help you locate the place in the text that contains the answer. For example, it's helpful to know that, say, the author's critique of a recommendation is in paragraph three. Doing so will allow you to zero in on the relevant information quickly. The art of *not* trying to understand every little thing in the passage brings us to our next principle.

4. Don't Obsess over Details

There are differences between the reading skills required in an academic environment and those useful on standardized tests. In school, you probably read to memorize information for an exam. This kind of reading most likely includes taking note of and memorizing details as well.

But this is not the type of reading that's good for getting points on LSAT Reading Comprehension. On the test, you'll need to read for short-term, as opposed to long-term, retention. When you finish the questions on a certain passage, that passage is over, gone, done with. You're free to promptly forget everything about it.

What's more, there's certainly no need to memorize details—it's an open-book test, after all. You always have the option to relocate details if a particular question requires you to do so. If you have a good sense of a passage's structure and paragraph topics, and your mental roadmap is clear in your mind, then you should have no problem navigating back through the text when the need arises.

5. Attack, Don't Just Read, the Passages

Always remember that you get no points for just "getting through" the passage. Don't be the kind of test taker who views reaching the end of a passage as a moral victory—this type of victory is short-lived when you find you can't answer any questions.

MAKE A MAP

Try labeling each paragraph, so you know what's covered in each and how it fits into the overall structure of the passage. This will help you get a fix on the passage as a whole, and it will help you locate specific details later.

HEY, IT'S AN OPEN BOOK TEST

Don't feel that you have to memorize or understand every little thing as you read the passage.

Remember, you can always refer back to the passage to clarify the meaning of any specific detail.

No, you must *attack*—not simply read—the passages. The former embodies the winning mindset: you're entering the passage for the sole purpose of picking up the author's key ideas that will enable you to rack up points. By thinking in terms of attack, you're less likely to be diverted from this mission or to let the densely worded prose distract you.

Attacking a passage involves the application of all of the strategies mentioned in the previously stated principles. It also means reading actively. Active readers keep their minds working at all times, while trying to anticipate where the author's points are leading. Typically when we read—say a newspaper—we start with the first sentence and read the article straight through. The words wash over us and are the only things we hear in our minds. This is typical of the passive approach to reading.

Active reading, on the other hand, involves doing more than just reading the words on the page—it means thinking about what you're reading as you read it. It means paraphrasing the complicated-sounding ideas and jargon. It means asking yourself questions as you read:

- What's the author's main point here?
- What's the purpose of this paragraph? Of this sentence?

When you read actively, there's a running commentary going on in your mind as you read. You may want to jot down notes or underline. When you read actively, you don't absorb the passage, you attack it!

6. Beware of Classic Wrong Answers

Knowing the most common types of wrong answer can help you eliminate wrong choices quickly, winning you extra time. Of course, ideally, you want to have prephrased an answer choice in your mind before looking at the choices. But in cases where that technique doesn't apply, you'll have to go to the choices and eliminate the bad ones to find the correct one. In such cases, you should always be on the lookout for:

- Choices that go beyond the author's scope
- Choices that are "half-right, half-wrong"
- Choices that use the wrong verb
- Choices that distort the passage's ideas
- Choices that say the exact opposite of what you are looking for

Being sensitive to these classic wrong choices will make it that much easier to zero in on the correct choice quickly and efficiently.

7. Read Critically

The single most important factor in Reading Comp success is the basic skill that underlies each of the preceding principles, as well as the rest of the test: critical reading.

Critical reading involves perspective—the ability to step back from a piece of prose and carefully evaluate it. On the Reading Comp section, critical reading echoes all of the principles we've been talking about, including:

- **Reading for purpose and idea**
  Why is the author writing? What's his/her point of view or main idea?

- **Reading for structure**
  How is the passage put together?

- **Reading between the lines**
  What is implied by the text?

The following are ways in which you can improve the specific critical reading skills necessary for success on Reading Comprehension:

- **Get a handle on the "spirit" of the passage.**
  Is it passionate? Neutral? Is it academic, conversational, or poetic in tone? What does the author favor? Disapprove of?

- **Keep paraphrasing key ideas.**
  Make sure you can put the author's most important concepts into your own words.

- **Keep anticipating where the author is going.**
  Each step of the way, ask yourself: "What could or must follow?"

- **Don't let complex-sounding words and sentences scare you.**
  Most passages consist of pretty simple ideas, written to sound impressive.

- **Connect abstract ideas to your own experience.**
  Visualize the subject matter if you can.

- **Read carefully for the gist or main point.**
  Read loosely for everything else—details, etcetera.

- **Remember that authors are repetitious.**
  Not every sentence they write adds a new idea.

- **Use keywords.**
  Like LR arguments, RC passages are full of structural signals—words or phrases whose main function is to help the author string ideas together logically. They allow you to infer a great deal about content, even if that content is obscure or difficult. Conclusion signals *(therefore, consequently, thus)* and evidence signals *(because, since)* are extremely helpful, as are contrast signals *(but, however, although, by contrast)* which indicate an opposition or shift in ideas.

The Three Crucial RC Question Types

While it might be convenient to break down the Reading Comprehension section into the types of *passages* that typically appear on it, Kaplan feels that that's not the best way to master the section. In Logic Games, categorizing the games is helpful because Sequencing games and Matching games, for instance, have their own sets of peculiarities, making a distinction between them useful. However, the same types of differences don't separate a humanities RC passage from a social science one, or even a natural science passage from a law passage. Their topics differ, but we read them in the same way, employing the same critical reading techniques for each.

For that reason, we find it more efficient to break the section down into the three main question types that accompany each passage: global, explicit text, and inference. Let's look at each of these more closely.

Global Questions

A global question asks us to sum up the author's overall intentions, ideas, or passage structure. It's basically a question whose scope is the entire passage. Global questions account for 25 to 30 percent of all Reading Comp questions.

In general, any global question choice that grabs onto a small detail—or zeros in on the content of only one paragraph—will be wrong. Often, scanning the verbs in the global question choices is a good way to take a first cut at the question. The verbs must agree with the author's tone and way in which he or she structures the passage, so scanning the verbs can narrow down the options quickly. The correct answer must be consistent with the overall tone and structure of the passage, whereas the wrong choices will go beyond the scope or focus on a detail or be inconsistent with the author's tone. You'll often find global questions at the beginning of question sets, and often one of the wrong choices will play on some side issue discussed at the tail end of the passage.

Main Idea and Primary Purpose Questions

The two main types of global questions are main idea and primary purpose questions. We discussed these types a little earlier, noting that main idea and purpose are inextricably linked, because the author's purpose is to convey his or her main idea. The formats for these question types are pretty self-evident:

- Which one of following best expresses the main idea of the passage?
- The author's primary purpose is to . . .

Title Questions

A very similar form of global question is one that's looking for a title that best fits the passage. (This question type disappeared for a while from the LSAT, but has started to make a comeback.) A title, in effect, is the main idea summed up in a brief, catchy way. This question may look like this: "Which of the following titles best describes the content of the passage as a whole?"

Be sure not to go with a choice that aptly describes only the latter half of the passage; a valid title, like a main idea and primary purpose, must cover the entire passage.

Structure Questions

Another type of global question is one that asks you to recognize a passage's overall structure. Here's what this type of question might sound like: "Which of the following best describes the organization of the passage?"

Answer choices to this kind of global question are usually worded very generally; they force you to recognize the broad layout of the passage as opposed to the specific content. For example, here are a few possible ways that a passage could be organized:

GLOBAL QUESTIONS AT A GLANCE

- GQs represent 25–30 percent of Reading Comp questions.
- GQs sum up author's overall intentions or passage structure.
- Nouns and verbs must be consistent with the author's tone and the passage's scope.
- Types of GQs: main idea, primary purpose, title, structure, logic, and tone.

- A hypothesis is stated and then analyzed.
- A proposal is evaluated and alternatives are explored.
- A viewpoint is set forth and then subsequently defended.

When choosing among these choices, literally ask yourself: "Was there a hypothesis here? Was there an evaluation of a proposal, or a defense of a viewpoint?" These terms may all sound similar, but in fact, they're very different things. Learn to recognize the difference between a proposal, a viewpoint, and so on. Try to keep an eye on what the author is doing as well as what the author is saying, and you'll have an easier time with this type of question.

Logic Questions

Logic questions are those that ask why the author does something—cite a source, bring up a detail, put one paragraph before another, etcetera. Choices that discuss the content or a detail will be wrong for these questions.

Tone Questions

The last type of global question is the tone question, which asks you to evaluate the style of the writing or how the author sounds. Is the author passionate, fiery, neutral, angry, hostile, opinionated, low-key? Here's an example: "The author's tone in the passage can best be characterized as. . . ."

Make sure you don't confuse the nature of the content with the tone in which the author presents the ideas—a social science passage based on trends in this century's grisliest murders may be presented in a cool, detached, strictly informative way. Once again, it's up to you to separate what the author says from how he or she says it.

Inference Questions

Inference questions make up 55 to 60 percent of the Reading Comprehension section, and are very similar to those found in Logical Reasoning. An inference is something that is almost certainly true, based on the passage, but that is contained "between the lines." The answer is something that the author strongly implies or hints at, but does not state directly. Furthermore, the Denial Test, which was introduced earlier for Logical Reasoning assumption and inference questions, works for inference questions on Reading Comp as well. The right answer, if denied, will contradict or significantly weaken the passage. So in those two respects,

Logical Reasoning and Reading Comp inferences are similar. The differences?

- RC inference questions can be on major points or small, whereas LR inference questions tend to focus on major elements of the stimulus.
- In RC, we can't always be sure where in the passage to look for the answer to an inference question.
- RC text is tougher to get through than LR prose, which is much briefer, so RC inference questions are tougher.

The same rules that apply to inferences in Logical Reasoning also apply to inferences in Reading Comp. A good inference:

- Stays in line with the gist of the passage
- Stays in line with the author's tone
- Stays in line with the author's point of view
- Stays within the scope of the passage and its main idea
- Is neither denied by, nor irrelevant to, the ideas stated in the passage
- Always makes more sense than its opposite

Extracting valid inferences from Reading Comp passages requires the ability to recognize that information in the passage can be expressed in different ways. The ability to bridge the gap between the way information is presented in the passage and the way it's presented in the correct answer choice is vital. In fact, inference questions often boil down to an exercise in translation.

Standard Inference Questions

The most common type of inference question simply asks what can be inferred from the passage, but does so in a variety of different ways:

- It can be inferred from the passage that . . .
- The passage/author suggests that . . .
- The passage/author implies that . . .
- The passage supports which one of the following statements . . .

Usually, some specific information will complete these question introductions, so you'll almost always have a clue as to which idea or set of ideas from the passage is the key to the answer. When evaluating the answer choices, keep the relevant ideas firmly in mind. The farther you stray from them to endorse a choice, the more likely it is that this choice will be wrong. Occasionally, the stem won't contain specific information, in which case you simply have to work your way through the choices until you find the one that's most consistent with the passage.

Agreement Questions

Another common form of inference question is one that asks you to find a statement that the author (or some character or group mentioned in the passage) would agree with. Once again, the question stem will usually provide a hint as to in which part of the passage the answer can be found.

Explicit Test Questions

The third major category of Reading Comprehension questions is the explicit test question. As the name implies, an explicit test question is one whose answer can be directly pinpointed and found in the text. This type makes up roughly 10 to 20 percent of the questions on the section. It's fairly simple to identify an explicit text question from its stem:

- According to the passage/author . . .
- The author states that . . .
- The author mentions which one of the following as . . .

Often, these questions provide very direct clues as to where an answer may be found, such as a line reference or some text that links up with the passage structure. (Just be careful with line references—they'll bring you to the right area, but usually the actual answer will be found in the lines immediately before or after the referenced line.) Detail questions are usually related to the main idea, and correct choices tend to be related to major points.

You may recall that we advised you to skim over details in Reading Comp passages in favor of focusing on the big idea, topic, and scope. So what do you do with a question type that's specifically concerned with details? The fact is, most of the details that appear in a passage aren't tested in the questions. With the few that are, you'll do one of the following:

- Remember them from your reading
- Be given a line reference to bring you right to them
- Simply have to find them on your own in order to track down the answer

EXPLICIT TEST QUESTIONS AT A GLANCE

- ETQs represent 10–20 percent of Reading Comp questions.
- ETQ answers can always be found in the text.
- ETQs sometimes include line references to help you locate the relevant material.
- ETQs are concrete, and therefore the easiest RC question type for most.

KAPLAN

If that's the case—if your mental roadmap and understanding of the purpose of each paragraph are both in the forefront of your mind—it shouldn't take long to locate the relevant detail and then choose an answer. And if even that fails, as a last resort, you have the option of putting that question aside and returning to it later, if and when you have the time to search through the passage. The point is, even with the existence of this question type, the winning strategy is still to note the purpose of details in each paragraph's argument, but not to attempt to memorize the details themselves.

Most students find explicit test questions to be the easiest type of Reading Comp question, since they're the most concrete. Unlike inferences, which hide somewhere between the lines, explicit details reside in the lines themselves. For this reason, we suggest placing explicit test questions high on your list of priorities, above inference questions but below global questions, when choosing the order in which you tackle the questions.

And speaking of setting priorities, this brings us to our next major topic, which should help bring all of these principles and strategies together.

The Kaplan Three-Step Method for Reading Comprehension

Now that you have the basics of LSAT Reading Comp under your belt, you'll want to learn our three-step method that allows you to orchestrate them all into a single modus operandi for RC questions:

1. Attack the first third of the passage.
2. Read the rest of the passage.
3. Do the questions in an efficient order.

1. Attack the First Third of the Passage
As outlined in the Basic Principles section, read the first part of the passage with care, in order to determine the main idea and purpose (via the zooming-in process we talked about earlier). Keep in mind two caveats, however. First, in some passages, the author's main idea doesn't become clear until the end of the passage. Second, occasionally a passage won't include a main idea, which in itself is a strong hint that the passage is more of a descriptive, storytelling type of passage, with an even-handed

tone and no strong opinions. Bottom line: don't panic if you can't immediately pin down the author's main idea and purpose. Read on.

2. Read the Rest of the Passage

Do so as we described in the Basic Principles section, making sure to take note of paragraph topics, location of details, etcetera.

3. Do the Questions in an Efficient Order

Quickly scan the question stems for global questions, specifically main idea or primary purpose questions. Doing these questions first will often help you solidify your conception of the author's main idea and purpose, and you're more likely to answer them correctly now, while the passage is still fresh in your mind.

If there are any other global types, such as questions regarding the author's overall tone or the organization of the passage, you may benefit from seeking out and handling those next. Explicit text questions, especially those with line references, are good candidates to tackle after that. Many test takers benefit from leaving the more difficult inference questions for last.

This, of course, is only a rough order based on question type. You may want to revise this order to account for the difficulty level of each individual question. For example, on any given passage, some inference questions may be easier than some explicit text questions. So, for each question, quickly ask yourself: "Can I answer this question quickly?" Shop around—tackle the questions that you think will get you quick points first, and leave the others for later. This reinforces the all-important LSAT mindset—your conscious decision to take control of the test.

Using the Kaplan Three-Step Method for Reading Comprehension

Now let's try the three-step method on an actual LSAT-strength RC passage. For the time being, we've just included the question stems of the questions attached to this passage, since you don't want to get into individual choices until later:

It has been suggested that post–World War II concepts of environmental liability, as they pertain to hazardous waste, grew out of issues regarding municipal refuse collection and disposal and industrial waste disposal in the period 1880–1940. To a great

(5) degree, the remedies available to Americans for dealing with the burgeoning hazardous waste problem were characteristic of the judicial, legislative, and regulatory tools used to confront a whole range of problems in the industrial age. At the same time, these remedies were operating in an era in which the problem of haz-

(10) ardous waste had yet to be recognized. It is understandable that an assessment of liability was narrowly drawn and most often restricted to a clearly identified violator in a specific act of infringement of the property rights of someone else. Legislation, for the most part, focused narrowly on clear threats to the public

(15) health and dealt with problems of industrial pollution meekly if at all.

Nevertheless, it would be grossly inaccurate to assume that the actions of American politicians, technologists, health officials, judges, and legislators in the period 1880–1940 have had little

(20) impact on the attempts to define environmental liability and to confront the consequences of hazardous waste. Taken as a whole, the precedents of the late nineteenth through the mid-twentieth century have established a framework in which the problem of hazardous waste is understood and confronted today. Efforts at

(25) refuse reform gradually identified the immutable connection between waste and disease, turning eyesores into nuisances and nuisances into health hazards. Confronting the refuse problem and other forms of municipal pollution forced cities to define public responsibility and accountability with respect to the envi-

(30) ronment. A commitment to municipal services in the development of sewers and collection and disposal systems shifted the burden of responsibility for eliminating wastes from the individual to the community. In some way, the courts' efforts to clarify and broaden the definition of public nuisance were dependent on

(35) the cities' efforts to define community responsibility itself.

The courts retained their role as arbiter of what constituted private and public nuisances. Indeed, fear that the courts would transform individual decisions into national precedents often contributed to the search for other remedies. Nonetheless, the

(40) courts remained an active agent in cases on the local, state, and

national level, making it quite clear that they were not going to be left out of the process of defining environmental liability in the United States. In the case of hazardous waste, precedents for behavior and remedial action were well developed by 1940. Even

(45) though the concept of *hazardous waste* is essentially a post–World War II notion, the problem was not foreign to earlier generations. The observation that the administrative, technical, and legal problems of water pollution in the 1920s were intertwined is equally applicable to today's hazardous waste problem.

1. According to the author, the efforts by cities to define public responsibility for the environment resulted in which of the following?

2. Which of the following, if substituted for the word *immutable* (line 25), would LEAST alter the author's meaning?

3. With which one of the following statements would the author be most likely to agree?

4. The author's primary purpose is to discuss . . .

5. The tone of the author's discussion of early attempts to deal with waste and pollution problems could best be described as . . .

6. According to the passage, judicial assessments of liability in waste disposal disputes prior to World War II were usually based on . .

7. The passage suggests that responses to environmental problems between 1880 and 1940 were relatively limited in part because of . . .

1. Attack the First Third of the Passage Carefully

The first few sentences introduce the topic: hazardous waste. The scope, as you recall, is the specific angle the author takes on the topic, and this seems to be the post–World War II concept of environmental liability associated with hazardous waste. The author points out that it's been suggested that this concept of liability has some connection to issues from the time period 1880–1940; latterday remedies for hazardous waste are "characteristic of the judicial, legislative, and regulatory tools used to confront a whole range of problems in the industrial age." Since hazardous waste liability concepts of the postwar era had their roots in an era that predated the recognition of hazardous waste problems, the author finds it understandable that liability assessment and the ensuing legislation regarding hazardous waste were both "narrowly drawn."

All of this comes out of the first paragraph. In some cases, this would be enough to cover the "first third of the passage" reading. However, the keyword *nevertheless* at the beginning of the next paragraph indicates that it may be helpful to include this sentence in your initial reading as well. This sentence harks back to and solidifies the connection between the actions and policies from the period 1880–1940 and the concept of environmental liability associated with hazardous waste. This connection is the author's main idea.

2. Read the Rest of the Passage

The sentence from lines 21 to 24—"Taken as a whole. . . ."—is simply another restatement of the main idea. It's followed by a description of the gradual recognition of the hazardous waste problem, and some of the repercussions of the cities' and courts' efforts to define the problem and to assign responsibility for it. Note that there's some talk in the paragraph about individual versus community responsibility, and the role of cities, but don't fuss over the specifics. If there's a question on these issues, you'll know where to look.

The first part of the last paragraph deals mainly with the courts' role in defining environmental liability. The last three sentences of the passage reinforce the main idea; namely that there's a historical context for the ways in which hazardous waste problems are viewed today.

3. Do the Questions in an Efficient Order

Let's look again at the seven question stems attached to this passage:

1. According to the author, the efforts by cities to define public responsibility for the environment resulted in which of the following?

2. Which of the following, if substituted for the word *immutable* (line 25), would LEAST alter the author's meaning?

3. With which one of the following statements would the author be most likely to agree?

4. The author's primary purpose is to discuss . . .

5. The tone of the author's discussion of early attempts to deal with waste and pollution problems could best be described as . . .

6. According to the passage, judicial assessments of liability in waste disposal disputes prior to World War II were usually based on . . .

7. The passage suggests that responses to environmental problems between 1880 and 1940 were relatively limited in part because of . . .

Global Questions
Quickly scan the question stems for global questions, specifically main idea or primary purpose. Upon inspection, if you come across the following question, you should attempt it at this point while the author's big idea is fresh in your mind:

4. The author's primary purpose is to discuss

   (A) contrasts in the legislative approaches to environmental liability before and after World War II
   (B) legislative trends which have been instrumental in the reduction of environmental hazardous wastes
   (C) the historical and legislative context in which to view post–World War II hazardous waste problems
   (D) early patterns of industrial abuse and pollution of the American environment
   (E) the growth of an activist tradition in American jurisprudence

Choice (C) has the elements of a right answer: the connection (denoted by "the historical and legislative context . . . to view . . . waste problems") that represents the author's main idea, and the correct topic and scope—hazardous waste, post–World War II.

Choice (B) is tempting; legislative trends were discussed, but not in enough depth to constitute the author's primary purpose. More damaging to (B) is the fact that the discussion hinges on defining liability for hazardous wastes, and doesn't specifically discuss any factor "instrumental in the *reduction of environmental wastes.*"

Meanwhile, (A) misinterprets the passage structure—there is no such contrast presented, while (D) and (E) both violate the topic and scope of the passage (notice that neither one even mentions the topic of hazardous wastes).

Question 5, focusing on tone, is another global question that you may wish to answer early on. Continuing to scan the question stems, the one with the line reference, question 2, may have caught your eye. This type simply tests your understanding of a certain word in a particular context, and since it tells us exactly where in the passage the word is, you'd be justified in trying this one next. Questions 1 and 6 are clearly explicit text questions, so you should do those next, beginning with the one that seems the most familiar. Questions 3 and 7, the inference questions, are good candidates to be saved for last.

We've already discussed one of the global questions, question 4, so let's now conclude this discussion with a brief look at one explicit text question and one inference question:

Explicit Text Question
Here's the complete form (with answer choices) of question 6:

6. According to the passage, judicial assessments of liability in waste disposal disputes prior to World War II were usually based on

    (A) excessively broad definitions of legal responsibility
    (B) the presence of a clear threat to the public health
    (C) precedents derived from well-known cases of large-scale industrial polluters
    (D) restricted interpretations of property rights infringements
    (E) trivial issues such as littering, eyesores, and other public nuisances

Pre–World War II judicial assessments of liability should ring a bell—they were discussed in the first paragraph. The correct answer, choice (D), is a direct paraphrase of the passage: ". . . an assessment of liability was narrowly drawn and most often restricted to a clearly identified violator in a specific act of *infringement of the property rights* of someone else."

Choice (E) is a common type of wrong answer; it consists of wording taken straight from the passage, but unfortunately, the wrong *part* of the passage. Don't choose an answer simply because you recognize some of the words or phrases in it; this is a common trap that snags many careless test takers.

Choice (B) is another classic wrong answer—the *au contraire* choice. This choice actually represents the *opposite* of what's stated or implied in the passage. According to the author, pre–World War II was "an era in which the problem of hazardous waste had yet to be recognized."

Inference Question
Finally, let's take a quick look at question 3, a complete inference question:

3. With which one of the following statements would the author be most likely to agree?

(A) The growth of community responsibility for waste control exemplifies the tendency of government power to expand at the expense of individual rights.

(B) Although important legal precedents for waste control were established between 1880 and 1940, today's problems will require radically new approaches.

(C) While early court decisions established important precedents involving environmental abuses by industry, such equally pressing matters as disposal of municipal garbage were neglected.

(D) Because environmental legislation between 1880 and 1940 was in advance of its time it failed to affect society's awareness of environmental problems.

(E) The historical role of U.S. courts in defining problems of hazardous waste and environmental liability provides valuable traditions for courts today.

WATCH FOR TRAPS

Same-wording and *au contraire* wrong choices are common. Recognize them and avoid them.

Remember the basic rule for inferences: an inference must stay in line with the author's tone as well as the passage's topic and scope. The author's tone in this passage—factual, evenhanded—doesn't seem to fit with choices (A) and (B).

Choice (A) offers a judgment taken from the community/individual responsibility issue, something the author never does; he or she simply says that the burden shifted from one to the other.

There's no reason to believe that the author would agree with (B), either. While he or she would certainly agree with the first part, there's nothing that indicates that the author would advocate radical new approaches for today's problems. Both of these choices fail to match the author's tone, and are slightly outside the scope of the passage as well.

Notice how correct choice (E) sounds like an offshoot of the author's main idea. The first sentence of the second paragraph says that it would be wrong to assume that the actions of judges and legislators, among others, had little impact on defining liability and confronting the issue of hazardous waste. This implies that the courts had a positive impact, which is bolstered by lines 39 to 43. Combine that with the statement in lines 21 to 24: "Taken as a whole, the precedents of the late nineteenth through the mid-twentieth century have established a framework in which the problem of hazardous waste is understood and confronted today." All of this points towards (E) as a statement that the author would agree with, and therefore the answer to this inference question.

Reading Comprehension Practice Set

Directions: Each passage in this test is followed by several questions. After reading the passage, choose the best answer to each question. Your replies are to be based on what is *stated* or *implied* in the selection. (The answer and explanation can be found at the end of each question.)

Passage for Questions 1–7:

Various factors influence voter preference in United States presidential elections, but perhaps none is so persuasive as a candidate's performance on nationally televised debates just prior to the
(5) election. Newspapers and television news programs generally attempt to provide thorough coverage of the debates, further augmenting the effect of good or bad candidate performances. In this way, the news media fulfill the traditional
(10) role of educating the public and enabling voters to make better informed decisions about elected officials. However, the same media that bring live debates into millions of living rooms across the nation also limit the availability of debate cover-
(15) age by use of "pool" coverage, the sharing of news coverage with other news organizations. When typical pool situations arise, one of the major networks covers the event, and a "feed" is created so other broadcasters may have access to the same
(20) coverage. Individual broadcasters are unable to convey a unique account to their viewers. The pool system limits the news-gathering ability of television news organizations and denies viewers an opportunity to gain maximum insight from
(25) the debate. The First Amendment freedoms afforded the press exist largely to ensure that the public benefits from the free flow of information.

Some commentators suggest that the purpose of a free press is to inform citizens about matters of
(30) public concern. Others, however, believe that the value of free press lies in its ability to foster a marketplace of ideas in which the best options prevail. Presidential debates embody all these considerations. Not only do candidates provide infor-
(35) mation about matters of utmost interest, they also offer diverse views on how to approach the major issues. Given television's ability to further informational and marketplace-of-ideas goals of the First Amendment, debate coverage should be
(40) diverse as possible.

What difference does it make whether viewers saw a "tight shot" of one candidate or a "two-shot" of both candidates at a given time? The answer depends on what happens, when it
(45) happens, and whether the pool director anticipated it or was fortunate enough to have captured it anyway. It may be argued that none of this matters. The important thing, the argument goes, is that viewers will know generally what happened.
(50) According to this line of reasoning, the number of news organizations covering an event—and even which ones—would be irrelevant. But courts have held differently: "It is impossible to treat two news services as interchangeable, and
(55) . . . it is only by cross lights from varying directions that full illumination can be secured." Undoubtedly, there are some circumstances in which pool coverage is the only way to cover an event. But these few situations must not foster a
(60) casual acceptance of pool implementation in other situations.

Question 1

It can be inferred that the author's primary objection to the pool system of covering presidential debates is that it

(A) restricts the public's access to a diversity of ideas and information
(B) limits the number of people who have access to debates on television
(C) undermines candidates' ability to persuade voters
(D) dissuades voters from exercising their right to choose between candidates
(E) contributes to an overreliance by the public on televised accounts of political issues

Ⓐ Ⓑ Ⓒ Ⓓ Ⓔ

Answer and Explanation

The first passage is pretty straightforward. It revolves around the author's argument that "pool" coverage of presidential debates stifles the news media's ability to gather and present news. Why does the author find such a limitation on the media so alarming? She feels that it denies viewers an opportunity to gain maximum insight from presidential debates—that is, it sets limits on the amount and variety of information that the public receives. That's the passage's main point. Be aware that the author is talking about the actual "shooting" of a news event—the visual image broadcast to the viewer. She feels that a diversity of images is needed to fully illuminate an event. Although she concedes at the end of the passage that pool coverage may be the only way to cover *some* events, she cautions against the indiscriminate use of such coverage.

Question 1 asks for the author's primary objection to pool coverage of presidential debates. As noted, the author is primarily concerned with the way pool coverage limits the public's exposure to a variety of view-

points and information. Choice (A) says exactly that, and is the correct answer. The author never charges the pool coverage system with limiting the *number* of people who have access to televised debates. Her point is that it limits the number of *versions* of a debate being offered to people, so choice (B) is wrong. The author discusses the impact of a candidate's debate performance in the first paragraph. But when examining the effects of pool coverage, the author clearly is thinking of the effect on the public's ability to judge, not on the candidates' ability to persuade, so choice (C) is out. Choice (D) involves a similar distortion of the passage's contents. The author claims that pool coverage, by limiting the information viewers receive, hampers the public's ability to choose between candidates, not its right to choose. As for choice (E), the author salutes TV's ability to bring live debates into millions of living rooms across the country. She sees this as an important factor in enabling voters to make better informed decisions about candidates. Her argument doesn't include a discussion of the dangers of an "overreliance" by the public on television, as choice (E) incorrectly suggests. Again, it's (A) for Question 1.

Question 2

The author would probably assert that the opinion of the court presented in the second paragraph is

(A) useful but biased
(B) reflective of an unfortunate trend
(C) overly permissive
(D) substantially correct
(E) commendable but ineffective

Ⓐ Ⓑ Ⓒ Ⓓ Ⓔ

Answer and Explanation

Take a look at the second paragraph and see what motivates the author's reference to court opinion. The author begins the paragraph by anticipating a possible counterargument—that it doesn't matter what specific images people see as long as they know generally what happened. This argument would lead a proponent of pool coverage to say that the number of news organizations covering an event is irrelevant. At the end of the paragraph, the author attacks this counterargument by quoting a court decision. That is, she's using the words of the court to defend her own views. If you realize this, you don't even have to look at the quote to infer the author's opinion of the court's findings. She must agree with them to a large extent, right? The only answer choice that reflects this level of agreement is choice (D)—"substantially correct." Choices (B) and (C) are way too negative, and choices (A) and (E) are not positive enough. So choice (D) is the answer for Question 2.

Question 3

In the first paragraph, the author cites two opinions concerning the benefits provided to society by a free press primarily in order to

(A) suggest the range of benefits that potentially would be provided by competitive coverage of presidential debates

(B) indicate that some of the defenses of pool coverage contradict one another

(C) criticize the assumptions held by some commentators on journalism

(D) contend that First Amendment freedoms do not apply to presidential debates

(E) reconcile different points of view in an effort to reach a more acceptable definition of press freedom

Ⓐ Ⓑ Ⓒ Ⓓ Ⓔ

Answer and Explanation

To answer Question 3, you need to take a close look at the second half of the first paragraph. The two benefits of a free press cited there are (1), its ability "to inform citizens about matters of public concern," and (2), its ability "to foster a marketplace of ideas in which the best options prevail." The author presents these not as contradictory benefits but as complementary ones. Both benefits are involved when television airs a presidential debate, and the author argues that diversity of coverage would maximize these benefits. Choice (A) paraphrases this argument, and is the correct choice. The author doesn't mention these benefits as proposed "defenses" of pool coverage and they certainly don't contradict each other, so choice (B) is off the mark. (C) is wrong—you more or less know this as soon as you see the verb *criticize*—it just doesn't fit what the author is doing in the first paragraph. The author is in no way critical of the benefits of a free press or of the commentators who have suggested them. The same goes for (E); the author does not "reconcile" anything here. In fact, there's no need to—the different views on free press benefits are presented here as being complementary. Finally, choice (D) is dead wrong—the point of this paragraph is that First Amendment freedoms have a whole lot to do with presidential debates. Once again, it was (A) for Question 3.

Question 4

It can be inferred from the passage that a proponent of the pool system of debate coverage would be most likely to defend her viewpoint with which of the following remarks?

(A) Broadcasters rarely betray their political preferences in debate coverage.
(B) Although imperfect, pool coverage is the only practical means of reporting most political events.
(C) Presidential debates are too complex to be covered thoroughly by any one broadcaster.
(D) Broadcasters are prevented by public opinion from presenting biased coverage.
(E) Small differences in style of coverage do not significantly affect the amount of information conveyed to viewers.

Ⓐ Ⓑ Ⓒ Ⓓ Ⓔ

Answer and Explanation

Question 4 asks how a proponent of the pool system would defend her viewpoint. Since the author argues that pool coverage limits the information provided to viewers, you need a choice that would challenge the author's point of view. Choice (A) doesn't address this position. So what if broadcasters only rarely betray their political preferences in debate coverage? Pool coverage still limits viewers to coverage by only one of these broadcasters. (B) could be tempting, too, but it also doesn't attack the author's main argument. The author already concedes that pool coverage may be the only way to cover some events. But the drawbacks of such coverage still exist for nonpolitical events—and you might have to forgo "practicality" at some point in deference to larger issues. Choice (C) only serves to strengthen the author's argument. If presidential debates are so complex that one broadcaster cannot cover them properly, pool coverage should be eliminat-

ed, allowing coverage by a number of broadcasters. Choice (D) is similar to choice (A) and is wrong for the same reason. (By the way, when you see that two or more answer choices on the LSAT are very similar, it's a strong signal that these choices are wrong. After all, there should be only one "right" answer to a given question.) Choice (E) is your last chance—and it's the right answer. If small differences in style of coverage don't affect the amount of information conveyed to viewers, then the premise to the author's argument is blown out of the water. (E) would be the best remark for a proponent of pool coverage to make in its defense.

Question 5

The author warns that the use of pool coverage in situations in which it may be needed may lead to other situations in which

(A) public events covered by the media are subjected to undue analytical scrutiny
(B) broadcasters accept further limitation of their First Amendment freedoms
(C) the informational content of news events is diminished
(D) pool coverage is relied upon when it is in fact undesirable
(E) broadcasters suffer increasing erosion of their capacity for news gathering

Ⓐ Ⓑ Ⓒ Ⓓ Ⓔ

Answer and Explanation

Question 5 is a detail question. The authorial warning occurs in the last paragraph. There the author expresses the hope that the few situations in which pool coverage is necessary will not "foster a casual acceptance of pool implementation in other situations." Unnecessary pool coverage translates to undesirable pool coverage for the author—so choice (D) is your answer. (A) comes out of left field—the author never mentions the dangers of analysis-crazed media. (Who knows, she might even welcome such a situation. It would provide the public with a lot of information, wouldn't it?) (B) calls attention to the author's fleeting reference—back in the first paragraph—to the First Amendment freedoms afforded the press. But in her discussion of these freedoms, the author never makes the specific argument that pool coverage violates them. So expanded use of pool coverage couldn't be referred to as a "further limitation."

Choice (C) could have been tempting if you made things difficult for yourself. If you thought, "Well, gee, the author thinks pool coverage limits the informational content of presidential debates, so she probably would claim that expanded use of pool coverage would reduce the informational content of other news events, too." But such logical gymnastics shouldn't be necessary on the LSAT. And remember, this is a specific-detail question—you've got to stick to what the author is doing in the last paragraph, where her warning occurs. The same thing goes for (E). The author does think pool coverage limits news gathering, but this point never arises in her final warning to you. Once again, it was (D) for Question 5.

Question 6

The author's argument that the pool system "denies viewers an opportunity to gain maximum insight from the debate" (lines 23–25) would be most WEAKENED if it could be shown that

(A) candidates' debate performances rarely make a difference of more than a few percent in voting results
(B) most debate viewers form their opinions primarily on the basis of post-debate commentary presented separately by each network

(C) candidates' posture and mannerisms during debates are as important in forming voter opinion as their actual words
(D) few viewers of televised debates bother to read followup commentary in newspapers and magazines
(E) competitive coverage would provide viewers with a wider variety of interpretations on which to base their opinions

Ⓐ Ⓑ Ⓒ Ⓓ Ⓔ

Answer and Explanation

Question 6 calls your attention to a specific part of the passage, namely lines 23–25, but you're actually dealing once again with the author's overall argument. The author feels that the pool system "denies viewers an opportunity to gain maximum insight from the debate" because the sharing of news coverage means that viewers are receiving only one set of images—only one version of the debate—not a wide variety representing various viewpoints. According to the author, this prevents individual broadcasters from conveying a unique account of the debate to their viewers. The question asks you to find an answer choice that would weaken the author's contention that this limitation adversely affects viewers' ability to make voting decisions.

Choice (A) might be tempting at first. If debate performances don't sway many voters one way or another, what difference does it make what version of the debate they saw? But choice (A) doesn't address the author's specific argument concerning the effects of the pool system on voter insight. It doesn't matter if a debate doesn't have a major impact on the outcome of an election. What matters—to the author at least—is that the public has access to as much information as possible when deciding how to vote. So (A) wouldn't weaken the author's argument. Choice (B) reveals a way to alleviate—if not make irrelevant—the limits that the pool system places on the public's access to a variety of ideas. If networks were to wrap up a debate with their own followup commentary, providing the public with a diversity of ideas that they then use as a basis for making voting decisions, then the author's objections to the pool system would be weakened. So (B) looks pretty good, but go on to the other choices. (C), (D), and (E) would all strengthen, not weaken, the author's argument. If (C) is correct, then the author's objections to pool coverage are right on the mark—no amount of postdebate coverage could make up for viewers' having access to only one visual version of a debate. If (D) is correct, the importance of televised coverage—and a variety of it—is emphasized all the more. Finally, (E) just restates the author's argument. "Competitive coverage" means the same thing as elimination of pool coverage. So it was choice (B) for Question 6.

Question 7

Which of the following titles best describes the content of the passage?

(A) Debate Coverage: How It Changes Voters' Opinions
(B) The "Pool" System: A Limitation on Public Access to Information
(C) The "Pool" System: Its Benefits Versus Its Impracticalities
(D) First Amendment Press Rights: How They Conflict with Presidential Politics
(E) Televised Debates: Their Role in Presidential Politics

Ⓐ Ⓑ Ⓒ Ⓓ Ⓔ

Answer and Explanation

Question 7 asks for the title that best describes the content of the passage. Wrong answer choices in such questions usually involve titles that are either too general or too specific—or those that are totally outside

the passage's scope. Take choice (A), for example. The author doesn't discuss how debate coverage changes voters' opinions, does she? Throw it out! The author also doesn't discuss the benefits or impracticalities of the pool system. Throw (C) out! Does the author discuss how First Amendment press rights conflict with presidential politics? Nope—forget (D). How about (E)? In the first paragraph, the author does touch on the influence exercised by televised presidential debates. But the brunt of the passage involves the pool system and the limitations it imposes on public access to information. That's (B), your answer—the only choice that accurately reflects the author's main concerns.

Passage for Questions 8–10:

It is crucial to question the assumption that for-profit health care institutions have special obligations to help subsidize care for the needy over and above their general obligation as taxpayers. As the
(5) for-profits are quick to point out, supermarkets are not expected to provide free food to the hungry poor, and real estate developers are not expected to let the poor live rent free in their housing. Yet food and housing, like health care,
(10) are basic necessities for even minimal subsistence. If there are basic human rights to some adequate level of health care, it is reasonable to think there are such rights to food and shelter as well.

Whose obligation is it, then, to secure some
(15) basic health care for those unable to secure it for themselves? Assuming that private markets and charity leave some without access to whatever amount of health care that justice requires be available to all, there are several reasons to believe
(20) that the obligation ultimately rests with the federal government. First, the obligation to secure a just or fair overall distribution of benefits and burdens across society is usually understood to be

a general societal obligation. Second, the federal
(25) government is the institution society commonly
employs to meet societywide distributive requirements. With its taxing power, it has the
revenue-raising capacities to finance what would
be a massively expensive program for an adequate
(30) level of health care to be guaranteed to all. This
taxing power also allows the burden of financing
health care for the poor to be spread fairly across
all members of society and not to depend on the
vagaries of how wealthy or poor a state or local
(35) area happens to be. The federal government also
has the power to coordinate programs
guaranteeing access to health care for the poor
across local and state boundaries. This is necessary both for reducing inefficiencies that allow
(40) substantial numbers of the poor to fall between
the cracks of the patchwork of local and state
programs, and for ensuring that there are not
great differences in the minimum of health care
guaranteed to all in different locales within our
(45) country.

If we are one society, a *United* States, then the
level of health care required by justice for all citizens should not vary greatly in different locales
because of political and economic contingencies.
(50) It is worth noting that food stamp programs and
housing subsidies, also aimed at basic necessities,
similarly are largely a federal responsibility. These
are reasons for the federal government having the
obligation to guarantee access to health care for
(55) those unable to secure it for themselves. It might
do this by directly providing the care itself, or by
providing vouchers to be used by the poor in the
health care marketplace. *How* access should be
guaranteed and secured—and in particular, to
(60) what extent market mechanisms ought to be uti-
lized—is a separate question.

Question 8

The author's primary concern in the passage is to
discuss

(A) the level of expenditures required to ensure equi-
table access to health care for all
(B) measures that might be enacted to carry out a program of subsidized health care
(C) differences among states and localities in the provision of basic social services
(D) whether a national commitment to health care
can be reconciled with the federal structure of the
United States
(E) which institutions bear the obligation for assuring
adequate health services for the poor

Ⓐ Ⓑ Ⓒ Ⓓ Ⓔ

Answer and Explanation

The main topic of this passage isn't immediately
apparent. The first paragraph leaves you expecting the
author to examine the obligations of for-profit health
care or the basic human rights to food and shelter.
The author's real topic becomes clear only when you
reach the second paragraph and its introductory
question—"Whose obligation is it to secure basic
health care for those unable to secure it for themselves?" According to the author, it's the federal government's obligation; the rest of the passage serves to
back up this claim. The second paragraph outlines the
powers that enable the federal government to guarantee access to health care for all those who need it.
Finally, the third paragraph reiterates the basic right to
an adequate level of health care and the government's
responsibility to provide it. The author ends by introducing the problem of how the federal government
should guarantee access to health care.

Question 8 is a main idea question that takes you
back to the beginning of the second paragraph.
Remember, that's where the author first introduces his

main topic—the question of whose obligation it is to secure basic health care for those unable to secure it for themselves. That's this passage's big idea, and choice (E), the correct choice, captures it well. Turning now to the wrong answers, choice (A) is way too specific. The author mentions in the second paragraph that the government's taxing power enables it to raise the money required for health care expenditures, but he doesn't delve into specifics, like the exact level of expenditures that would be required. The same goes for choices (B) and (C). In the last paragraph, the author only fleetingly discusses the how of his argument, choice (B). He also mentions that differences among various states and localities in the provision of basic social services could arise, choice (C), but these differences aren't specifically described, and they don't take up the bulk of the discussion. As for choice (D), the author's argument presupposes that a national commitment to health care can be reconciled with the federal structure of the United States. Indeed, the author's whole argument is that the federal structure is ideal for assuring access to health care. Again, the correct answer is choice (E).

Question 9

The author mentions federal "food stamp programs and housing subsidies" (lines 50–51) primarily in order to

(A) modify a previous point in response to new information

(B) support his argument by mentioning a comparable situation

(C) argue that these programs should be modified

(D) make a concession to a contrasting opinion

(E) acknowledge that not all programs would benefit from the approach he favors

Ⓐ Ⓑ Ⓒ Ⓓ Ⓔ

Answer and Explanation

Look at lines 50–51, where the author mentions federal food stamp programs and housing subsidies. Why are these mentioned? The author notes that the food stamp programs and housing subsidies, both of which are aimed at basic necessities, are largely a federal responsibility. He mentions these two already established federal programs in order to support his argument that the federal government should start a *similar* program involving access to health care—another basic necessity. Now, keeping that in mind, you probably could have picked the correct answer, choice (B), by looking solely at the verbs of the answer choices.

But take a closer look at the wrong answers. As for (A), the author certainly doesn't modify a previous point—in fact, he reiterates his main argument wholesale. And he doesn't argue for the modification of the aforementioned programs, either. He just wishes that a federal health care program would join them, so (C) gets eliminated. The author's reference to food stamp programs and housing subsidies does not involve a "contrasting opinion." As you know, the author sees the existence of these programs as support for his own argument. Since no contrasting opinion is presented, no "concession" can be made to it, and choice (D) is wrong. The "approach" favored by the author is federal support of programs involving basic human necessities. Food stamps and housing subsidies are examples of programs that have already benefited from this approach, so (E) doesn't make sense. Again, choice (B) is the answer.

Question 10

According to the passage, the federal government possesses all the following powers in regard to health care EXCEPT the power to

(A) raise the revenue to finance health care expenditures
(B) distribute the costs of health care equitably among different sectors of the country
(C) ensure that the poor have access to health care regardless of state and local boundaries
(D) compel private businesses and charities to assume greater responsibility for financing health care for the needy
(E) set comparable standards for the minimum level of health care in different areas

Answer and Explanation

This is a detail question, and the second paragraph provides you with all the information you need. It is there that the author lists the federal government's powers regarding health care. If you managed to remember the nature of these powers, it might have been fairly easy for you to run down through the choices and pick out the one that looked suspicious. Assuming you didn't, compare each choice with the information in the second paragraph. Choice (A) corresponds to the first power cited—the federal government's ability to tax. This power enables it to raise the revenue needed to finance health care expenditures. Choice (B), conveniently enough, corresponds to the second power cited. The government's taxing power ensures that the burden of financing health care would be spread equitably across all members of society. Choice (C) corresponds nicely to the third power—the power to coordinate programs guaranteeing access to health care for the poor across local and state boundaries. The ability to ensure that there are not great differences in the minimum of health care guaranteed to all is the last power cited and one that is paraphrased in choice (E). This leaves you with choice (D). Nowhere does the author mention a state power that can compel private businesses and charities to assume greater responsibility for financing health care for the needy. By virtue of being wrong, choice (D) is the answer to Question 10.

THE WRITING SAMPLE

The Writing Sample comes at the end of your LSAT day. Typically, it consists of a scenario followed by two possible courses of action. You'll have thirty minutes to make a written case that one of the two courses of action is superior.

This section tests your ability to write a clear, concise, persuasive argument. No outside knowledge whatsoever is required.

You'll receive a pen to write the essay, as well as scrap paper to plan out your response before you actually write it. Your essay must be confined to the space provided, which is roughly the equivalent of one sheet of standard lined paper. You won't be given additional paper, so you'll have to keep your argument concise. Usually, two or three paragraphs will be enough. Note that there's really no time or space to change your mind or radically alter your essay once you've begun writing, so *plan your argument out carefully before beginning to write*. Make sure to write as legibly as you can.

The Writing Sample is ungraded, but it is sent to law schools along with your LSAT score. Many law schools use the Writing Sample to help make decisions on borderline cases, or to decide between applicants with otherwise comparable credentials. Granted, it may not carry the same weight as the scored sections of the test, but since it can impact on your admission chances, your best bet is to take it seriously.

Sample Topic

The structure of every Writing Sample topic is the same: a brief introduction first outlines the choice to be made. That's followed by two bullet-pointed criteria that should guide your decision. Finally, the two alternatives that you're to choose from are described in a paragraph each.

The following is an example of a Writing Sample topic:

> The *Daily Tribune*, a metropolitan newspaper, is considering two candidates for promotion to business editor. Write an argument for one candidate over the other with the following considerations in mind:
>
> • The editor must train new writers and assign stories.
> • The editor must be able to edit and rewrite stories under daily deadline pressure.

DOES IT REALLY MATTER?

The Writing Sample may not matter in some admissions decisions, but in others, it will be crucial. If you take it seriously, therefore, you'll be covered either way.

Laura received a B.A. in English from a large university. She was managing editor of her college newspaper and served as a summer intern at her hometown daily paper. Laura starting working at the *Tribune* right out of college and spent three years at the city desk covering the city economy. Eight years ago the paper formed its business section and Laura became part of the new department. After several years covering state business, Laura began writing on the national economy. Three years ago, Laura was named senior business and finance editor on the national business staff; she is also responsible for supervising seven writers.

Palmer attended an elite private college where he earned both a B.S. in business administration and an M.A. in journalism. After receiving his journalism degree, Palmer worked for three years on a monthly business magazine. He won a prestigious national award for a series of articles on the impact of monetary policy on multinational corporations. Palmer came to the *Tribune* three years ago to fill the newly created position of international business writer. He was the only member of the international staff for two years and wrote on almost a daily basis. He now supervises a staff of four writers. Last year, Palmer developed a bimonthly business supplement for the *Tribune* that has proved highly popular and has helped increase the paper's circulation.

The Eight Basic Principles of Writing Sample Success

Here are the most important rules-of-thumb to remember when attacking the Writing Sample:

1. Use Scrap Paper to Plan Your Essay
The proctors give you scrap paper for a reason. Use it! Make yourself a rudimentary outline, listing the points you want to make in each paragraph. Ideally, you should know what you want to say and how you want to say it before putting pen to paper.

2. Don't Obsess over Making Your Choice of Alternative
Nobody really cares which choice you make (for example, whether you choose to support Laura or Palmer in the sample above). What's

NOBODY CARES

The admissions officers don't care what you think here; they care *how* you think. Make your choice of alternative quickly and then stick with it.

NO POINTS FOR SPONTANEITY

Since the Writing Sample topic always takes the same basic form, you can decide in advance exactly how you will structure your response to that topic. That will save time, giving you more time to devote to your deathless prose.

important is how well you support the choice you make. Generally, the alternatives are written to be pretty evenly matched, so there's no right or wrong answer, just a well-supported or ill-supported position.

3. Get Right to the Point
The first sentence should immediately offer a solid endorsement of one choice over the other. Assume that the reader is already familiar with the situation; there's no need to waste time describing the scenario and the alternatives.

4. Use a Clear, Simple Essay Format
Since all the essay topics have the same structure, you can decide in advance how you will structure your response. One possibility is the "winner/loser" format, in which the first paragraph begins with a statement of choice and then discusses the reason why your choice (the winner) is superior. The next paragraph focuses on why the other alternative (the loser) is not as good, and should end with a concluding sentence reaffirming your decision. Another possibility is the "according to the criteria" format, in which the first paragraph would discuss both the winner and the loser in light of the first criterion, and the second paragraph would discuss them both in light of the second criterion.

Whether you adopt one of these formats or use one of your own, the most important thing is that your essay be coherent, and not all over the map in its reasoning. The more organized your essay is, the more persuasive it will be.

5. Mention, but Downplay, the Loser's Strengths and the Winner's Weaknesses
Use sentence structures that allow you to do this, such as, "Even though Palmer won a prestigious national award. . . ." and then attempt to demonstrate why this is really no big deal. This is an example of mentioning yet downplaying one of the loser's strengths. Try to do the same thing for at least one of the winner's obvious weaknesses. Doing so demonstrates that you see the full picture. Recognizing and dealing with possible objections makes your argument that much stronger.

6. Don't Simply Repeat Facts about the Candidates
Try instead to offer an *interpretation of the facts in light of the stated criteria*. If you're arguing for Laura in the topic above, you can't state simply that "Laura was named senior business and finance editor on the national

But Doctors Have Bad Handwriting . . .

If you don't think your poor handwriting will work against you, guess again. Many people will be prejudiced against your Writing Sample if it's hard to decipher.

Plan Out Your Thirty Minutes

You'll probably want to break down your time like so:

• Five to seven minutes: planning and outlining
• Twenty minutes: writing
• Three to five minutes: proofreading and correcting

business staff" and expect the reader to infer that that's a good thing. For all we know, being in that position may be a detriment when it comes to the criteria—training new writers and working under daily deadline pressure. It's up to you to indicate why certain facts about the winner are positive factors in light of the criteria, and vice versa for facts about the loser. Merely parroting what's written in the topic won't win you any points with the law schools.

7. Write Well

It sounds obvious, of course, but you should try to make your prose as clean and flawless as you can. Some people get so entangled in content that they neglect the mechanics of essay writing. But spelling, grammar, and writing mechanics are important. Use structural signals to keep your writing fluid and clear, and use transitions between paragraphs to keep the entire essay unified. Above all, write legibly. Nothing annoys essay readers more than an illegible essay.

8. Budget Your Time Wisely

We suggest spending roughly five to seven minutes reading the topic, making a decision, and planning out your essay. As we suggested, use the scrap paper provided to jot down a quick outline of the points you intend to make. Then spend about twenty minutes writing the essay. This should be plenty of time; remember, we're only looking at two or three paragraphs at the most. This schedule will leave about three to five minutes at the end to proofread your essay for spelling and grammar.

Sample Essay

At this point, you'll probably want to try your hand at writing an essay on the above-mentioned topic. Please do so (observing the thirty-minute time limit, of course). Then check your essay, making sure it observes the basic principles outlined above.

The following is a sample response to the essay topic above:

> Both candidates are obviously qualified, but Laura is the better choice. For one thing, Laura has been working at the *Tribune* for eleven years, and has therefore had plenty of opportunity to learn the workings of the paper. For another, her experience has been in national rather than international business, and national

business will certainly be the focus of the *Tribune*'s financial coverage. In her current capacity, she is responsible for writing and editing articles while simultaneously overseeing the work of a staff of seven. Clearly, then, Laura can work under deadline pressure and manage a staff, a capability she demonstrated at an early age as the managing director of her college newspaper. Although Laura's academic credentials may not measure up to Palmer's, her background in English, her history of steady promotions, and her work as senior national business writer—combined with a solid business knowledge and obvious drive for accomplishment—will certainly spur the department to journalistic excellence.

Palmer's résumé is admirable but is nonetheless inferior to Laura's. True, Palmer has evidently done a fine job managing the international section, but his staff numbers only four, and the scope of the venture is smaller than Laura's. True, Palmer's articles on the impact of monetary policy did win an award in the past, but since he has been working for the *Tribune* no such honors have been forthcoming. Not only does Palmer lack the English literature background that Laura has, but he also lacks her long experience at the *Tribune*. Furthermore, Palmer's editing experience seems slight, considering the length of his current tenure and the size of his staff, and while he demonstrates competence in the area of international business, he has little experience in the national business area.

In light of these circumstances, the newspaper would meet its stated objectives best by promoting Laura to the position of business editor.

This generally well-reasoned and well-written essay would be an asset to any applicant's law school admissions file. The writer states his choice in the first sentence and then substantiates this choice in a paragraph on the winner and a paragraph on the loser. Notice the way this writer acknowledges, yet rebuts, the winner's flaws and the loser's strengths. Whether or not one agrees with the choice of Laura over Palmer, the essay definitely makes a strong, well-reasoned case for the choice—and that, after all, is what the law schools will be looking for.

SO CLEARLY THE JOB MUST BE GIV . . .

Don't let yourself get cut off. It's a big mistake to leave the Writing Sample unfinished. Be strict with yourself, so that you'll have at least a few minutes left at the end to read over what you've written.

A Note on Finishing

Before leaving the topic of the Writing Sample, we want to make one more important point—make sure you finish your essay. Some students find that time is called while they're still writing. Bad move. Not only does that leave you with an incomplete essay, it also hints to the admissions officers that your organization and time-management skills aren't stellar.

So don't make this classic error. Give yourself plenty of time to finish the essay.

KAPLAN

CHAPTER 3

TEST EXPERTISE

The first year of law school is a frenzied experience for most law students. In order to meet the requirements of a rigorous work schedule, they either learn to prioritize and budget their time or else fall hopelessly behind. It's no surprise, then, that the LSAT, the test specifically designed to predict success in the first year of law school, is a time-intensive test, demanding excellent time-management skills as well as that *sine qua non* of the successful lawyer—grace under pressure.

As we saw, it's one thing to answer a Logical Reasoning question correctly; it's quite another to answer twenty-five of them correctly in thirty-five minutes. And the same goes for Reading Comp and Logic Games—it's a whole new ballgame once you move from doing an individual game or passage at your leisure to handling a full Logic Games or Reading Comp section under actual timed conditions. In fact, the only section of the test that's not very time intensive is the Writing Sample; most test takers find they have ample time to write the essay. But when it comes to the scored sections, time pressure is a factor that affects virtually every test taker.

So when you're comfortable with the content of the test, namely, the type of material discussed in the previous chapter, your next challenge will be to take it to the next level, test expertise, which will enable you to manage the all-important time element of the test.

IT'S NOT JUST ABOUT CORRECT ANSWERS

For complete LSAT success, you've got to get as many correct answers as possible in the time you're given. Knowing the strategies is not enough. You've got to perfect your time management skills so that you get a chance to use those strategies on as many questions as possible.

BE A TEST EXPERT

In order to meet the stringent time requirements of the LSAT, you've got to cultivate the following elements of test expertise:

- A sense of timing
- An ability to skip around without getting mixed up
- An ability to assess the difficulty level of a question or passage or game
- A cool head

POP QUIZ

Every question is worth exactly one point. But questions vary dramatically in difficulty level. Given a shortage of time, which questions should you work on—easy or hard?

The Four Basic Principles of Test Expertise

On most of the tests you take in school, you wouldn't dream of not taking at least a try at every single one of the questions. If a question seems particularly difficult, you spend significantly more time on it, since you'll probably be given more points for correctly answering a hard question. Not so on the LSAT. Remember, every LSAT question, no matter how hard, is worth a single point. And since there are so many questions to do in so little time, you'd be a fool to spend three minutes getting a point for a hard question and then not have time to get a couple of quick points from two easy questions later in the section.

Given this combination—limited time, all questions equal in weight—you've got to develop a way of handling the test sections to make sure you get as many points as you can as quickly and easily as you can. Here are the principles that will help you do that:

Attack the Questions in Any Order That Strikes You as Logical

One of the most valuable strategies to help you finish the sections in time is to learn to recognize and deal first with the questions, games, and passages that are easier and more familiar to you. That means temporarily skipping those that promise to be difficult and time consuming. You can always come back to these at the end, and if you run out of time, you're much better off not getting to questions you may have had difficulty with, rather than missing potentially doable material. Of course, since there's no wrong-answer penalty, always fill in an answer to every question on the test, whether you get to it or not.

Learn to Recognize and Seek out Questions You're Good At

Another thing to remember about managing the sections is that LSAT questions, games, and passages, unlike items on the SAT and other standardized tests, are not presented in order of difficulty. There's no rule that says that you have to work through the sections in any particular order; in fact, the test makers scatter the easy and difficult questions throughout the section, in effect rewarding those who actually get to the end. Don't lose sight of what you're being tested for along with your reading and thinking skills—efficiency and cleverness. If you find sequencing games particularly easy, for example, seek out the sequencing game on the LG section and do it first. Similarly, if you just love formal logic questions, head straight for such questions when you first turn to the LR sections.

Know That the Test Questions Are Written to Different Levels of Difficulty

It's imperative that you remain calm and composed while working through a section. You can't allow yourself to be rattled by one hard logic game or reading passage, so that it throws off your performance on the rest of the section. Expect to find at least one difficult passage or game on every section, but remember, you won't be the only one to have trouble with it. The test is curved to take the tough material into account. Having trouble with a difficult logic game isn't going to ruin your score—but getting upset about it and letting it throw you off-track will. When you understand that part of the test maker's goal is to reward those who keep their composure, you'll recognize the importance of not panicking when you run into challenging material.

Control Time Instead of Letting Time Control You

Of course, the last thing you want to happen is to have time called on a particular section before you've gotten to half the questions. It's essential, therefore, that you pace yourself, keeping in mind the general guidelines for how long to spend on any individual question, passage, or game (we'll give you those guidelines below). No one is saying that you should spend, for instance, exactly one and a quarter minutes on every Logical Reasoning question. But you should have a sense of how long you have to do each question, so you know when you're exceeding the limit and should start to move faster.

Keeping track of time is also important for guessing. Remember, there's no penalty for a wrong answer on the LSAT! So it pays to leave a little time at the end to guess on the questions you couldn't answer. For instance, let's say you never get a chance to do the last logic game on an LG section. If you just leave the grids for those questions blank, you're going to get no points for that entire game. If, on the other hand, you give yourself a little time at the end to fill in a guess for each of those questions, you'll have a very good chance of getting lucky on at least one or two questions. That would up your raw score by one or two points—which translates into a higher scaled score.

So, when working on a section, always remember to keep track of time. Don't spend a wildly disproportionate amount of time on any one question or group of questions. Also, give yourself thirty seconds or so at the end of each section to fill in answers for any questions you didn't get to. After all, a correct guess is worth just as much as any other correct answer.

DON'T BE MACHO!

It's difficult for some of us to give up on a tough, time-consuming question, but it must be done occasionally. Remember, there's no point of honor at stake here, but there are LSAT points at stake.

GUESS!

We've said it before and we'll say it again: If you can't do a question or can't get to it, guess! Fill in an answer—any answer—on the answer grid. There's no penalty if you're wrong, but there's a big fat point if you're right.

Section-Specific Strategies

Let's now look at the section-specific timing requirements and some tips for meeting them.

Logical Reasoning

Time Per Question

Twenty-four to twenty-six questions in thirty-five minutes works out to roughly a minute and a quarter per question. Keep in mind that this is only an average; there are bound to be some questions that take less time and some that take more. It's okay if the occasional question takes you two minutes, if you're able to balance it out with a question that takes forty-five seconds. Remember, too, that every question is worth the same, so don't get hung up on any one question. No single point on this section is worth three minutes of your valuable time, that's for sure. And think about it—if a question is so hard that it takes you that long to answer it, chances are you may get it wrong anyway. In that case, you'd have nothing to show for your extra time but a lower score.

Managing the Section

What kind of Logical Reasoning questions should you skip? Certainly questions containing stimuli that are indecipherable to you after a quick reading. Questions containing extra-long stimulus arguments may be good to skip initially as well, especially if you're running behind on time. But don't automatically be intimidated by the sheer length of a stimulus; often, the long ones are uncomplicated and easy to understand.

If you adhere to our strategy of reading the question stem first, you may be able to single out questions to postpone based solely on question type. This is a matter of recognizing your own strengths and weaknesses. For example, if a question involves finding a principle that lends credence to an argument, and you know historically that principle questions are a problem for you, then that's a good question to postpone.

A good stimulus is one that comes with two questions attached. There are usually anywhere from two to four double-question stimuli on each Logical Reasoning section. Working through these, as opposed to single question arguments, saves a little time, as you can potentially rack up two points for reading only one stimulus.

Logic Games

Time Per Game

There are four games to get through in thirty-five minutes, which works out to roughly eight and a half minutes per game. Remember, just as in Logical Reasoning, this is an average—some games may take a little more time, while some may take a little less.

Managing the Section

There are definitely some things to keep in mind when it comes to working through an entire Logic Games section. First, and most important, is the necessity of previewing the section. By this, we mean that you should literally flip through the pages, having a glance at each game in order to decide which games look the easiest and most familiar to you. Previewing, of course, is not foolproof; a game that looks fairly straightforward at first glance could easily turn out to be a killer. But it works more often than not.

The ideal goal is to tackle the games in order of difficulty, from easiest to hardest. But if you achieve nothing more than saving the hardest game for last, then the strategy is a winner.

So how do you tell which games may be difficult? The best way is to know the game types discussed in the Logic Games section cold, and to have a feeling for which types you're strong in and which ones you should avoid like the plague (until the end, of course). A game that doesn't look familiar at all could simply be an oddball game—a good candidate to postpone. And don't necessarily be scared off by games with a lot of rules; sometimes, this works to your advantage. The more rules they give you, the more definite and concrete the game situation is, and the easier it will be to answer the questions. It's the games with few rules that often turn out to be tough, because they're inherently ambiguous.

If you have several Logic Games to practice on, you may wish to build gradually to the point where you're ready to take full-length sections. Begin by attempting one game in eight or nine minutes. Next, try two games in seventeen minutes. When you're ready to move on, try three games in about twenty-six to twenty-seven minutes, until finally you can handle a full four-game section in thirty-five minutes.

Finally, remember what we said about the way the test makers test efficiency. They're crafty—they'll sometimes throw an intentionally time-consuming question at the end of a game, possibly one involving a rule change that requires you to backtrack and set the game up all over again. Bear in mind that when this happens, they may not be testing who's smart

LOGIC GAMES EXPERTISE

Here's how best to manage your time on the LG section:

- Spend about eight and a half minutes per game.
- Preview the section so you know what you're up against.
- Do the easiest game first; save the toughest for last.
- Skip rule-change questions and others that promise to be especially time consuming.

enough to get the right answer, but who's clever enough to skip the killer question in order to devote their precious time to the next game, with a possible payoff of six or seven new points.

If you apply the principles regarding making deductions and working through questions discussed earlier, and combine that with these tips on how to approach a full Logic Games section, you'll be well on your way to an excellent Logic Games performance on the day of the test.

Reading Comprehension

Time Per Passage
The Reading Comp section format is similar to that of the Logic Games section: four passages in thirty-five minutes, which means about eight and a half minutes per passage. The Reading Comp strategies and techniques in the previous chapter should help you to get through each passage as quickly as possible, but here are a few additional points about tackling a full section.

Managing the Section
It's a little more difficult to preview the Reading Comp section than it is to preview a Logic Games section, but it is possible to know that it's time to move on if the first third of a passage is extraordinarily confusing or simply really boring to the point of distraction. Concentration is a major key in Reading Comp, and if you simply can't "lock into" the ideas in a particular passage, then it's time to put that one aside and look for friendlier territory. As in Logic Games, the goal is to save the most difficult stuff for last.

Quite often, you'll encounter Reading Comprehension passages that contain a preponderance of technical details or difficult concepts, only to find that few if any questions deal with the part of the passage that's so dense. Just as in the Logic Games example above, the test makers aren't necessarily testing to see who's smart enough to understand that section of the passage; they may be looking to see who's clever enough to skim past those details and focus on the more important aspects of the passage instead. If you keep this in mind, you'll be less likely to get mired in extraneous details.

READING COMP EXPERTISE

Some suggestions for maximizing your time on the RC section:

- Spend about eight and a half minutes per passage (including questions).
- Preview the section, as in LG, to assess difficulty levels.
- Save any passages that look daunting for last.
- Remember not to get mired in details. Read for structure and main idea and come back for the details if necessary to answer questions.

Answer Grid Expertise

An important part of LSAT test expertise is knowing how to handle the answer grid. After all, you not only have to pick the right answers; you also have to mark those right answers on the answer grid in an efficient and accurate way. It sounds simple, but it's extremely important: *Don't make mistakes filling out your answer grid!* When time is short, it's easy to get confused going back and forth between your test book and your grid. If you know the answer, but misgrid, you won't get the points. Here are a few methods of avoiding mistakes on the answer grid.

Always Circle Questions You Skip

Put a big circle in your test book around the number of any question you skip (you may even want to circle the whole question itself). When you go back, such questions will then be easy to locate. Also, if you accidentally skip a box on the grid, you can more easily check your grid against your book to see where you went wrong.

Always Circle Answers You Choose

Circle the correct answers in your test booklet, but don't transfer the answers to the grid right away. That wastes too much time, especially if you're doing a lot of skipping around. Circling your answers in the test book will also make it easier to check your grid against your book.

Grid Five or More Answers at Once

As we said, don't transfer your answers to the grid after every question. Transfer your answers after every five questions, or at the end of each Reading Comp passage or Logic Game (find the method that works best for you). That way, you won't keep breaking your concentration to mark the grid. You'll save time and improve accuracy. Just make sure you're not left at the end of the section with ungridded answers!

DON'T UNDERESTIMATE THE IMPORTANCE OF GRID TECHNIQUE

Yes, it's pure bookkeeping, but you won't get the points if you put your answers in the wrong place, or if you waste time searching for the right place to put your answers. Take the time now to develop some good answer grid habits.

Save Time at the End for a Final Grid Check
Make sure you have enough time at the end of every section to make a quick check of your grid, to make sure you've got an oval filled in for each question in the section. Remember, a blank grid has no chance of earning a point, but a guess does.

CHAPTER 4

TEST MENTALITY

We first looked at the content that makes up each specific section of the LSAT, focussing on the strategies and techniques you'll need to tackle individual questions, games, and passages. Then we discussed the test expertise involved in moving from individual items to working through full-length sections. Now we're ready to turn our attention to the often overlooked aspect of test mentality, and to combine these factors with what we learned in Levels One and Two to put the finishing touches on your comprehensive LSAT approach.

The Four Basics of Good Test Mentality

We've already armed you with the weapons you need to do well on the LSAT. But you must wield those weapons with the right frame of mind and in the right spirit. This involves taking a certain stance toward the entire test. Here's what's involved:

1. Test Awareness

To do your best on the LSAT, you must always keep in mind that the test is like no other test you've taken before, both in terms of content and in terms of scoring system. If you took a test in high school or college and got a quarter of the questions wrong, you'd probably receive a pretty lousy grade. But on the LSAT, you can get a quarter of the questions wrong (about twenty-five) and still score higher than the eightieth percentile! The test is geared so that only the very best test takers are able to finish every section. But even these people rarely get every question right. As

WHAT MAKES FOR GOOD TEST MENTALITY?

We're glad you asked. The important elements are:

- Test awareness
- Stamina
- Confidence
- The right attitude

NOBODY'S PERFECT

Remember that the LSAT isn't like most tests you've taken. You can get a lot of questions wrong and still get a great score. So don't get rattled if you miss a few questions. Even those with "perfect" scores of 180 get some questions wrong.

BE COOL

Losing a few extra points here and there won't do serious damage to your score, but losing your head will. Keeping your composure is an important test-taking skill.

mentioned earlier, you can get a "perfect" score of 180 and still get a handful of questions wrong.

What does this mean for you? Well, just as you shouldn't let one bad game or passage ruin an entire section, you shouldn't let what you consider to be a below par performance on one section ruin your performance on the entire test. A lousy performance on one single section will not by itself spoil your score (unless you miss almost every question). However, if you allow that poor section to rattle you, it can have a cumulative negative effect, setting in motion a downward spiral. It's the kind of thing that could potentially do serious damage to your score. Losing a few extra points won't do you in, but losing your head will.

Remember, if you feel you've done poorly on a section, don't sweat it. Who knows, it could be the experimental. And even if it's not, chances are it's just a difficult section—a factor that will already be figured into the scoring curve anyway. The point is, you must remain calm and collected. Simply do your best on each section, and once a section is over, forget about it and move on.

While we're on the topic of the experimental section, we'd like to reiterate an important point: never, never try to figure out which section is unscored. This practice has caused trouble for countless test takers. They somehow convince themselves that a certain section is the one that doesn't count, and then don't take it seriously. And they're pretty upset when they find out they guessed wrong. You can't know which section is the experimental section, so handle each section as if it counts. That way, you're covered no matter what. If a section you had trouble with turns out to be experimental, it's gravy. If it turns out to be scored—well, think how much worse you'd have done if you blew it off entirely.

2. Stamina

The LSAT is a fairly grueling experience, and some test takers simply run out of gas before it's over. To avoid this, take as many full-length practice tests as possible in the week or two before the test. That way, five sections plus a writing sample will seem like a breeze (well, maybe not a breeze, but at least not a hurricane).

One option is to buy PrepTests, which are the actual released exams published by Law Services. The available PrepTests are listed in the LSAT Registration and Information Book, which is available at most colleges and law schools, or you can call Law Services at 215-968-1001 for information. (Try to send away for them early, since they take two to three weeks for delivery.)

Another option, if you have some time, would be to take the full Kaplan course. We'll give you access to every released test plus loads of additional material, so you can really build up your LSAT stamina. As a bonus, you'll also have the benefit of our expert live instruction in every aspect of the LSAT. If you decide to go this route, call 1-800-KAP-TEST for the Kaplan Center location near you.

3. Confidence

Confidence feeds on itself, and unfortunately, so does self-doubt. Confidence in your ability leads to quick, sure answers and a sense of well-being that translates into more points. If you lack confidence, you end up reading sentences and answer choices two, three, or four times, to the point at which you confuse yourself and get off-track. This leads to timing difficulties, which only perpetuate the downward spiral, causing anxiety and a tendency to rush in order to finish sections.

If you subscribe to the LSAT mentality we've described, however, you'll gear all of your practice toward the major goal of taking control of the test. When you've achieved that goal—armed with the principles, techniques, strategies, and methods set forth in this book—you'll be ready to face the LSAT with supreme confidence. And that's the one sure way to score your best on the day of the test.

4. The Right Attitude

Those who approach the LSAT as an obstacle, and who rail against the necessity of taking it, usually don't fare as well as those who see the LSAT as an opportunity to show off the reading and reasoning skills that the law schools are looking for. Those who look forward to doing battle with the LSAT—or, at least, who enjoy the opportunity to distinguish themselves from the rest of the applicant pack—tend to score better than do those who resent or dread it.

It may sound a little dubious, but take our word for it: attitude adjustment is a proven test-taking technique. Here are a few steps you can take to make sure you develop the right LSAT attitude:

- Look at the LSAT as a challenge, but try not to obsess over it; you certainly don't want to psyche yourself out of the game.
- Remember that, yes, the LSAT is obviously important, but this one test will not single-handedly determine the outcome of your life.
- Try to have fun with the test. Learning how to match your wits against the test makers can be a very satisfying experience, and the

GET TOUGH

You wouldn't run a marathon without working on your stamina well in advance of the race, would you? The same goes for taking the LSAT.

DEVELOP AN ATTITUDE

It sounds New-Agey, we know. But your attitude toward the test really does affect your performance. We're not asking you to "think nice thoughts about the LSAT," but we are recommending that you change your mental stance toward the test.

reading and thinking skills you'll acquire will benefit you in law school as well as in your future legal career.

- Remember that you're more prepared than most people. You've trained with Kaplan. You have the tools you need, plus the know-how to use those tools.

A Final Word

Let's conclude with a recap of some of the most important global principles and strategies for success on the LSAT:

- The test questions are not necessarily presented in order of difficulty. Answer the questions in any order that seems effective.
- There is no penalty for wrong answers on the LSAT. *Always guess if you can't answer a question*, or if you can't get to it! Never leave a question blank.
- All questions are worth the same amount, so don't spend an excessive amount of time on any one question.
- You are rewarded for correctly identifying the "credited answer." Learn to think like the test maker—follow the test maker's reasoning to that credited answer.

Follow this advice—and all the rest that you've learned in this section—when you take the Practice Test.

CHAPTER 5

TIPS FOR THE FINAL WEEK

And Now the Real Thing . . .

Is it starting to feel like your whole life is a buildup to the LSAT? You've known about it for years, worried about it for months, and now spent at least a few weeks in solid preparation for it. As the test gets closer, you may find your anxiety is on the rise. You shouldn't worry. After the preparation you've received from this book, you're in good shape for the test.

To calm any pretest jitters you may have, though, let's go over a few strategies for the days before the test.

The Week Before Test Day

In the week or so leading up to the test, you should do the following:

- Recheck your admission ticket for accuracy; call Law Services if corrections are necessary.
- Visit the testing center if you can. Sometimes seeing the actual room where your test will be administered and taking notice of little things—like the kind of desk you'll be working on, whether the room is likely to be hot or cold, etcetera—may help to calm your nerves. And if you've never been to the campus or building where your test will take place, this is a good way to ensure that you don't get lost on the day of the test. Remember, you must be on time—the proctors won't wait for you.

- Practice getting up early and working on test material, preferably a full-length test, as if it were the real day of the test.
- Time yourself accurately, with the same device and in the same manner in which you plan to keep track of time on the test.
- Evaluate thoroughly where you stand. Use the time remaining before the test to shore up your weak points, rereading the appropriate sections of this book. But don't neglect your strong areas; after all, this is where you'll rack up most of your points.

The Day Before the Test

Try to avoid doing intensive studying the day before the test. There's little you can do to help yourself at this late date, and you may just wind up exhausting yourself and burning out. Our advice is to review a few key concepts, get together everything you'll need for test day, and then take the night off entirely. Go to see a movie or watch some TV. Try not to think too much about the test.

The Day of the Test

Get up early, leaving yourself plenty of time. Read something to warm up your brain—you don't want the LSAT to be the first written material your brain tries to assimilate that day.

Dress in layers for maximum comfort. That way, you'll be able to adjust to the testing room's temperature.

In traveling to the test center, leave yourself enough time for traffic and mass transit delays.

Be ready for a long day. Total testing time, remember, is three hours and twenty-five minutes. When you add the administrative paperwork before and after, and the ten- to fifteen-minute break in the middle, you're looking at an experience of four and a half to six hours.

Don't get flustered when they fingerprint you as you enter the testing room—this is standard operating procedure and is not intended for your FBI file. The test administrators do this because occasionally they have reason to believe that some test takers are not exactly who they say they are. If you're on the up and up, you'll have nothing to worry about.

After the test booklets are handed out, and you've filled out all of the required information, the test will begin. Your proctor should write the

---

KNOW WHEN TO QUIT

Don't try to cram a lot of studying into the last day before the test. It probably won't do you much good, for one thing, and it could bring on a case of test burnout.

PACK A SURVIVAL KIT

On the night before the test, get together an "LSAT survival kit" containing the following items:

- A watch
- A few #2 pencils (pencils with slightly dull points fill the ovals better)
- Erasers
- Photo ID card
- Your admission ticket
- A snack—there's a break and you'll probably get hungry

starting and ending time of each section on a blackboard in front of the room, and will usually announce the time remaining at specified intervals, such as when there's ten minutes remaining, five minutes remaining, and one minute remaining.

Most test centers have a clock on the wall that the proctor will use to time the test, but don't take anything for granted—your test center may not (stranger things have been known to happen). You should definitely bring along your own timing device, such as a watch or a stopwatch, so long as it doesn't make any noise (devices that beep on the hour or sound an alarm at specified times are prohibited from the testing site).

It's also best to practice using a timing routine that you'll follow during the real test. For example, some students find it helpful to set their watches at twenty-five past the hour for the scored sections, often 11:25. This way, they know that the section will end exactly when their watch says 12:00. Others reset their watches exactly on the hour at the beginning of each section, and know that every section will end at thirty-five minutes after the hour (except for the Writing Sample, of course, which will end on the half-hour). Still others synchronize their watches with the room clock and follow the proctor's timing guidelines. It doesn't matter which one of the these procedures you adopt, or even if you come up with one of your own that you're comfortable with, just as long as you use it consistently, so that keeping track of time during test is second nature.

Here are some other last-minute reminders to help guide your work on the test:

- Read each question stem carefully, and reread it before making your final selection. Also, to make sure your answer sheet is gridded accurately, say the question number and choice to yourself (silently, of course) as you grid.
- Give all five choices a fair shot in Logical Reasoning and Reading Comp, time permitting. For Logic Games, go with the objectively correct answer as soon as you find it and blow off the rest.
- Don't get bogged down in the middle of any section. At the end of *every* section are questions that may be really easy and manageable. Make sure that you get to them! Conversely, don't be alarmed if you run across extra-tough questions at the beginning, especially in Logical Reasoning. It happens. Skip past tough ones and come back to them later, making sure to circle them in the test booklet so you can find them fast.
- Preview the LG and RC sections before you launch into them. The third or fourth game or reading passage could be the easiest one. Take a brief look at all four before you decide where to begin.

DON'T RELY ON PROCTORS

Hey, they're usually nice people, but nobody's perfect. Be your own timer.

I AM NOT A CROOK

No, they don't fingerprint you because they expect you to cheat. They do it to have some way of making sure you're who you say you are.

Don't Heed the Intermission Pundits

During the break, there will undoubtedly be those who want to talk about the test—how hard or easy it is, which section is "definitely experimental," etcetera. Don't listen to these people. They will probably be wrong, for one thing. And their comments will just hurt your concentration on the rest of the test.

Do You Really Want to Cancel?

The key question to ask yourself when deciding whether to cancel is this, "Will I really do significantly better next time?"

- Don't bother trying to figure out which section is unscored. It can't help you, and you might very well be wrong. Instead, just determine to do your best on every section.
- Confidence is key. *Accentuate the positives, and don't dwell on the negatives!* Your attitude and outlook are crucial to your performance on test day.
- During the exam, try not to think about how you're scoring. It's like a baseball player who's thinking about the crowd's cheers and the sportswriters and his contract as he steps up to the plate. There's no surer way to strike out. Instead, focus on the question-by-question task of picking (A), (B), (C), (D), or (E). The correct answer is there. You don't have to come up with it; it's sitting right there in front of you! Concentrate on each question, each passage, each game—on the mechanics, in other words—and you'll be much more likely to hit a home run.

Test Rhythm

Between sections 1 and 2, 2 and 3, and 4 and 5, the proctor will say only: "Time's up on this section. Go on to the next section." Notice that there's no break here—you must go immediately from one section to the next. Also, if you finish a section early, you're not allowed to move on to another section. They're pretty strict about this one, so watch your step. If you have extra time, spend it looking back over your work on that section alone.

After section 3, you'll be instructed to close your test booklets and take a ten- to fifteen-minute break. Pay no attention to people's nervous chatter during the break. Some will say it's the hardest test since the dawn of time; others will say it's so easy they can't believe it. Either kind of comment can rattle you. Instead, bring a Walkman, headphones, and some tunes that'll pump you up and some that'll relax you, to use as needed.

After the break, you'll return to the testing room for the remaining sections. Then, after section 5, your test materials will be collected and the Writing Sample materials and pens to write the essays will be handed out (no pens are allowed on the scored sections).

After the Writing Sample is collected, the test ends and you're free to get on with your life. For most of you, this means getting back to the rest of the application and admission process we talked about earlier. In the short term, however, this signals the beginning of a well-deserved night out to unwind.

After the Test

Cancellation and Multiple Scores Policy

Unlike many things in life, the LSAT allows you a second chance. If you walk out of the test feeling that you've really not done as well as you could have, you have the option of canceling your score—as long as you notify Law Services within five business days after the day of the test. Canceling a test means that it won't be scored. It will just appear on your score report as a cancelled test. No one will know how well or poorly you really did—not even you.

There's been a recent change in the LSAT cancellation policy. Previously, in order to cancel a test, you had no option except to mail or fax the signed cancellation form to Law Services within five business days. While you still have that option, it's now possible to cancel your score immediately after the test, right at the test center. However, we strongly advise against this. When deciding whether to cancel your score, a good rule of thumb is to make an honest assessment of whether you'll do better on the next test. Wishful thinking doesn't count; you need to have a valid reason to believe that the next time would be different. Remember, no test experience is going to be perfect. If you were distracted by the proctor's hacking cough this time around, next time you may be even more distracted by construction noise, or a cold, or the hideous lime-green sweater of the person sitting in front of you.

Two legitimate reasons to cancel your test are illness and personal circumstances that cause you to perform poorly on that particular day. Also, if you feel that you didn't prepare sufficiently, then it may be advisable to cancel your score and approach your test preparation a little more seriously the next time.

But keep in mind that test takers historically underestimate their performance, especially immediately following the test. They tend to forget about all of the things that went right, and focus on everything that went wrong. So unless your performance is terribly marred by unforeseen circumstances, don't cancel your test immediately—at least sleep on the decision for one or two nights, and if you still feel you want to do it again, then send in the form. Just remember, cancellations are permanent. Once the form is sent, you can't change your mind.

What the Schools Will See

If you do cancel your test and then take it again for a score, your score report will indicate that you've canceled a previous score. Since it won't be scored, you don't have to worry about this score showing up on any

ABOUT CANCELING

While we hope you won't find it necessary to cancel your LSAT score, here are a few points to keep in mind:

- Students sometimes underestimate their performance immediately after the test and think they should cancel their scores. But doing poorly on one part of the test does not necessarily mean you've bombed. Scores should be canceled only after giving the issue careful thought and deciding that overall performance was poorer than usual.
- Scores can be canceled on the spot or within five working days after the test date.
- To avoid anxiety, use a mailgram, telegram, fax, or overnight letter.
- A form is provided at the test site, or write your own letter with name, address, social security number, signature, test date, test center name, test center code number.
- Send to: Law Service Score Cancellation, Box 2000-T, 661 Penn St., Newton, PA 18940-0995, or fax (215) 968-1277.
- Scores can now be canceled at the site of the test. But we recommend that you not do so except in extreme cases of performance disaster. Better to sleep on it and cancel later if necessary.

subsequent score report. If you take more than one test without canceling, then all the scores will show up on each score report, so the law schools will see them all. Most law schools average LSAT scores, although there are a few exceptions. Check with individual schools for their policy on multiple scores.

Post-LSAT Festivities

After all the hard work you've done preparing for and taking the LSAT, you want to make sure you take time to celebrate afterwards. Plan to get together with friends the evening after the test. Relax, have fun, let loose. After all, you've got a lot to celebrate. You prepared for the test ahead of time. You did your best. You're going to get a good score.

So start thinking about all of the great parties you'll be attending at the law school of your choice!

CHAPTER 6

THE KAPLAN ADVANTAGE™ STRESS MANAGEMENT SYSTEM

The countdown has begun. Your date with THE TEST is looming on the horizon. Anxiety is on the rise. The butterflies in your stomach have gone ballistic. Perhaps you feel as if the last thing you ate has turned into a lead ball in your stomach. Your thinking is getting cloudy. Maybe you think you won't be ready. Maybe you already know your stuff, but you're going into panic mode anyway. Worst of all, you're not sure of what to do about it.

Don't freak! It is possible to tame that anxiety and stress—before and during the test. We'll show you how. You won't believe how quickly and easily you can deal with that killer anxiety.

Making the Most of Your Prep Time

Lack of control is one of the prime causes of stress. A ton of research shows that if you don't have a sense of control over what's happening in your life you can easily end up feeling helpless and hopeless. So, just having concrete things to do and to think about—taking control—will help reduce your stress. This section shows you how to take control during the days leading up to taking the LSAT—or any other test.

Identify the Sources of Stress

The first step in gaining control is identifying the sources of your test-related stress. The idea is to pin down that free-floating anxiety so that you can take control of it. Here are some examples:

- I always freeze up on tests.
- I'm nervous about the Logic Games section (or the Logical Reasoning section or the Reading Comprehension section).
- I need a good/great score to go to Acme Law School.
- My older brother/sister/best friend/girl- or boyfriend did really well. I must match their scores or do better.
- My parents, who are paying for school, will be really disappointed if I don't test well.
- I'm afraid of losing my focus and concentration.
- I'm afraid I'm not spending enough time preparing.
- I study like crazy but nothing seems to stick in my mind.
- I always run out of time and get panicky.
- I feel as though thinking is becoming like wading through thick mud.

Take a few minutes to think about your own particular sources of test-related stress. Then write them down in some sort of order. List the statements you most associate with your stress and anxiety first, and put the least disturbing items last. As you write the list, you're forming a hierarchy of items so you can deal first with the anxiety-provokers that bug you most. Very often, taking care of the major items from the top of the list goes a long way toward relieving overall testing anxiety. You probably won't have to bother with the stuff you placed last.

Take Stock of Your Strengths and Weaknesses

Take one minute to list the areas of the test that you are good at. They can be general (Logical Reasoning) or specific (inference questions). Put down as many as you can think of, and if possible, time yourself. Write for the entire time; don't stop writing until you've reached the one-minute stopping point.

Next, take one minute to list areas of the test you're not so good at, just plain bad at, have failed at, or keep failing at. Again, keep it to one minute, and continue writing until you reach the cutoff. Don't be afraid to identify

VERY SUPERSTITIOUS

Stress expert Stephen Sideroff, Ph.D., tells of a client who always stressed out before, during, and even after taking tests. Yet she always got outstanding scores. It became obvious that she was thinking superstitiously—subconsciously believing that the great scores were a result of her worrying. She also didn't trust herself, and believed that if she didn't worry she wouldn't study hard enough. Sideroff convinced her to take a risk and work on relaxing before her next test. She did, and her test results were still as good as ever—which broke her cycle of superstitious thinking.

and write down your weak spots! In all probability, as you do both lists you'll find you are strong in some areas and not so strong in others. Taking stock of your assets *and* liabilities lets you know the areas you don't have to worry about, and the ones that will demand extra attention and effort.

Now, go back to the "good" list, and expand it for two minutes. Take the general items on that first list and make them more specific; take the specific items and expand them into more general conclusions. Naturally, if anything new comes to mind, jot it down. Focus all of your attention and effort on your strengths. Don't underestimate yourself or your abilities. Give yourself full credit. At the same time, don't list strengths you don't really have; you'll only be fooling yourself.

Every area of strength and confidence you can identify is much like having a reserve of solid gold at Fort Knox. You'll be able to draw on your reserves as you need them. You can use your reserves to solve difficult questions, maintain confidence, and keep test stress and anxiety at a distance. The encouraging thing is that every time you recognize another area of strength, succeed at coming up with a solution, or get a good score on a test, you increase your reserves. And, with a plan to strengthen a weak area or get a good score on a practice test, there is absolutely no limit to how much self-confidence you can have or how good you can feel about yourself.

What Do You Want to Accomplish in the Time Remaining?

The whole point of this next exercise is sort of like checking out a used car you might want to buy. You'd want to know up front what the car's weak points are, right? Knowing that influences your whole shopping-for-a-used-car campaign. So it is with your conquering-test-stress campaign: Knowing your weak points ahead of time helps you prepare.

So let's get back to the list of your weak points. Take two minutes to expand it just as you did with your "good" list. Be honest with yourself without going overboard. It's an accurate appraisal of the test areas that give you troubles.

Facing your weak spots gives you some distinct advantages. It helps a lot to find out where you need to spend extra effort. Increased exposure to tough material makes it more familiar and less intimidating. (After all, we mostly fear what we don't know and are probably afraid to face.) You'll feel better about yourself because you're dealing directly with areas of the test that bring on your anxiety. You can't help feeling more confident

STRESS TIP

Don't work in a messy or cramped area. Before you sit down to study, clear yourself a nice, open space. And make sure you have books, paper, pencils—whatever tools you will need—within easy reach before you sit down to study.

LINK YOUR THOUGHTS

When you're committing new information to memory, link one fact to another, much as elephants are linked trunk to tail in a circus parade. Visualize an image (preferably a bizarre one) that connects the thoughts. You'll remember them in the same linked way, with one thought easily bringing the next to your mind.

THE "NEW AGE" OF RELAXATION

Here are some more tips for beating stress:

- Find out if massage, especially shiatsu, is offered through your school's phys ed department, or at the local "Y."
- Check out a book on acupressure, and find those points on your body where you can press a "relax button."
- If you're especially sensitive to smells, you might want to try some aromatherapy. Lavender oil, for example, is said to have relaxing properties. Health food stores, drug stores, and New Age bookstores may carry aromatherapy oils.
- Many health food stores carry herbs and supplies that have relaxing properties, and they often have a specialist on staff who can tell you about them.

STRESS TIP

If you want to play music, keep it low and in the background. Music with a regular, mathematical rhythm—reggae, for example—aids the learning process. A recording of ocean waves is also soothing.

when you know you're actively strengthening your chances of earning a higher overall test score.

Imagine Yourself Succeeding

This next little group of exercises is both physical and mental. It's a natural followup to what you've just accomplished with your lists.

First, get yourself into a comfortable sitting position in a quiet setting. Wear loose clothes. If you wear glasses, take them off. Then, close your eyes and breathe in a deep, satisfying breath of air. Really fill your lungs until your rib cage is fully expanded and you can't take in any more. Then, exhale the air completely. Imagine you're blowing out a candle with your last little puff of air. Do this two or three more times, filling your lungs to their maximum and emptying them totally. Keep your eyes closed, comfortably but not tightly. Let your body sink deeper into the chair as you become even more comfortable.

With your eyes shut you can notice something very interesting. You're no longer dealing with the worrisome stuff going on in the world outside of you. Now you can concentrate on what happens inside you. The more you recognize your own physical reactions to stress and anxiety, the more you can do about them. You may not realize it, but you've begun to regain a sense of being in control.

Let images begin to form on the "viewing screens" on the back of your eyelids. You're experiencing visualizations from the place in your mind that makes pictures. Allow the images to come easily and naturally; don't force them. Imagine yourself in a relaxing situation. It might be in a special place you've visited before or one you've read about. It can be a fictional location that you create in your imagination, but a real-life memory of a place or situation you know is usually better. Make it as detailed as possible and notice as much as you can.

If you don't see this relaxing place sharply or in living color, it doesn't mean the exercise won't work for you. Some people can visualize in great detail, while others get only a sense of an image. What's important is not how sharp the details or colors, but how well you're able to manipulate the images. If you can conjure up finely detailed images, great. If you only have a faint sense of the images, that's okay—you'll still experience all the benefits of the exercise.

Think about the sights, the sounds, the smells, even the tastes and textures associated with your relaxing situation. See and feel yourself in this special place. Say you're special place is the beach, for example. Feel how warm the sand is. Are you lying on a blanket, or sitting up and looking out at the water? Hear the waves hitting the shore, and the occasional seagull. Feel a comfortable breeze. If your special place is a garden or park, look up and see the way sunlight filters through the trees. Smell your favorite flowers. Hear some chimes gently playing and birds chirping.

Stay focused on the images as you sink farther back into your chair. Breathe easily and naturally. You might have the sensations of any stress or tension draining from your muscles and flowing downward, out your feet and away from you.

Take a moment to check how you're feeling. Notice how comfortable you've become. Imagine how much easier it would be if you could take the test feeling this relaxed and in this state of ease. You've coupled the images of your special place with sensations of comfort and relaxation. You've also found a way to become relaxed simply by visualizing your own safe, special place.

Now, close your eyes and start remembering a real-life situation in which you did well on a test. If you can't come up with one, remember a situation in which you did something (academic or otherwise) that you were really proud of—a genuine accomplishment. Make the memory as detailed as possible. Think about the sights, the sounds, the smells, even the tastes associated with this remembered experience. Remember how confident you felt as you accomplished your goal. Now start thinking about the upcoming test. Keep your thoughts and feelings in line with that successful experience. Don't make comparisons between them. Just imagine taking the upcoming test with the same feelings of confidence and relaxed control.

This exercise is a great way to bring the test down to earth. You should practice this exercise often, especially when the prospect of taking the exam starts to bum you out. The more you practice it, the more effective the exercise will be for you.

Exercise Your Frustrations Away

Whether it is jogging, walking, biking, mild aerobics, pushups, or a pick-up basketball game, physical exercise is a very effective way to stimulate both your mind and body and to improve your ability to think and concentrate. A surprising number of students get out of the habit of regular exercise, ironically because they're spending so much time prepping for exams. Also, sedentary people—this is medical fact—get less oxygen to

OCEAN DUMPING

Visualize a beautiful beach, with white sand, blue skies, sparkling water, a warm sun, and seagulls. See yourself walking on the beach, carrying a small plastic pail. Stop at a good spot and put your worries and whatever may be bugging you into the pail. Drop it at the water's edge and watch it drift out to sea. When the pail is out of sight, walk on.

TAKE A HIKE, PAL

When you're in the middle of studying and hit a wall, take a short, brisk walk. Breathe deeply and swing your arms as you walk. Clear your mind. (And don't forget to look for flowers that grow in the cracks of the sidewalk.)

NUTRITION AND STRESS: THE DOS AND DON'TS

Do eat:

- Fruits and vegetables (raw is best, or just lightly steamed or nuked)
- Low-fat protein such as fish, skinless poultry, beans, and legumes (like lentils)
- Whole grains such as brown rice, whole wheat bread, and pastas

Don't eat:

- Refined sugar; sweet, high-fat snacks (simple carbohydrates like sugar make stress worse, and fatty foods lower your immunity)
- Salty foods (they can deplete potassium, which you need for nerve functions)

the blood and hence to the head than active people. You can live fine with a little less oxygen; you just can't think as well.

Any big test is a bit like a race. Thinking clearly at the end is just as important as having a quick mind early on. If you can't sustain your energy level in the last sections of the exam, there's too good a chance you could blow it. You need a fit body that can weather the demands any big exam puts on you. Along with a good diet and adequate sleep, exercise is an important part of keeping yourself in fighting shape and thinking clearly for the long haul.

There's another thing that happens when students don't make exercise an integral part of their test preparation. Like any organism in nature, you operate best if all your "energy systems" are in balance. Studying uses a lot of energy, but it's all mental. When you take a study break, do something active instead of raiding the fridge or vegging out in front of the TV. Take a five- to ten-minute activity break for every fifty or sixty minutes that you study. The physical exertion gets your body into the act which helps to keep your mind and body in sync. Then, when you finish studying for the night and hit the sack you won't lie there, tense and unable to sleep, because your head is overtired and your body wants to pump iron or run a marathon.

One warning about exercise, however: It's not a good idea to exercise vigorously right before you go to bed. This could easily cause sleep-onset problems. For the same reason, it's also not a good idea to study right up to bedtime. Make time for a "buffer period" before you go to bed: For thirty to sixty minutes, just take a hot shower, meditate, simply veg out.

Get High . . . Naturally

Exercise can give you a natural high, which is the only kind of high you can afford right now. Using drugs (prescription or recreational) specifically to prepare for and take a big test is definitely self-defeating. Except for the drugs that occur naturally in your brain, every drug has major drawbacks—and a false sense of security is only one of them.

You may have heard that popping uppers helps you study by keeping you alert. If they're illegal, definitely forget about it. You're just wasting your time. Amphetamines make it hard to retain information. So you'll stay awake, but you probably won't remember much of what you read. And, taking an upper before you take the test could really mess things up. You're already going to be a little anxious and hyper; adding a strong stimulant could easily push you over the edge into panic. Remember, a little anxiety is a good thing. The adrenaline that gets pumped into your bloodstream helps you stay alert and think more clearly. But, too much anxiety and you can't think straight at all.

Mild stimulants, such as coffee, cola, or over-the-counter caffeine pills can sometimes help as you study, since they keep you alert. On the down side, they can also lead to agitation, restlessness, and insomnia. Some people can drink a pot of high-octane coffee and sleep like a baby. Others have one cup and start to vibrate. It all depends on your tolerance for caffeine.

Alcohol and other depressants are out, too. Again, if they're illegal, forget about it. Depressants wouldn't work, anyway, since they lead to the inevitable hangover/crash, the fuzzy thinking, and lousy sense of judgment. These are not going to help you ace the test.

Instead, go for endorphins—the "natural morphine." Endorphins have no side effects and they're free—you've already got them in your brain. It just takes some exercise to release them. Running around on the basketball court, bicycling, swimming, aerobics, power walking—these activities cause endorphins to occupy certain spots in your brain's neural synapses. In addition, exercise develops staying power and increases the oxygen transfer to your brain. Go into the test naturally.

Take a Deep Breath . . .

Here's another natural route to relaxation and invigoration. It's a classic isometric exercise that you can do whenever you get stressed out—just before the test begins, even *during* the test. It's very simple and takes just a few minutes.

Close your eyes. Starting with your eyes and—*without holding your breath*—gradually tighten every muscle in your body (but not to the point of pain) in the following sequence:

1. Close your eyes tightly.
2. Squeeze your nose and mouth together so that your whole face is scrunched up. (If it makes you self-conscious to do this in the test room, skip the face-scrunching part.)
3. Pull your chin into your chest, and pull your shoulders together.
4. Tighten your arms to your body, then clench your hands into tight fists.
5. Pull in your stomach.

STRESS TIP

Don't study on your bed, especially if you have problems with insomnia. Your mind may start to associate the bed with work, and make it even harder for you to fall asleep.

THE RELAXATION PARADOX

Forcing relaxation is like asking yourself to flap your arms and fly. You can't do it, and every push and prod only gets you more frustrated. Relaxation is something you don't work at. You simply let it happen. Think about it. When was the last time you tried to force yourself to go to sleep, and it worked?

6. Squeeze your thighs and buttocks together, and tighten your calves.
7. Stretch your feet, then curl your toes (watch out for cramping in this part).

At this point, every muscle should be tightened. Now, relax your body, one part at a time, in reverse order, starting with your toes. Let the tension drop out of each muscle. The entire process might take five minutes from start to finish (maybe a couple of minutes during the test). This clenching and unclenching exercise should help you to feel very relaxed.

And Keep Breathing

Conscious attention to breathing is an excellent way of managing test stress (or any stress, for that matter). The majority of people who get into trouble during tests take shallow breaths. They breathe using only their upper chests and shoulder muscles, and may even hold their breath for long periods of time. Conversely, the test taker who by accident or design keeps breathing normally and rhythmically is likely to be more relaxed and in better control during the entire test experience.

So, now is the time to get into the habit of relaxed breathing. Do the next exercise to learn to breathe in a natural, easy rhythm. By the way, this is another technique you can use during the test to collect your thoughts and ward off excess stress. The entire exercise should take no more than three to five minutes.

With your eyes still closed, breathe in slowly and deeply through your nose. Hold the breath for a bit, and then release it through your mouth. The key is to breathe slowly and deeply by using your diaphragm (the big band of muscle that spans your body just above your waist) to draw air in and out naturally and effortlessly. Breathing with your diaphragm encourages relaxation and helps minimize tension.

As you breathe, imagine that colored air is flowing into your lungs. Choose any color you like, from a single color to a rainbow. With each breath, the air fills your body from the top of your head to the tips of your toes. Continue inhaling the colored air until it occupies every part of you, bones and muscles included. Once you have completely filled yourself with the colored air, picture an opening somewhere on your body, either natural or imagined. Now, with each breath you exhale, some of the colored air will pass out the opening and leave your body. The level of the air (much like the water in a glass as it is emptied) will begin to drop. It will descend progressively lower, from your head down to your feet. As you

BREATHE LIKE A BABY

A baby or young child is the best model for demonstrating how to breathe most efficiently and comfortably. Only its stomach moves as it inhales and exhales. The action is virtually effortless.

STRESS TIP

A lamp with a 75-watt bulb is optimal for studying. But don't put it so close to your study material that you create a glare.

continue to exhale the colored air, watch the level go lower and lower, farther and farther down your body. As the last of the colored air passes out of the opening, the level will drop down to your toes and disappear. Stay quiet for just a moment. Then notice how relaxed and comfortable you feel.

Thumbs Up for Meditation

Once relegated to the fringes of the medical world, meditation, biofeedback, and hypnosis are increasingly recommended by medical researchers to reduce pain from headaches, back problems—even cancer. Think of what these powerful techniques could do for your test-related stress and anxiety.

Effective meditation is based primarily on two relaxation methods you've already learned: body awareness and breathing. A couple of different meditation techniques follow. Experience them both, and choose the one that works best for you.

Breath Meditation

Make yourself comfortable, either sitting or lying down. For this meditation you can keep your eyes open or close them. You're going to concentrate on your breathing. The goal of the meditation is to notice everything you can about your breath as it enters and leaves your body. Take three to five breaths each time you practice the meditation, which should take about a minute for the entire procedure.

Take a deep breath and hold it for five to ten seconds. When you exhale, let the breath out very slowly. Feel the tension flowing out of you along with the breath that leaves your body. Pay close attention to the air as it flows in and out of your nostrils. Observe how cool it is as you inhale and how warm your breath is when you exhale. As you expel the air, say a cue word such as *calm* or *relax* to yourself. Once you've exhaled all the air from your lungs, start the next long, slow inhale. Notice how relaxed feelings increase as you slowly exhale and again hear your cue words.

Mantra Meditation

For this type of meditation experience you'll need a mental device (a mantra), a passive attitude (don't try to do anything), and a position in which you can be comfortable. You're going to focus your total attention on a mantra you create. It should be emotionally neutral,

THINK GOOD THOUGHTS

Create a set of positive, but brief affirmations and mentally repeat them to yourself just before you fall asleep at night. (That's when your mind is very open to suggestion.) You'll find yourself feeling a lot more positive in the morning. Periodically repeating your affirmations during the day makes them even more effective.

repetitive, and monotonous, and your aim is to fully occupy your mind with it. Furthermore, you want to do the meditation passively, with no goal in your head of how relaxed you're supposed to be. This is a great way to prepare for studying or taking the test. It clears your head of extraneous thoughts and gets you focused and at ease.

Sit comfortably and close your eyes. Begin to relax by letting your body go limp. Create a relaxed mental attitude and know there's no need for you to force anything. You're simply going to let something happen. Breathe through your nose. Take calm, easy breaths and as you exhale, say your mantra (*one, ohhm, aah, soup*—whatever is emotionally neutral for you) to yourself. Repeat the mantra each time you breathe out. Let feelings of relaxation grow as you focus on the mantra and your slow breathing. Don't worry if your mind wanders. Simply return to the mantra and continue letting go. Experience this meditation for ten to fifteen minutes.

Quick Tips for the Days Before the Exam

- The best test takers do less and less as the test approaches. Taper off your study schedule and take it easy on yourself. You want to be relaxed and ready on the day of the test. Give yourself time off, especially the evening before the exam. By that time, if you've studied well, everything you need to know is firmly stored in your memory banks.
- Positive self-talk can be extremely liberating and invigorating, especially as the test looms closer. Tell yourself things such as, "I choose to take this test" rather than "I have to"; "I will do well" rather than "I hope things go well"; "I can" rather than "I cannot." Be aware of negative, self-defeating thoughts and images and immediately counter any you become aware of. Replace them with affirming statements that encourage your self-esteem and confidence. Create and practice doing visualizations that build on your positive statements.
- Get your act together sooner rather than later. Have everything (including choice of clothing) laid out days in advance. Most important, know where the test will be held and the easiest, quickest way to get there. You will gain great peace of mind if you know that all the little details—gas in the car, directions, etcetera—are firmly in your control before the day of the test.

- Experience the test site a few days in advance. This is very helpful if you are especially anxious. If at all possible, find out what room your part of the alphabet is assigned to, and try to sit there (by yourself) for a while. Better yet, bring some practice material and do at least a section or two, if not an entire practice test, in that room. In this case, familiarity doesn't breed contempt; it generates comfort and confidence.

- Forego any practice on the day before the test. It's in your best interest to marshal your physical and psychological resources for twenty-four hours or so. Even race horses are kept in the paddock and treated like princes the day before a race. Keep the upcoming test out of your consciousness; go to a movie, take a pleasant hike, or just relax. Don't eat junk food or tons of sugar. And—of course—get plenty of rest the night before. Just don't go to bed too early. It's hard to fall asleep earlier than you're used to, and you don't want to lie there thinking about the test.

Handling Stress During the Test

The biggest stress monster will be the day of the test itself. Fear not; there are methods of quelling your stress during the test.

- Keep moving forward instead of getting bogged down in a difficult question or passage. You don't have to get everything right to achieve a fine score. So, don't linger out of desperation on a question that is going nowhere even after you've spent considerable time on it. The best test takers skip (temporarily) difficult material in search of the easier stuff. They mark the ones that require extra time and thought. This strategy buys time and builds confidence so you can handle the tough stuff later.

- Don't be thrown if other test takers seem to be working more busily and furiously than you are. Continue to spend your time patiently but doggedly thinking through your answers; it's going to lead to higher-quality test taking and better results. Don't mistake the other people's sheer activity as signs of progress and higher scores.

WHAT ARE "SIGNS OF A WINNER," ALEX?

Here's some advice from a Kaplan instructor who won big on *Jeopardy!*™ In the green room before the show, he noticed that the contestants who were quiet and "within themselves" were the ones who did great on the show. The contestants who did not perform as well were the ones who were fact-cramming, talking a lot, and generally being manic before the show. Lesson: Spend the final hours leading up to the test getting sleep, meditating, and generally relaxing.

- *Keep breathing!* Weak test takers tend to share one major trait: they forget to breathe properly as the test proceeds. They start holding their breath without realizing it, or they breathe erratically or arrhythmically. Improper breathing hurts confidence and accuracy. Just as importantly, it interferes with clear thinking.
- Some quick isometrics during the test—especially if concentration is wandering or energy is waning—can help. Try this: Put your palms together and press intensely for a few seconds. Concentrate on the tension you feel through your palms, wrists, forearms, and up into your biceps and shoulders. Then, quickly release the pressure. Feel the difference as you let go. Focus on the warm relaxation that floods through the muscles. Now you're ready to return to the task.
- Here's another isometric that will relieve tension in both your neck and eye muscles. Slowly rotate your head from side to side, turning your head and eyes to look as far back over each shoulder as you can. Feel the muscles stretch on one side of your neck as they contract on the other. Repeat five times in each direction.

With what you've just learned here, you're armed and ready to do battle with the test. This book and your studies will give you the information you'll need to answer the questions. It's all firmly planted in your mind. You also know how to deal with any excess tension that might come along, both when you're studying for and taking the exam. You've experienced everything you need to tame your test anxiety and stress. You are going to get a great score.

PRACTICE TEST FOR THE LSAT

How to Take This Practice Test

Before taking this test, find a quiet place where you can work uninterrupted for about two and a half hours. Make sure you have a comfortable desk and several No. 2 pencils.

This Practice Test includes four scored multiple choice sections. Keep in mind that on the actual LSAT, there will be an additional multiple choice section—the experimental section—which will not contribute to your score, plus an unscored Writing Sample.

Use the grid on the following page to record your answers.

Once you start the Practice Test, don't stop until you've gone through all four sections. Remember, you can review any questions within a section, but you may not go back or forward a section.

You'll find the answer key, score converter, and explanations following the test.

Good luck.

PRACTICE TEST

Remove or photocopy this answer sheet and use it to complete the Practice Test.
See the answer key immediately following the test to correct your answers when you're finished.

Start with number 1 for each new section. If a section has fewer questions than answer spaces, leave the extra spaces blank.

SECTION 1

1 (A) (B) (C) (D) (E)	11 (A) (B) (C) (D) (E)	21 (A) (B) (C) (D) (E)	31 (A) (B) (C) (D) (E)
2 (A) (B) (C) (D) (E)	12 (A) (B) (C) (D) (E)	22 (A) (B) (C) (D) (E)	32 (A) (B) (C) (D) (E)
3 (A) (B) (C) (D) (E)	13 (A) (B) (C) (D) (E)	23 (A) (B) (C) (D) (E)	33 (A) (B) (C) (D) (E)
4 (A) (B) (C) (D) (E)	14 (A) (B) (C) (D) (E)	24 (A) (B) (C) (D) (E)	34 (A) (B) (C) (D) (E)
5 (A) (B) (C) (D) (E)	15 (A) (B) (C) (D) (E)	25 (A) (B) (C) (D) (E)	35 (A) (B) (C) (D) (E)
6 (A) (B) (C) (D) (E)	16 (A) (B) (C) (D) (E)	26 (A) (B) (C) (D) (E)	36 (A) (B) (C) (D) (E)
7 (A) (B) (C) (D) (E)	17 (A) (B) (C) (D) (E)	27 (A) (B) (C) (D) (E)	37 (A) (B) (C) (D) (E)
8 (A) (B) (C) (D) (E)	18 (A) (B) (C) (D) (E)	28 (A) (B) (C) (D) (E)	38 (A) (B) (C) (D) (E)
9 (A) (B) (C) (D) (E)	19 (A) (B) (C) (D) (E)	29 (A) (B) (C) (D) (E)	39 (A) (B) (C) (D) (E)
10 (A) (B) (C) (D) (E)	20 (A) (B) (C) (D) (E)	30 (A) (B) (C) (D) (E)	40 (A) (B) (C) (D) (E)

SECTION 2

1 (A) (B) (C) (D) (E)	11 (A) (B) (C) (D) (E)	21 (A) (B) (C) (D) (E)	31 (A) (B) (C) (D) (E)
2 (A) (B) (C) (D) (E)	12 (A) (B) (C) (D) (E)	22 (A) (B) (C) (D) (E)	32 (A) (B) (C) (D) (E)
3 (A) (B) (C) (D) (E)	13 (A) (B) (C) (D) (E)	23 (A) (B) (C) (D) (E)	33 (A) (B) (C) (D) (E)
4 (A) (B) (C) (D) (E)	14 (A) (B) (C) (D) (E)	24 (A) (B) (C) (D) (E)	34 (A) (B) (C) (D) (E)
5 (A) (B) (C) (D) (E)	15 (A) (B) (C) (D) (E)	25 (A) (B) (C) (D) (E)	35 (A) (B) (C) (D) (E)
6 (A) (B) (C) (D) (E)	16 (A) (B) (C) (D) (E)	26 (A) (B) (C) (D) (E)	36 (A) (B) (C) (D) (E)
7 (A) (B) (C) (D) (E)	17 (A) (B) (C) (D) (E)	27 (A) (B) (C) (D) (E)	37 (A) (B) (C) (D) (E)
8 (A) (B) (C) (D) (E)	18 (A) (B) (C) (D) (E)	28 (A) (B) (C) (D) (E)	38 (A) (B) (C) (D) (E)
9 (A) (B) (C) (D) (E)	19 (A) (B) (C) (D) (E)	29 (A) (B) (C) (D) (E)	39 (A) (B) (C) (D) (E)
10 (A) (B) (C) (D) (E)	20 (A) (B) (C) (D) (E)	30 (A) (B) (C) (D) (E)	40 (A) (B) (C) (D) (E)

SECTION 3

1 (A) (B) (C) (D) (E)	11 (A) (B) (C) (D) (E)	21 (A) (B) (C) (D) (E)	31 (A) (B) (C) (D) (E)
2 (A) (B) (C) (D) (E)	12 (A) (B) (C) (D) (E)	22 (A) (B) (C) (D) (E)	32 (A) (B) (C) (D) (E)
3 (A) (B) (C) (D) (E)	13 (A) (B) (C) (D) (E)	23 (A) (B) (C) (D) (E)	33 (A) (B) (C) (D) (E)
4 (A) (B) (C) (D) (E)	14 (A) (B) (C) (D) (E)	24 (A) (B) (C) (D) (E)	34 (A) (B) (C) (D) (E)
5 (A) (B) (C) (D) (E)	15 (A) (B) (C) (D) (E)	25 (A) (B) (C) (D) (E)	35 (A) (B) (C) (D) (E)
6 (A) (B) (C) (D) (E)	16 (A) (B) (C) (D) (E)	26 (A) (B) (C) (D) (E)	36 (A) (B) (C) (D) (E)
7 (A) (B) (C) (D) (E)	17 (A) (B) (C) (D) (E)	27 (A) (B) (C) (D) (E)	37 (A) (B) (C) (D) (E)
8 (A) (B) (C) (D) (E)	18 (A) (B) (C) (D) (E)	28 (A) (B) (C) (D) (E)	38 (A) (B) (C) (D) (E)
9 (A) (B) (C) (D) (E)	19 (A) (B) (C) (D) (E)	29 (A) (B) (C) (D) (E)	39 (A) (B) (C) (D) (E)
10 (A) (B) (C) (D) (E)	20 (A) (B) (C) (D) (E)	30 (A) (B) (C) (D) (E)	40 (A) (B) (C) (D) (E)

SECTION 4

1 (A) (B) (C) (D) (E)	11 (A) (B) (C) (D) (E)	21 (A) (B) (C) (D) (E)	31 (A) (B) (C) (D) (E)
2 (A) (B) (C) (D) (E)	12 (A) (B) (C) (D) (E)	22 (A) (B) (C) (D) (E)	32 (A) (B) (C) (D) (E)
3 (A) (B) (C) (D) (E)	13 (A) (B) (C) (D) (E)	23 (A) (B) (C) (D) (E)	33 (A) (B) (C) (D) (E)
4 (A) (B) (C) (D) (E)	14 (A) (B) (C) (D) (E)	24 (A) (B) (C) (D) (E)	34 (A) (B) (C) (D) (E)
5 (A) (B) (C) (D) (E)	15 (A) (B) (C) (D) (E)	25 (A) (B) (C) (D) (E)	35 (A) (B) (C) (D) (E)
6 (A) (B) (C) (D) (E)	16 (A) (B) (C) (D) (E)	26 (A) (B) (C) (D) (E)	36 (A) (B) (C) (D) (E)
7 (A) (B) (C) (D) (E)	17 (A) (B) (C) (D) (E)	27 (A) (B) (C) (D) (E)	37 (A) (B) (C) (D) (E)
8 (A) (B) (C) (D) (E)	18 (A) (B) (C) (D) (E)	28 (A) (B) (C) (D) (E)	38 (A) (B) (C) (D) (E)
9 (A) (B) (C) (D) (E)	19 (A) (B) (C) (D) (E)	29 (A) (B) (C) (D) (E)	39 (A) (B) (C) (D) (E)
10 (A) (B) (C) (D) (E)	20 (A) (B) (C) (D) (E)	30 (A) (B) (C) (D) (E)	40 (A) (B) (C) (D) (E)

SECTION ONE
Time—35 minutes
25 questions

Directions: This test is composed of questions that ask you to analyze the logic of statements or short paragraphs. You are to choose as the answer to each question the one choice you consider <u>best</u> on the basis of your common-sense evaluation of the statement and its assumptions. Although a question may seem to have more than one acceptable answer, there is only one *best* answer, and it is the one that does not entail making any illogical, extraneous, or conflicting assumptions about the question.

1. If we must refrain from liberating the conquered islands simply because the lives of some civilians would be endangered, then we must never engage in any kind of armed conflict near populated areas.

   The author of the argument above assumes that

   (A) armed conflict invariably endangers the lives of civilians
   (B) the conquered islands can be liberated without conflict
   (C) one cannot engage in armed conflict near populated areas without endangering civilians
   (D) the liberation of the conquered islands is less important than the lives of a few civilians
   (E) the conquered islands should be liberated despite the risk to civilians

2. Marybeth will go shopping only when she has her mother's permission. Her mother allows her to go shopping alone at the mall down the street, but she insists that Marybeth take Sue and Desiree along for any shopping expeditions to the downtown department stores.

   Which one of the following conclusions can be logically inferred from the statements above?

   (A) If Marybeth is shopping alone, then she is not shopping at a department store.
   (B) If Marybeth is shopping, then Sue and Desiree are with her.
   (C) If Desiree is not with Marybeth, then Marybeth is not shopping.
   (D) If Marybeth is shopping at the downtown department stores, then Sue is with her.
   (E) If Desiree and Sue are with her, then Marybeth is shopping at the downtown department stores.

3. The owners of an Italian bicycle manufacturing company, unhappy that 20 percent of their new "Street Fleet" bicycles came back for repair within six months of purchase, recalled every "Street Fleet" bicycle and altered them to make them less susceptible to ordinary wear and tear. They improved the construction by switching to an equally lightweight but sturdier metal, and by increasing the number of spokes supporting the rim. The company renamed the new bikes "Rough Rider," and in six months sold roughly the same number of these as the original "Street Fleets." Despite the improvements, 50 percent of the "Rough Riders" came back for repairs within six months of purchase.

   Which one of the following, if true, most helps to explain the unexpected results noted in the passage?

   (A) The higher costs of the new manufacturing process have forced the owners to close one of their two service centers.
   (B) The company's new promotional literature on the "Rough Rider" now appeals to customers more apt to ride the bikes on unusually rough terrain.
   (C) The company has broadened its warranty on the "Rough Rider" so that it now covers parts as well as labor.
   (D) The aerodynamic design, initially suspected to cause the "Street Fleet" to veer slightly leftward at top speeds, was not corrected in the "Rough Rider."
   (E) The bikes still use a braking system that puts an unusually large amount of pressure on both the front and back rims.

GO ON TO THE NEXT PAGE.

Questions 4–5

Ms. Maloney: Drug X is effective only when its cumulative effects are allowed to work on the body over several months. Drug Y, however, works much more quickly and is just as powerful as drug X. I know that drug Y has side effects, but it will cure my daughter more quickly, so it's the best thing for her. I demand that you replace her current dosage of drug X with the same dosage of drug Y.

Doctor Ortiz: Yes, drug Y is as effective as drug X, but it has not yet been thoroughly tested for use with children. Side effects that are merely inconvenient for adults may prove to be very harmful for children. Drug X has been very successful so far, and it's a better choice in this case.

4. Which one of the following is the main point at issue between Ms. Maloney and Dr. Ortiz?

   (A) whether the use of drug Y should be discontinued for use in treatment because of its side effects
   (B) whether the patient's current dosage of medicine is inappropriate for children
   (C) whether it is justifiable to try a drug that may be harmful when a safer drug is available
   (D) whether the patient would be a viable test subject for an experiment on drug Y's effects on children
   (E) whether parents should be able to recommend changes in medication prescribed for their children

5. Doctor Ortiz's position most closely conforms to which one of the following principles?

   (A) Doctors are more qualified to prescribe treatment than are even the most well-informed parents.
   (B) When there is a choice between two similar treatments, the patient's potential safety should be the primary factor in the decision.
   (C) Adults and children have very different medical needs, and doctors must base treatment recommendations on the age of the patient in question.
   (D) If a certain treatment is found to be effective, it is unwise to change to another treatment without a valid medical reason.
   (E) Drugs that work by accumulating in the body are less jarring to a patient's immune system than are quick-acting drugs.

6. Botanists have found that a certain wildflower that is known to have bordered the cart paths of New England in colonial times does not grow on the modern roadsides that cover the same tracts of land. Obviously, the botanists have concluded, these particular flowers could not tolerate the auto emissions, since other wildflower species have continued to flourish on roadsides without any perceptible change in number.

The botanists' argument presupposes which one of the following?

   (A) No disease specific to the wildflowers in question could have caused their disappearance, while leaving other species intact.
   (B) Pollution has been shown to be the cause of the demise of many botanical species since the invention of the automobile.
   (C) The flowers are not found in areas of New England that are sheltered from auto emissions.
   (D) Auto emissions have grown steadily more toxic as the evolution of the automobile has progressed.
   (E) Most botanical species are able to adapt to changing environments without undergoing drastic evolutionary change.

7. Vegetables, in the proper combinations, can provide all of the nutrients necessary for human life. A mixture of whole grains and legumes, for instance, contains protein of a quality at least as high as that of animal protein, and the major vitamin and mineral groups can easily be represented in an all-vegetable diet. What's more, a little culinary imagination can make a vegetarian feast as varied and interesting as any meal based around meat. Given these facts, it's certainly time that we outlaw the raising and slaughtering of domestic livestock and turn to the wider cultivation of high-nutrition crops.

Which one of the following is a major flaw of the argument above?

   (A) The author does not provide a full definition of the terms used in the argument.
   (B) The author bases the conclusion on an inappropriate analogy.
   (C) The evidence provided by the author does not sufficiently support the conclusion.
   (D) The author does not demonstrate that a wider cultivation of high-nutrition crops is feasible.
   (E) The author employs circular reasoning in making the argument.

GO ON TO THE NEXT PAGE.

Questions 8–9

Public speaker: When Daphne LaBranche was caught littering in the state park she was given a stiff fine, which the judge said would go toward the park's upkeep. When Ewell McTavish was caught doing the same thing, he was let off with a reprimand and a nominal fine. Granted, Daphne's litter spread out over a wider area and was harder to pick up, but that was only because it was a windy night when she littered, not because she dumped more litter. The offenses were virtually identical. The judge only gave Daphne a stiffer fine because she's wealthy, and he was using a court case to do a little fund raising. That's patently unjust. The judge punished Daphne for her wealth rather than for her crime.

8. Which one of the following best describes the function performed in the argument by the statement that Daphne's litter was harder to pick up than Ewell's?

    (A) It presents additional evidence that directly supports the argument's conclusion that Daphne was treated unfairly.

    (B) It shows the author is aware of a reason for a possible objection to his contention that Daphne and Ewell deserved equal punishment.

    (C) It deliberately characterizes the judge's position in an opposing argument in an unfair way so as to discredit it.

    (D) It explains the reasoning that led the judge to impose a harsher fine on Daphne.

    (E) It emphasizes the difference between the seriousness of Daphne's offense and Ewell's offense.

9. Which one of the following principles, if established, would do most to justify the speaker in concluding from the evidence presented that Daphne was treated unfairly?

    (A) A judge should not treat crimes against state property more severely than crimes against public property.

    (B) The desire to do good often causes a judge to violate the letter of the law.

    (C) The only consideration in punishing a criminal should be the seriousness of his or her crime.

    (D) A person cannot be held legally responsible for natural phenomena and "acts of God."

    (E) The primary purpose of a legal sentence should be deterrence of future crime rather than punishment of the convicted criminal.

10. Delgado's hiring policy is fundamentally unsound for a large corporation like our own. She insists that we should fill executive positions with recent business school graduates because "their grasp of theory more than makes up for a lack of hands-on experience, even though they may not yet be presidential material." That kind of thinking is extremely dangerous. Readers of flying manuals may know a lot about flying, but that hardly qualifies them to pilot a jumbo jet.

    Which one of the following methods of argumentation is most central to the passage above?

    (A) using a specific example in order to illustrate and support a general principle

    (B) illustrating a judgment by drawing an analogy between two situations

    (C) attacking an opponent's belief by impugning the motives of that opponent

    (D) showing that an existing policy will lead to a conflict of interest

    (E) making a judgment about one type of situation by alluding to findings in another type of situation

GO ON TO THE NEXT PAGE.

11. In seeking indisputable proof that the continents as we know them today are in fact the result of millions of years of drift and collision, one scientist noted that marsupials are generally found only in South America and Australia. In fact, even the parasites of marsupials on the two continents are the same. He concluded that at one time these two great land masses were joined, with Antarctica as the link, and that marsupials and other mammals migrated to Australia from South America.

Which one of the following, if true, would most probably be cited by a scientist wishing to dispute the claim that marsupials came to Australia from South America?

(A) Its present ice and snow cover make travel across Antarctica difficult at best.

(B) An Australian marsupial captured in the wild and flown to a South American country is unlikely to thrive there.

(C) Years of intensive work on the rich fossil fields of Antarctica have yielded many kinds of bones, but none of marsupials.

(D) The oldest known marsupial fossil is of a North American animal that resembles today's opossum.

(E) Marsupial bones discovered in Antarctica resemble neither those of South American nor those of Australian marsupials.

12. **Student:** Dismissing Ms. Geschwitz because of her known advocacy of drug legalization amounts to a denial of her constitutional rights. Her personal views are her own business and have nothing to do with her work as a guidance counselor.

School administrator: Ms. Geschwitz is free to proclaim her views in private. As an administrator, it is my responsibility to balance her rights against those of the parents of our students, who do not want their children unduly influenced by someone whose views they do not agree with.

Which one of the following would be most relevant to investigate in evaluating the validity of the school administrator's position?

(A) whether Ms. Geschwitz could be persuaded to take another position at the school that would require no contact with students

(B) whether Ms. Geschwitz has ever used her authority to convince students to adopt her views

(C) what the student population thought of Ms. Geschwitz's work as a guidance counselor

(D) whether Ms. Geschwitz is the only school employee who espouses controversial opinions

(E) whether any parents of the students share Ms. Geschwitz's controversial views regarding drug legalization

13. **Director:** I know that our bylaws prohibit the inclusion in the festival of plays that have received more than five full productions, but I think we should make an exception in the case of *The Green Light Revue*, since all seven of its productions were short runs staged in tiny theaters with very small audiences.

The bylaws are most probably intended to ensure that the festival includes plays that

(A) have already proven their appeal in previous productions

(B) are actual narrative plays rather than revues

(C) have not already received wide exposure

(D) are suitable for production in small theaters

(E) are not running elsewhere simultaneously

GO ON TO THE NEXT PAGE.

14. **Advertisement:** The residents of East Hollow, New Jersey, were given free samples of Treegro feed for their oaks. As a result of this distribution of Treegro over the past ten years, the oaks in East Hollow are 4 inches taller than the average New Jersey oak. For taller oaks, try Treegro today.

    Which one of the following, if true, is the strongest criticism of the suggestion made in the above advertisement that the product will cause oaks to grow taller?

    (A) Most oaks in East Hollow were already ten years old when the distribution of Treegro was begun.
    (B) Half of the trees in New Jersey were recently planted under a federally sponsored reforestation program.
    (C) Many New Jersey residents living outside of East Hollow also used Treegro on their oaks.
    (D) Many oaks in New Jersey grow in heavily industrialized towns.
    (E) The average age of East Hollow oaks is substantially greater than that of other New Jersey oaks.

15. Polychlorinated biphenyls, a versatile group of chemicals used in Michigan in recent years to aid in the cultivation of animal feed grain, should be banned immediately lest they cause more harm to humans. Residual traces of the biphenyls used in the cultivation of feed grain have been found in the cow feed distributed to hundreds of Michigan farmers over the past ten years.

    Which one of the following, if true, most conclusively strengthens the argument above?

    (A) Scientists have observed an unusually high rate of intestinal cancer among consumers of Michigan dairy products over the past two years.
    (B) Traces of polychlorinated biphenyls have been found in the blood and urine of many Michigan cows.
    (C) Michigan has one of the highest cancer rates in the country.
    (D) Industrial scientists who contributed to the research and development of polychlorinated biphenyls conducted extensive tests to ascertain the safety of the chemicals.
    (E) The rate of sterility among Michigan cows greatly exceeds the national average.

Questions 16–17

Esmeralda: According to environmentalists, personality traits are determined and molded by the growing child's home environment. Yet identical twins who are separated at birth and reared by adoptive families of different socioeconomic and educational levels are often found later in life to have the same tastes, temperaments, and patterns of behavior. Obviously, environment has little to do with the development of personality.

Lothar: Environment is a factor that must work upon the genetic material at hand, and the significant aspect of environment is not so much the family's socioeconomic and educational background as its level of commitment to nurturing the individual child.

16. Lothar's response has which one of the following relations to Esmeralda's views?

    (A) It presents a logical consequence of her views.
    (B) It strengthens her views by pointing out supporting evidence that had not been mentioned.
    (C) It supplies a premise for Esmeralda's argument that had not been stated explicitly.
    (D) It cannot be true if Esmeralda's assertion concerning the development of adoptive identical twins is true.
    (E) It weakens Esmeralda's argument by pointing out its lack of precision.

17. The point at issue between Esmeralda and Lothar is

    (A) whether genetics or environment plays more of a role in the development of personality
    (B) whether Esmeralda's evidence about adopted identical twins necessarily demonstrates that environment has little effect on personality development
    (C) whether families of less privileged educational and socioeconomic backgrounds are as capable of nurturing their children as are families of more privileged educational and socioeconomic backgrounds
    (D) whether personality traits predetermined by genetics can be overcome through the proper environmental influences
    (E) whether families are as committed to nurturing their adopted children as they are to nurturing their biological children

GO ON TO THE NEXT PAGE.

18. If Larry studied harder, he would have more confidence in his abilities. He would feel better about himself, and he would be glad that he had made the decision to study harder. His whole outlook on school would improve. Clearly, then, Larry's increase in study time will lead to increased confidence.

Which one of the following arguments contains flawed reasoning that most closely parallels the flawed reasoning in the argument above?

(A) If voters were to research our candidate's background, they would understand why she is the best person for the job. She has made great strides in the area of human rights, she has lowered taxes, and she has improved our school system. Clearly, therefore, if voters make a well-informed choice, they will probably choose our candidate.

(B) If students with difficulties in specific subject areas seek tutoring, they will probably improve. Tutoring also allows superior students to review their own work while helping classmates to learn. Tutoring leads to overall scholastic improvement. Thus, all schools should implement tutoring programs.

(C) If television were made more educational, more parents would approve of it. Parents would recommend programs for their children, and let them choose their own viewing patterns. Their entire opinion of TV would be revised. Obviously, therefore, a rise in educational programming will lead to an increase in parental approval of television.

(D) If historians want to know how people lived, they should stage reenactments of historical events. They would learn more about customs, while coping with some of the same hardships that historical personages had to cope with. Therefore, reenactments are one of the most powerful tools that historians can use.

(E) Obviously we should pay more attention to the effects of workplace pollutants on our employees. Not only will the number of insurance claims rise if we continue to ignore health hazards, but we will also be faced with an increasing number of lawsuits. Clearly, therefore, we should form a committee to investigate the sources of workplace pollutants.

19. Four out of five people who filled out our questionnaire about solar energy indicated that they would strongly support any decision to direct more federal resources toward solar energy research, even if it involved cutting funds to synthetic fuel research. How, then, can the Administration claim that interest in solar energy is waning? The direction of public opinion is clear.

The argument above would be most conclusively weakened if it could be demonstrated that

(A) people who oppose solar energy research are far less likely to fill out a questionnaire than are people who support it

(B) synthetic fuel is a cheaper and cleaner source of energy than is solar power

(C) those who filled out questionnaires were not knowledgeable about energy issues

(D) the Administration has never been known in the past to willfully mislead the public

(E) the need for alternative energy sources will increase significantly in the future

20. Newspapers have completely overemphasized Dalyville's rate of violent deaths for this year. One isolated incident, a bus crash, was the cause of more than three-fourths of the violent deaths in the city this year. Meanwhile, papers are printing headlines like, "Violent Death Rate Skyrockets in Dalyville This Year!" This is hurting our tourism industry and making some citizens of Dalyville afraid to walk the streets at night.

If the statements above are true, which one of the following conclusions is most strongly supported by them?

(A) Dalyville has never before had an accident as major as this year's bus crash.

(B) Newspapers should never print statistics without the prior approval of city tourism associations.

(C) Citizens of Dalyville are apt to react strongly to statistics published by the news media.

(D) The term *violent death* is too vague to allow for appropriate interpretation of these statistics.

(E) Misuse of statistics on the part of news media has given Dalyville an undeservedly poor reputation.

GO ON TO THE NEXT PAGE.

21. Barbara Weston is a travel agent whose agency deals exclusively with business travel packages. Her agency had advertised only in *People and Places*, a monthly magazine, since its beginning, but she realized that this magazine did not reach many of her potential clients. Therefore, she changed all of her advertising to *Paper Money*, a weekly newspaper. Many of *Paper Money*'s readers are international business travelers, and it has lower advertising rates than *People and Places*. After one year, however, she discovered that the amount of revenue generated by advertising for her business had plummeted.

Which one of the following, if true, does most to explain the steep drop in revenue generated by advertising?

(A) *People and Places* has a much higher total readership and serves a more diverse population than does *Paper Money*.

(B) The ad in *People and Places* would be seen by many people who take frequent family trips to resorts and amusement areas.

(C) The amount of money spent on a business trip by a *People and Places* reader is likely to be far greater than the amount spent by a reader of *Paper Money*, a "budget" travel publication.

(D) The circulation of *People and Places* has risen steadily for the last five years, and will probably surpass that of *Paper Money* within two years.

(E) Although *People and Places* has higher advertising rates, the cost of advertising over a year would work out to be approximately the same as that of advertising in *Paper Money* for a year.

Questions 22–23

A study of women between the ages of thirty and fifty-five found that even those who are moderately overweight run a substantially higher risk of heart disease. Of the women observed, even the moderately overweight were at an 80 percent higher risk than were the thinnest women. Thus, at weights considered average on the height-and-weight charts issued by insurance companies, there was an increased risk of heart disease. This is the first time that being moderately overweight has been alleged to be a health risk.

22. If all of the statements in the passage are true, which one of the following must also be true on the basis of them?

(A) Insurance premiums for moderately overweight women will rise.

(B) Weights listed as average on insurance company charts may in fact be in excess of what is healthy.

(C) Obesity poses as serious a risk to health as do heavy smoking and excessive alcohol consumption.

(D) Overweight women are at as great a risk for heart disease as are comparably overweight men.

(E) Overweight women aged thirty to fifty-five are more likely to suffer from heart disease than are overweight women in any other age group.

23. A group of doctors is deciding whether to recommend that their overweight female patients aged thirty to fifty-five lose weight. In addition to the information in the passage, it would also be useful for the doctors to consider which one of the following?

(A) the risk, if significant, of heart disease for women aged fifty-five and older

(B) the risk, if significant, of heart disease for women between the ages of fifteen and thirty

(C) the percentage of women between the ages of thirty to fifty-five who are overweight

(D) the risk of heart disease for women between the ages of thirty to fifty-five who are very overweight

(E) the benefits, if any, of a woman aged thirty to fifty-five being slightly overweight

GO ON TO THE NEXT PAGE.

24. If human beings attempt to understand their lives, then they will be faced with certain unanswerable questions. That will lead them to admit the uncertainty underlying all things. If they make that admission, they will conclude that their lives are necessarily without meaning. Thus, if human beings attempt to understand their lives, they will conclude that their lives are without meaning.

    Which one of the following uses reasoning most similar to that used in the argument above?

    (A) If people believe that their lives are meaningful, they must admit that life itself has a discernible purpose, and thus that life itself can be understood. If people believe that life can be understood, they will never give up trying to understand their lives. As a result, if people believe that their lives are meaningful, they will never give up trying to understand their lives.

    (B) If human beings attempt to answer unanswerable questions, they will be faced with a decision between admitting that their understanding is limited or that the world is unknowable. If they decide the former, they must admit that their lives are meaningless; if the latter, that the world is meaningless.

    (C) Because human beings attempt to understand their lives, they ask themselves unanswerable questions. Because they ask themselves unanswerable questions, they conclude that the world is unknowable and therefore meaningless. Thus, human beings should not attempt to understand their lives.

    (D) If human beings attempt to understand that which is incomprehensible, they will have to admit defeat. If they admit defeat, they will soon regard their lives as meaningless. If they regard their lives as meaningless, they will no longer attempt to understand that which is incomprehensible. Therefore, it is impossible to attempt to understand that which is incomprehensible.

    (E) Whenever people attempt to find meaning in their lives, they ask unanswerable questions. When they ask unanswerable questions, they must provide themselves with false answers. False answers, therefore, are incompatible with the attempt to find meaning in life.

25. Between November and April, Fairvale's city pound collected an average of twenty-five stray animals per month. Yet between May and October the average dropped to seven strays per month. It's clear that fewer animals roam the streets of Fairvale during the warmer months from May to October than during the colder months, November through April, since the pound employs the same number of people all year long.

    For the conclusion that fewer animals roam the streets of Fairvale during the warmer as opposed to the colder months to be valid based on the evidence cited, the author must assume which one of the following?

    (A) The pound facilities have room to handle at least thirty-five animals at a time, including those who remain there for several months.

    (B) The pound does not have any temporary or seasonal employees who substitute for employees on leave or vacation.

    (C) Diseases such as rabies and distemper tend to be more prevalent in Fairvale during the summer months.

    (D) The drop in the number of animals impounded was not caused by a change in animal impoundment regulations.

    (E) A similar drop in impoundings during the summer months has been observed in many other pounds across the country.

STOP
**IF YOU FINISH BEFORE TIME IS CALLED, YOU MAY CHECK YOUR WORK ON THIS SECTION ONLY.
DO NOT WORK ON ANY OTHER SECTION IN THE TEST.**

SECTION TWO
Time—35 minutes
27 questions

<u>Directions</u>: Each selection in this test is followed by several questions. After reading the selection, choose the best response to each question and mark it on your answer sheet. Your replies are to be based on what is <u>stated</u> or <u>implied</u> in the selection.

In recent years biology has undergone a revolution that has attracted wide attention. Controversy centered initially on whether genetic cloning techniques could create new, possibly dangerous forms of life. Attention next focused on the power
(5) of genetic engineering to produce valuable new medical and agricultural products. Largely overlooked, however, are developments that will ultimately have far greater social impact: the ability to analyze genetic information will allow the prediction of human traits. While some fear that by analyzing the entire
(10) library of human gene sequences we will discover the essence of humanity, this is unlikely. Our bodies are complex networks of interacting components, influenced by a variable environment. Nevertheless, genes do help determine aspects of human form and function. Herein lie the seeds of future
(15) problems.

By about the year 2000, barring unforeseen technical obstacles, scientists will have fully mapped the complex human genetic terrain. Before this, however, new information will make possible techniques that will engender a host of eth-
(20) ical issues. Imagine that investigators could predict with some accuracy such aspects of human behavior or functioning as intelligence, shyness, aggressiveness, or heat tolerance. Consider the power this would give to some—and the vulnerable position in which it would put others.

(25) Even if society can anticipate and control most misuse of genetic data, we face a more insidious problem: a rising ethic of genetic determinism. For the past century, ideological currents have closely affected the nature versus nurture debate. Widespread rejection of social Darwinism and institutional-
(30) ized racism has buoyed the strong nurturist sentiments of the past half century, but a growing proportion of the public, impressed by the successes of genetics, is likely to come to view genes as determinants of the human condition. Such an uncritical embrace of genetics will not be deterred by scien-
(35) tists' reminders that the powers of genetic predictions are limited. Environmental variations can cause genetically similar individuals to develop in dramatically different ways, and

genetics will at best suggest only a probability of development for complex traits, such as those involved in behavior and cog-
(40) nition. Those overlooking this will disastrously misjudge individual ability.

What a tragedy this would be. We Americans have viewed our roots as interesting historical relics, hardly as rigid molds dictating all that we are and will be. Moreover, a belief
(45) that each of us is responsible for our own behavior has woven our social fabric. Yet in coming years we will hear increasingly from those attributing "bad" behavior to inexorable biological forces. As a biologist, I find this a bitter prospect. The biological revolution of the past decades will spawn enormous
(50) benefits, but we will pay a price unless we craft an ethic that cherishes our spontaneity, unpredictability, and individual uniqueness.

1. Which one of the following best expresses the main idea of the passage?

   (A) The relationship between science and society leads to complex ethical questions that may either benefit or impair the development of each.
   (B) Society should understand that environmental conditions may cause genetically similar individuals to develop in dramatically different directions.
   (C) The effort to analyze humans' genetic makeup could lead to a dangerous belief in genes as determinants of who we are and how we think.
   (D) The ability to analyze complex genetic information will ultimately lead to a fundamental understanding of human form and function.
   (E) Scientific research has often been influenced by public values and attitudes in ways that have had important results.

GO ON TO THE NEXT PAGE.

2. The author suggests that an "uncritical embrace" (line 34) of advances in genetics will tend to

(A) obscure the degree of complexity of many human traits

(B) diminish the public's ability to halt illicit use of genetic data

(C) further the chance that genetic cloning may lead to hazardous life forms

(D) enlarge the magnitude of technical problems occurring in genetics studies

(E) increase the potential for negligence on the part of geneticists

3. With which one of the following predictions about the biological revolution discussed in the passage would the author be most likely to agree?

(A) The revolution will lead to gross injustices in society.

(B) The revolution will bring greater good than harm to society.

(C) The revolution will not be as far-reaching as some believe.

(D) The revolution will lead to needless anxiety on the part of the public.

(E) The revolution will be problematic as well as beneficial.

4. The author mentions the nature-versus-nurture debate primarily in order to

(A) demonstrate the difficulty of predicting and preventing misuse of scientific data

(B) supply a point of reference for an assessment of the validity of recent advances in genetics

(C) cast doubt on the moral integrity of society

(D) illustrate that political interests have largely determined public interpretations of scientific issues

(E) point out a distinction between scientific conclusions based on facts and those based on assumptions

5. The author's attitude toward the revolution discussed in the passage can best be characterized as

(A) concerned that the revolution will suffer technical setbacks

(B) apprehensive about some of the revolution's likely effects

(C) encouraged about the material benefits society will derive from it

(D) surprised that the revolution enjoys wide public support

(E) anxious that the revolution's accomplishments be fully recognized

6. The author implies that recent advances in genetics would pose fewer problems if which one of the following were true?

(A) The public was more circumspect in its response to those advances.

(B) Scientists conducting research were more sensitive to public concerns.

(C) The public was less skeptical of innovative scientific techniques.

(D) Scientists were less influenced in their work by public opinion.

(E) Scientists were more willing to admit the limitations of their work.

7. Which of the following sentences would best complete the last paragraph of the passage?

(A) Biologists must assist in a search for a community of common purpose just as they must assist in the design of a society of mutual advantage.

(B) Routine tests will soon detect predispositions to diseases as well as indicate a range of normal human traits.

(C) In particular, the tangible fruits of the revolution will greatly improve our society's health and economic productivity.

(D) By studying and enumerating individual genes, we will only begin to penetrate the surface of human complexity.

(E) Even biologists having valid access to genetic profiles may misinterpret data made available by new procedures.

GO ON TO THE NEXT PAGE.

When Gwendolyn Brooks published her first collection of poetry, *A Street in Bronzeville,* in 1945 most reviewers recognized Brooks's versatility and craft as a poet. Yet, while noting her stylistic successes few of her contemporaries discussed
(5) the critical question of Brooks's relationship to the Harlem Renaissance. How had she addressed herself, as a poet, to the literary movement's assertion of the folk and African culture, and its promotion of the arts as the agent to define racial integrity?

(10) The New Negro poets of the Harlem Renaissance expressed a deep pride in being black; they found reasons for this pride in ethnic identity and heritage; and they shared a common faith in the fine arts as a means of defining and reinforcing racial pride. But in the literal expression of this
(15) impulse, the poets were either romantics or realists and, quite often within the same poem, both. The realistic impulse, as defined best in the poems of McKay's *Harlem Shadows* (1922), was a sober reflection upon blacks as second-class citizens, segregated from the mainstream of American socio-
(20) economic life, and largely unable to realize the wealth and opportunity that America promised. The romantic impulse, on the other hand, as defined in the poems of Sterling Brown's *Southern Road* (1932), often found these unrealized dreams in the collective strength and will of the folk masses.

(25) In comparing the poems in *A Street in Bronzeville* with various poems from the Renaissance, it becomes apparent that Brooks brings many unique contributions to bear on this tradition. The first clue that *A Street in Bronzeville* was, at its time of publication, unlike any other book of poems by a
(30) Black American is its insistent emphasis on demystifying romantic love between black men and women. During the Renaissance, ethnic or racial pride was often focused with romantic idealization upon the black woman. A casual streetwalker in Hughes's poem, "When Sue Wears Red," for exam-
(35) ple, is magically transformed into an Egyptian queen. In *A Street in Bronzeville,* this romantic impulse runs headlong into the biting ironies of racial discrimination. There are poems in which Hughes, McKay, and Brown recognize the realistic underside of urban life for black women. But for Brooks,
(40) unlike the Renaissance poets, the victimization of poor black women becomes not simply a minor chord but a predominant theme. Brooks's relationship with the Harlem Renaissance poets, as *A Street in Bronzeville* ably demonstrates, was hardly imitative. As one of the important links with the black
(45) poetic tradition of the 1920s and 1930s, she enlarged the element of realism that was an important part of the Renaissance world view. Although her poetry is often conditioned by the

optimism that was also a legacy of the period, Brooks rejects outright their romantic prescriptions for the lives of black
(50) women. And in this regard, she serves as a vital link with the black arts movement of the 1960s that, while it witnessed the flowering of black women as poets and social activists as well as the rise of black feminist aesthetics in the 1970s, brought about a curious revival of romanticism in the Renaissance
(55) mode.

8. Which of the following best expresses the main idea of the passage?

    (A) The evolution of realism in black women's poetry can be traced from Gwendolyn Brooks to the present day.
    (B) Gwendolyn Brooks's first poems were unique in the context of early twentieth-century poetry.
    (C) Contemporary scholars misinterpreted the crucial issue of Gwendolyn Brooks's relationship to the Harlem Renaissance.
    (D) Gwendolyn Brooks's poetry brought a new emphasis on the realistic elements of the Harlem Renaissance tradition.
    (E) The poets of the Harlem Renaissance were not sufficiently realistic in their portrayal of women.

9. According to the passage, the poems in *A Street in Bronzeville* are similar to the poems in *Harlem Shadows* because they each

    (A) portray black women in early twentieth-century America as resourceful individuals who were able to make successes of themselves
    (B) influenced the poetry and social activism of black women poets during the black arts movement of the 1960s
    (C) are based entirely on the romantic impulse of the New Negro poets of the Harlem Renaissance
    (D) illustrate the grim realities of suffering and discrimination faced by black Americans in early twentieth-century America
    (E) present an optimistic view of race relations in early twentieth-century America

GO ON TO THE NEXT PAGE.

10. The passage suggests that the author would be most likely to agree with which one of the following statements about the poetry of the Harlem Renaissance?

    (A) The movement was inspired by a revival of folk and African culture.
    (B) The Harlem Renaissance poets portrayed a common heritage in different ways.
    (C) The movement has been widely criticized for its lack of realism.
    (D) Brooks was more technically accomplished than other Harlem Renaissance poets.
    (E) The importance of the movement is rarely acknowledged by critics.

11. The author most probably mentions Hughes's poem, "When Sue Wears Red" (line 34) in order to

    (A) prove that Brooks had not simply imitated the Harlem Renaissance poets
    (B) highlight the critical role of the imagination in the creative process
    (C) contrast the irony of Brooks's poetry with the naivety of earlier poetry
    (D) provide an example of the romanticized portrayal of black women
    (E) cite an author whose work particularly influenced Gwendolyn Brooks

12. With which one of the following statements about *A Street in Bronzeville* would the author most likely agree?

    (A) It was an authentic replication of Harlem Renaissance styles.
    (B) It was marred by an optimism inherited from Harlem Renaissance poetry.
    (C) It completely rejected the poetic conventions of the Harlem Renaissance.
    (D) It was the first significant work of a black feminist writer.
    (E) It further developed the realistic impulse of the Harlem Renaissance tradition.

13. According to the passage, critics praised the quality of Brooks's first collection of poetry but

    (A) rejected her description of the plight of poor black women in urban America
    (B) argued that she had neglected to demystify romantic love between black men and women
    (C) assumed incorrectly that she had borrowed many ideas from the poems of Sterling Brown
    (D) failed to consider the links between her work and the work of earlier black poets
    (E) decried her unwillingness to support the New Negro poets in their quest for political change

14. Which of the following would best complete the last paragraph of the passage?

    (A) For many readers, however, Brooks will best be remembered for her virtuosity in poetic technique.
    (B) In many ways, Brooks's poetry owes more to the influence of the black arts movement than to the poets of the Harlem Renaissance.
    (C) For while poets of the black arts movement would often idealize their culture, their work was tempered by realism.
    (D) But while her importance for later movements is established, Brooks's relationship to the Harlem Renaissance remains open to question.
    (E) Thus despite her early anonymity, Gwendolyn Brooks's feminist poetry finally reached a wide audience.

GO ON TO THE NEXT PAGE.

(This passage was written in 1988.)

Nearly twenty years ago, former President Nixon signed the National Environmental Policy Act, this nation's first major federal environmental law. Although the nation has now witnessed almost twenty years of continuing debate
(5) about environmental law, a relatively new element has recently entered the controversy: the use of risk assessment procedures to determine levels of acceptable risk from threats of hazardous wastes.

Before the development of risk assessment as a decision-
(10) making tool, when a spill of a pollutant occurred, a government agency often simply told a responsible party to remove the pollutant. Inspections after cleanup often relied on visual observations to determine compliance with a cleanup order. Most environmental professionals consider risk assessment an
(15) improvement over what was done in the past because it provides a factual and scientific basis for the cleanup decision rather than an intuitive or emotional basis. Accordingly, many environmental professionals regard risk assessment procedures to be neutral policy tools that can be employed by the gov-
(20) ernment to make sound technical judgments that assure efficient and appropriate cleanups.

But are risk assessments really neutral scientific procedures? Analysis of the choices that must be made in risk assessment makes the answer clear. Because risk assessment depends
(25) on choices for which there is no *a priori* scientific method of deciding from among available assumptions, risk assessment ultimately depends largely, if not predominantly, on values positions rather than on science. Each of the four components of risk assessment methodology—hazard identification, a
(30) determination of whether a substance will cause an adverse health effect; dose-response assessment, an analysis of the relationship between an administered dose and the incidence of the adverse health effect; exposure assessment, an analysis of the processes and pathways by which contact with a substance
(35) creates opportunity for exposure; and risk characterization, the process of identifying the incidence of adverse health effects under various exposure pathways—requires the application of some judgment that must ultimately rely on something less than scientifically proven principles. Indeed, many
(40) of the choices that must be made in completing a risk assessment must be viewed as pure values judgments. For example, in the hazard identification portion of an assessment, the decision on picking a confidence level to determine statistically whether there has been a positive determination of whether a
(45) substance is a hazard is a pure values judgment.

Environmental decisions based on current risk assessment procedures should therefore be viewed primarily as ethical choices rather than as technically dictated conclusions. It is important in an age of increasing scientific complexity that
(50) interested parties attempt to understand the values positions and ethical issues that underlie scientifically derived policy choices. Government must bring greater clarity to the debate about environmental cleanup through identification of the embedded values positions and issues in risk assessment
(55) procedures.

15. Which one of the following best expresses the main point of the passage?

(A) Risk assessment is an improvement over past cleanup methods because it is based more on factual evidence than on intuition.

(B) Former President Nixon did more than his predecessors to protect the environment from pollutants by approving the use of risk assessment.

(C) Though perhaps more scientific than previous pollution control measures, the claim that risk assessment is a value-free process is not wholly credible.

(D) While the concept of risk assessment is enticing from a scientific viewpoint, this method is so expensive that its use is impractical on a large scale.

(E) Since past cleanup procedures were effective in cleaning up the environment, the government should not have approved the use of risk assessment.

16. All of the following are explicitly mentioned in the passage as part of the risk assessment process EXCEPT

(A) visual observation

(B) exposure assessment

(C) hazard identification

(D) risk characterization

(E) dose-response assessment

GO ON TO THE NEXT PAGE.

17. The author most probably mentions "confidence level" (line 43) in order to

    (A) demonstrate that risk assessment is more scientific than past cleanup methods
    (B) question the accuracy of postcleanup visual observations
    (C) suggest that government should eliminate ambiguities in its environmental cleanup agenda
    (D) show that nonscientific principles can affect the results of scientific processes
    (E) strengthen the notion that the National Environmental Policy Act needs to be modified

18. The author suggests which one of the following about pollution cleanup methods that predated the development of risk assessment?

    (A) They are considered to be completely ineffective in protecting the environment.
    (B) President Nixon's National Environmental Policy Act was based on their success.
    (C) Many environmental professionals are not satisfied with the results produced by these methods.
    (D) They are often difficult to apply because they depend on precise scientific measurements.
    (E) The best features of these methods should be integrated into the risk assessment process.

19. Which of the following words, as it appears in the passage, best supports the author's view of the role of nonscientific components in the risk assessment process?

    (A) *improvement* (line 15)
    (B) *neutral* (line 19)
    (C) *adverse* (line 33)
    (D) *opportunity* (line 35)
    (E) *underlie* (line 51)

20. The passage's reference to the "factual and scientific basis" of the risk assessment process in line 16 serves which of the following functions?

    (A) It explains the government's unwillingness to choose between older pollution cleanup methods and risk assessment.
    (B) It outlines the differences among environmentalists over the practicality of visual observation techniques.
    (C) It underscores the belief of environmentalists that risk assessment is a useful method for controlling pollution.
    (D) It introduces pollution control policy choices for which there is no *a priori* assessment method.
    (E) It highlights the attitude of environmentalists toward the National Environmental Policy Act.

21. The author of the passage is primarily concerned with

    (A) comparing risk assessment with earlier methods of pollution cleanup
    (B) explaining why government should make explicit the ethical choices involved in environmental cleanup
    (C) highlighting government's inability to deal effectively with pollution cleanup
    (D) reviewing the evolution of pollution cleanup methods over the past two decades
    (E) proposing a new method for environmental cleanup that incorporates the best features of risk assessment

GO ON TO THE NEXT PAGE.

In order to understand the hostility that has surrounded the idea of comparable worth, it is necessary to examine the opponents' arguments. These involve three related contentions: the male/female earnings gap results, largely, from (5) factors unrelated to discrimination by particular employers; comparable worth analysis is logistically impossible since there is no objective basis for establishing comparisons between different jobs; and, third, pay equity based on comparable worth would cripple the free market.

(10) The argument that the male/female wage gap results from nondiscriminatory factors is clearly expressed in a report by the U.S. Civil Rights Commission. The Commission essentially argues three propositions: women choose low-paying jobs because of sociological predisposition; women make (15) educational choices that lead to low-paying jobs; and the interrupted participation of women in the labor force leads to lower pay. Each contention is misguided or flawed, but the report's most serious shortcoming is that it mistakenly assumes that the validity of comparable worth theory depends (20) upon a demonstration that discrimination accounts for the entire wage gap between men and women workers. The issue in comparable worth litigation is not some generalized assertion about any overall wage gap, but a specific complaint that particular disparities between men and women working for (25) one employer, in enumerated positions, are the result of discrimination.

The second major argument mounted against comparable worth is that no objective technique exists for comparing jobs that are not identical in content. The Civil Rights (30) Commission contends that job evaluations are inherently subjective and cannot establish jobs' intrinsic worth. This objection, though partially valid, goes too far. While evaluation techniques are not absolutely objective, job evaluation is a well-established technique in American industry for deter- (35) mining relative wage levels. Even a cursory examination of industrial relations practice demonstrates that business and industry have long used specific techniques to determine the relative wage rates of jobs that are dissimilar in content.

The third argument raised against comparable worth is (40) that it requires an unwarranted intrusion into the market. This argument's proponents insist that supply and demand curves create the wage disparity at issue. Thus, comparable worth theory is not a legitimate response to discrimination but rather a specious definition of discrimination. If there is (45) no discrimination, there is no justification for interference with market forces. This argument would cloak impermissible

sex-based discrimination in the putative legality of "market operation." Yet, the argument sidesteps the contention of comparable worth proponents that, despite a pay differential, (50) the jobs are equivalent according to a rational standard. The market-based argument is instructive in that it links criticisms of the allegedly spurious nature of comparable worth with antipathy to the remedy—interference with the market. It is this connection that is critical to an understanding of judicial (55) opinions in the comparable worth area, since judges often defer to the operation of the market.

22. Which of the following, if true, would most strengthen the author's belief about the relationship between discrimination and the male/female wage gap?

(A) An experienced female patent attorney employed by a law firm earns less money than an inexperienced male patent attorney employed by a rival firm.

(B) A female computer programmer working for an engineering company earns less money than her junior male co-worker who is also a computer programer.

(C) A female airline pilot with ten years on the job earns less money than her male counterpart with twenty years on the job.

(D) A female corporate vice president earns less money than the male corporate president, even though she must work longer hours.

(E) A highly regarded female plastic surgeon in private practice earns less money than a mediocre male vascular surgeon employed by the local hospital.

23. The author's assertion that job evaluation is a justifiable technique for comparing dissimilar jobs is qualified by an admission that

(A) risks to a company's economic health cannot be ruled out

(B) the technique can cause divisiveness among a company's employees

(C) subjectivity cannot be entirely avoided in making the evaluations

(D) the technique is a recent, relatively untested procedure

(E) objectivity is not desirable in establishing comparable worth

GO ON TO THE NEXT PAGE.

24. It can be inferred that opponents of the idea of comparable worth have concluded which of the following?

(A) Interference with market forces is involved in all social reform.
(B) Application of the idea would be economically beneficial, but socially harmful.
(C) The legal opinions of judges often reflect an unwillingness to interfere with market forces.
(D) Sex-based wage discrimination is a widespread phenomenon that should be dealt with by individual employers.
(E) Wage disparities between men and women result primarily from sociological factors and the effects of supply and demand.

25. According to the author's argument, opinions of the Civil Rights Commission in regard to comparable worth have included all of the following assertions EXCEPT:

(A) The unequal pay of women does not stem primarily from discriminatory practice on the part of employers.
(B) It is not feasible to measure the relative value of dissimilar jobs.
(C) Women are paid at lower rates because their participation in the labor force is intermittent.
(D) Women are predisposed to choosing poorly paying employment positions.
(E) There can never be justification for judicial interference with the functioning of a free market.

26. The author suggests that the argument that wage disparities are a legitimate result of supply and demand fails to take into account the

(A) notion that a job's intrinsic worth can be measured only subjectively
(B) possibility that two jobs with dissimilar pay can be determined to possess equal value
(C) idea that market forces should never be manipulated for political purposes
(D) legitimate role of the courts in shaping an appropriate response to wage disparities
(E) occurrence of social injustice in America

27. The author's attitude toward the U.S. Civil Rights Commission's finding that discrimination is not a factor in the male/female wage gap can best be described as

(A) totally dismissive
(B) fervently enthusiastic
(C) somewhat bewildered
(D) quietly opposed
(E) politely supportive

STOP
IF YOU FINISH BEFORE TIME IS CALLED, YOU MAY CHECK YOUR WORK ON THIS SECTION ONLY.
DO NOT WORK ON ANY OTHER SECTION IN THE TEST.

SECTION THREE
Time—35 minutes
24 questions

Directions: Each group of questions is based on a set of conditions. You may wish to draw a rough sketch to help you answer some of the questions. Choose the best answer for each question and fill in the corresponding space on your answer sheet.

Questions 1–6

A basketball coach is forming two three-person teams to play against each other in a scrimmage game. The coach can choose from the following players: Charles, Edna, Greg, Jerrod, Katya, Mort, Paulina, and Terence. Each person chosen for a team plays opposite a specific player chosen for the other team. Those not chosen sit on the bench.

Charles, Edna, Katya, and Paulina are tall; the rest of the players are short.
A tall player can play only opposite another tall player.
If Paulina is chosen, Charles is chosen to play opposite her.
If Terence is chosen, Charles is chosen and plays on the same team as Terence.

1. Which one of the following players must be chosen for a team?

   (A) Edna
   (B) Terence
   (C) Katya
   (D) Charles
   (E) Jerrod

2. Which one of the following is an acceptable team?

   (A) Paulina, Jerrod, Charles
   (B) Charles, Jerrod, Mort
   (C) Jerrod, Mort, Greg
   (D) Mort, Paulina, Greg
   (E) Edna, Katya, Charles

3. Which one of the following pairs of players CANNOT sit together on the bench?

   (A) Edna and Katya
   (B) Jerrod and Paulina
   (C) Mort and Jerrod
   (D) Paulina and Edna
   (E) Greg and Terence

4. Paulina can play on the same team as any one of the following EXCEPT:

   (A) Edna
   (B) Greg
   (C) Katya
   (D) Terence
   (E) Mort

5. If one team consists of Katya, Charles, and one other player, how many possible combinations are there for the other team?

   (A) 1
   (B) 2
   (C) 3
   (D) 4
   (E) 5

6. Which one of the following CANNOT be true?

   (A) Paulina and Mort are chosen for different teams, while Edna sits on the bench.
   (B) Paulina is chosen while Greg sits on the bench.
   (C) Paulina and Edna are chosen for different teams, while Jerrod and Greg sit on the bench.
   (D) Charles is chosen for the same team as Mort and Terence, while Paulina sits on the bench.
   (E) Terence and Edna are chosen for the same team, while Katya sits on the bench.

GO ON TO THE NEXT PAGE.

Questions 7–12

A laboratory is testing six chimps for acquisition of communication skills. The six chimps are Alonzo, Bobo, Carlo, Dingo, Elmo, and Frank. A technician will work with one chimp at a time for a single time slot—defined as an entire morning or an entire afternoon. Each chimp will be tested exactly once. Time slots not filled by chimp testing are considered free. The tests will be conducted during a single week from Monday to Friday.

Alonzo is tested on Thursday morning.
Bobo, Elmo, and Frank sleep late, and can be tested only in the afternoon.
No testing is conducted on Monday morning.
Elmo is not tested on Monday or Tuesday.
The time slot immediately preceding that in which Alonzo is tested is free.
Alonzo is tested after Dingo but before Frank.
Carlo is tested on Tuesday.

7. Which one of the following must be true?

    (A) Bobo is tested on Monday.
    (B) Alonzo is the fourth chimp tested.
    (C) Carlo is the second chimp tested.
    (D) Alonzo is tested immediately before Frank.
    (E) There are exactly three free morning time slots.

8. Which one of the following pairs of chimps CANNOT be tested on the same day?

    (A) Bobo and Dingo
    (B) Carlo and Dingo
    (C) Carlo and Bobo
    (D) Alonzo and Elmo
    (E) Alonzo and Frank

9. If Dingo is tested on Tuesday morning, which one of the following must be true?

    (A) Elmo is tested on Thursday.
    (B) Frank is tested on Friday.
    (C) Bobo is tested on Monday.
    (D) There are exactly two free morning time slots.
    (E) There are exactly two free afternoon time slots.

10. If Frank is tested two days after Bobo is tested, which one of the following can be false?

    (A) Frank is tested immediately after Alonzo.
    (B) Bobo is tested immediately after Carlo.
    (C) The free time slots are only on Monday, Wednesday, and Friday.
    (D) Elmo is the last chimp tested.
    (E) Dingo is the first chimp tested.

11. If Dingo is tested in the afternoon, in how many different ways can the chimps be scheduled for testing?

    (A) 1
    (B) 2
    (C) 3
    (D) 4
    (E) 5

12. If at least one chimp is tested each day, and if Elmo is tested on the same day as another chimp, which one of the following must be true?

    (A) Bobo is tested in the time slot immediately preceding the time slot in which Carlo is tested.
    (B) Elmo is tested on the day after Dingo is tested.
    (C) Carlo is tested in the time slot immediately preceding the time slot in which Dingo is tested.
    (D) No other chimp is tested between Bobo and Dingo.
    (E) Exactly one other chimp is tested between Carlo and Elmo.

GO ON TO THE NEXT PAGE.

Questions 13–18

A teacher instructs her class to create four separate pictures to be used as scenery for a school play. There are to be one dog picture, one house picture, and two tree pictures. Each picture is done in one of two media, paint or crayon. Each picture is done in one of three colors—blue, red, or yellow.

There is exactly one blue and one yellow picture.
The two tree pictures are done in different colors but in the same medium.
The blue and yellow pictures are not done in the same medium.
The dog picture is done in crayon.
One tree picture is done in red.

13. Which one of the following is an acceptable group of four pictures?

   (A) Blue crayon dog, red painted house, red painted tree, yellow crayon tree
   (B) Yellow crayon dog, red painted house, blue painted tree, red crayon tree
   (C) Blue crayon dog, red painted house, red painted tree, yellow painted tree
   (D) Yellow crayon dog, blue painted house, red crayon tree, red crayon tree
   (E) Yellow painted dog, red painted house, blue crayon tree, red crayon tree

14. If the maximum number of pictures is done in crayon, which one of the following must be true?

   (A) A tree is done in blue.
   (B) A tree is done in yellow.
   (C) The dog is done in red.
   (D) The house is done in blue.
   (E) The house is done in yellow.

15. If the dog picture is done in blue, which one of the following must be FALSE?

   (A) There are more crayon pictures than painted pictures.
   (B) There are more painted pictures than crayon pictures.
   (C) The house is done in crayon.
   (D) The house is done in paint.
   (E) One tree is done in yellow.

16. If the house is done in yellow, which one of the following CANNOT be true?

   (A) The trees are done in paint.
   (B) The trees are done in crayon.
   (C) There is an equal number of pictures done in crayon and in paint.
   (D) Both red pictures are done in paint.
   (E) The yellow picture is done in crayon.

17. If neither of the tree pictures is done in yellow, and if there are more painted pictures than those done in crayon, then which one of the following is true?

   (A) The dog picture must be done in blue paint.
   (B) The house picture could be done in red crayon.
   (C) The house picture could be done in yellow paint.
   (D) The dog picture must be done in red crayon.
   (E) The house picture must be done in red paint.

18. Which one of the following pieces of additional information would make it certain that the dog picture is done in blue or yellow?

   (A) Exactly three pictures are done in crayon.
   (B) Exactly three pictures are done in paint.
   (C) The house is done in blue.
   (D) A tree is done in blue.
   (E) The house is done in yellow.

GO ON TO THE NEXT PAGE.

Questions 19–24

Nine chairs are arranged in a circle, with each chair facing the center of the circle. Lisa, Marvin, Naomi, Oliver, Pam, Randi, and Sybil each sit in one of the chairs. The other two chairs are empty.

Sybil sits immediately to Marvin's left.
Randi sits three chairs to Sybil's right.
Neither Randi nor Sybil sits next to empty chairs.
Lisa sits in a chair immediately next to Oliver.

19. Which one of the following must be true?

   (A) Pam sits next to Randi.
   (B) Naomi sits next to Randi.
   (C) Lisa sits next to an empty chair.
   (D) The empty chairs are immediately next to each other.
   (E) Oliver sits next to Sybil.

20. If Oliver sits two chairs to the right of Randi, which one of the following could be false?

   (A) Randi sits three chairs away from an empty chair.
   (B) Oliver sits next to an empty chair.
   (C) Lisa sits next to Randi.
   (D) Exactly two people sit between Pam and Naomi.
   (E) Pam sits next to Sybil.

21. Which one of the following CANNOT be true?

   (A) Pam sits next to neither Randi nor Sybil.
   (B) Oliver sits next to neither Randi nor Sybil.
   (C) Pam sits immediately between Randi and Marvin.
   (D) Sybil sits next to Lisa.
   (E) Sybil sits next to Naomi.

22. If Lisa sits next to an empty chair, how many different arrangements of people in chairs are possible?

   (A) 2
   (B) 3
   (C) 4
   (D) 5
   (E) 6

23. Which one of the following statements would allow one to determine the exact positions of all seven people?

   (A) Exactly two people sit between Lisa and Pam.
   (B) Oliver sits next to Sybil.
   (C) Exactly one person sits between Lisa and Naomi.
   (D) Lisa sits next to Randi.
   (E) Exactly two people sit between Oliver and Naomi.

24. If Sybil sits two chairs to Marvin's right, but all of the other conditions remain the same, which one of the following statements CANNOT be true?

   (A) Marvin sits next to an empty chair.
   (B) Pam sits next to an empty chair.
   (C) Randi sits next to Oliver.
   (D) Naomi sits exactly three chairs away from Lisa.
   (E) Sybil sits exactly three chairs away from Lisa.

STOP

IF YOU FINISH BEFORE TIME IS CALLED, YOU MAY CHECK YOUR WORK ON THIS SECTION ONLY. DO NOT WORK ON ANY OTHER SECTION IN THE TEST.

SECTION FOUR
Time—35 minutes
25 questions

<u>Directions</u>: This test is composed of questions that ask you to analyze the logic of statements or short paragraphs. You are to choose as the answer to each question the one choice you consider best on the basis of your common-sense evaluation of the statement and its assumptions. Although a question may seem to have more than one acceptable answer, there is only one best answer, and it is the one that does not entail making any illogical, extraneous, or conflicting assumptions about the question. These questions do not pre-suppose any knowledge of formal logic on your part.

1. Mass public education in the past half-century has clearly failed at the most basic level. In fact, it has been detrimental to the public welfare. Recent studies show that only about half of the country's graduating high school seniors can compose a simple business letter.

   Which one of the following, if true, gives the strongest support to the author's argument?

   (A) A larger percentage of high school seniors than ever before are able to write a business letter correctly.
   (B) At least 15 percent of today's high school seniors speak English as a second language.
   (C) Fewer than half of the high school seniors graduating today can do the math necessary to complete an income tax return.
   (D) More accurate data show that only 46 percent of the nation's high school seniors can compose a simple business letter.
   (E) A survey taken five decades ago showed that four out of five graduating seniors could write an acceptable business letter.

2. **Editorial:** Residents who accept miserable air quality and dangerous levels of pollution as unavoidable concomitants of living in a city the size of Eastchester should consider recent history. Five years ago we all accepted a crumbling infrastructure and hopeless traffic congestion as inevitable, until Mayor Angel made transportation his top priority and spent the necessary money to fix the system. The mayor doesn't seem to place the same value on clean air, but there is a candidate who has promised to make it her top priority. Those citizens who share her concern should remember what determination can accomplish and should vote for Inge Schwartz.

   Which one of the following best describes the argumentative strategy employed by the editorial?

   (A) It draws a causal connection between the city's former inefficient transportation system and its current problem with air pollution.
   (B) It contrasts Schwartz's willingness to spend money on programs she considers to be important with the mayor's unwillingness to do the same.
   (C) It demonstrates that air pollution in Eastchester is not an inevitable result of the city's size, but instead is a correctable problem.
   (D) It exhorts the readers to place clean air at the top of their list of priorities and therefore to vote for Schwartz.
   (E) It compares Eastchester's pollution problem to its former transportation problem in order to imply that the current problem can be solved by city government.

GO ON TO THE NEXT PAGE.

3. Wisdom does not come from a life of untrammeled ease but only from adversity. Constanza is a very wise old woman—therefore she must have suffered a great deal in her life.

Which one of the following most closely parallels the reasoning in the above argument?

(A) Character is a result of early training in patience and fortitude. Leon is a man of exemplary character so he must have had dutiful parents.

(B) Denise won the gold medal at the Olympics, so she must have had an excellent coach, since such a high level of performance can come only with the very best training and preparation.

(C) Good health cannot develop without attention to proper nutrition. Farley will remain healthy throughout his life since he is a fanatic about eating a healthy diet.

(D) Francois is a brilliant musician; he must have been surrounded by other excellent musicians from the day he was born, since musical ability flourishes only among people who have some steady exposure to good music.

(E) A society that does not provide for its poor stands condemned as a failure, despite its other political and cultural achievements. Therefore our own society will be judged harshly by history.

4. Economists can directly compare how effectively different economic systems perform specific tasks—for example, the number of automobiles or tons of steel produced at what cost in labor—simply by referring to the relevant statistics. Assuming the statistics are accurate, one system then can be fairly judged better or worse than others in terms of its operational effectiveness. In comparing systems as a whole, however, the difficulty of comparing their unquantifiable aspects—such as what constitutes an acceptable level of unemployment or a fair distribution of income—may produce widely diverging opinions among economists who otherwise concur in their analyses of the systems' relative operational merits.

If all of the statements in the passage are true, which one of the following must also be true on the basis of them?

(A) An economic system's effectiveness in performing specific tasks cannot be accurately determined by statistical analysis alone.

(B) The statistics on unemployment and income distribution within a given economic system are frequently considered unreliable by economic analysts.

(C) In comparing economic systems as a whole, economists must inevitably make value judgments about certain aspects of the systems' performances.

(D) Most economists would agree that the relative merits of different economic systems should not be assessed on the basis of their productive capabilities.

(E) Comparative analysis of different economic systems depends on agreement among economists about how statistics should be correctly interpreted.

GO ON TO THE NEXT PAGE.

KAPLAN

5. Although we tend to measure the phenomenon of aging in a casual way by referring to the passing of chronological time, this really provides an incomplete description of an animal's or a human being's real physiological age. Physiological, or "true," age relates the physiological changes brought about in the animal by the passing of chronological time to the whole aging process of its species. A fifteen-year-old cat could aptly be described as "very old," which would not be true of a horse younger than twenty years, while a fifty-year-old human being nowadays could be considered still relatively young.

It can be most properly inferred from the above that

(A) people are better able to make an accurate determination of another person's age than of an animal's age

(B) the idiosyncrasies of animal physiology preclude any meaningful use of words such as *old* or *young* in descriptions of age

(C) evaluating an animal's physiological condition is not the most accurate way of determining its true age

(D) definitions of the adjectives "old" and "young" depend on whether they are applied to humans or to other animals

(E) knowing the chronological age of any animal is meaningful as a measure of true age only when its species' life span is also known

6. The city council's policy of granting contracts for construction projects to companies filing the lowest bid is an invitation to disaster. The effect of the policy is that bridges, buildings, and other public works are built with inferior materials and workmanship, creating a situation which is not only dangerous but financially self-defeating. Extra maintenance costs on poorly constructed projects are excessive, often negating within a few years the savings on original building costs. This misguided policy must be changed if we are to maintain a safe and efficient infrastructure in this city.

Which one of the following, if true, would significantly weaken the argument above?

(A) The need to rebuild poorly constructed buildings provides many jobs for the city's residents.

(B) The city's building contracts rarely specify the quality of the materials or workmanship to be employed.

(C) The policy requires that the city entertain bids only from firms whose plans meet very stringent standards of workmanship and materials.

(D) Even buildings that are constructed with the finest materials and workmanship can be dangerous if their architectural design is faulty.

(E) The city is already operating with an enormous budget deficit and cannot afford to spend more money on the construction and maintenance of the projects in question.

GO ON TO THE NEXT PAGE.

7. Evidently, the director's intention here was to draw a contrast between the social status of the military and that of the working classes during the second World War. The drab, simple clothing of the charwomen and chimney sweeps indicates a debased socioeconomic position, whereas the crisp, neat, colorful uniform of General Von Vandt denotes the respect and honor accorded to German fighting men. We must not allow the conversational allusions to social equality to blind us to the film's powerful visual message.

The author's argument presupposes which one of the following?

(A) Film is fundamentally a visual medium.
(B) Moviegoers are frequently misled by filmmakers' subtle messages.
(C) Viewers are prone to ignore the visual aspects of a film.
(D) A film's true message can be conveyed visually rather than verbally.
(E) Social distinctions between working people and the military were unique to Germany during the second World War.

8. The government is considering two different sites—one on the Abaco River and one on the Bornos River—for the multibillion dollar hydroelectric plant. Although the technical expertise exists to build roughly the same plant in either place, producing roughly the same amount of electricity per hour, building the plant on the Abaco site will cost over twice as much money. With the federal budget currently in deficit, it is clear why they should choose to build the dam at the Bornos site.

Which one of the following would be most useful in explaining the difference in building costs for the two proposed dam sites?

(A) Many farms along the lower Bornos River valley would benefit from the controlled flow of water a dam would make possible.
(B) The Abaco site is in an inaccessible area, requiring the building of new roads and the importation of nonlocal labor.
(C) The Bornos site is near a large city whose residents could use the resulting lake for inexpensive recreation.
(D) The Abaco site is in an area that contains many endangered species that would be threatened by the new dam.
(E) The Abaco River has a relatively low volume of flow, making it impossible to expand an Abaco plant to meet future electricity needs.

GO ON TO THE NEXT PAGE.

Questions 9–10

Menendez: My mother stated in her living will that she would refuse life-saving treatment if she became terminally ill. Yet when she stopped breathing, you attached her to a respirator. Your refusal to let her die despite her repeated requests to be taken off the machine amounts to a breach of your duty as a physician.

Doctor: Although this state honors living wills, my duty as a physician is nonetheless to intervene, if necessary, in order to save lives. I cannot "play God," even if it means acting against patients' wishes.

9. Which one of the following principles, if established, would determine that attaching Mrs. Menendez to a respirator was the right decision or instead would determine that her wishes should have been heeded?

   (A) If a patient whose life is being artificially sustained has expressed the desire to die, the physician is morally obliged to facilitate that desire.

   (B) If a terminally ill patient has expressed the desire to die, the physician is obliged to intervene medically to facilitate that desire.

   (C) When a patient with a living will is in a persistent vegetative state, the physician is obliged to carry out the desires expressed in that will, regardless of the family's wishes.

   (D) When a terminally ill patient has expressed a clear wish to die, the physician is obliged to honor that request, regardless of when the request was originally expressed.

   (E) If a terminally ill patient's desires contradict what she originally expressed in her living will, the physician is obliged to carry out the wishes of the patient's closest living relative.

10. Which one of the following characterizations of the doctor's response would contribute most to a defense by Menendez against the doctor's position?

    (A) It leads to the further but unacceptable conclusion that only those who can afford life-saving treatment should be eligible to receive it.

    (B) It draws a false distinction between the patient's desire and the physician's professional obligation.

    (C) It is imprecise in that it fails to demonstrate that artificially prolonging someone's life is different from "playing God."

    (D) It overlooks the possibility that the patient could later change her mind regarding her desire to die.

    (E) It assumes without warrant that the patient did not make her request when she was mentally competent.

11. A single remark can mean many different things in different contexts, its connotations changing with the situation in which it is uttered and the person uttering it. However, most remarks contain objective information that is not subject to interpretation.

    Which one of the following is most similar in principle to the situation described above?

    (A) Many athletes compete to be the best in their sport, but only one can actually win that honor.

    (B) A particular tie can look different with many different suits, but most ties have definite, individual traits.

    (C) A single work of art can provoke many different reactions from different people, but most artwork cannot easily be classified as good or bad.

    (D) A particular person may behave differently in different situations, but most people find that consistency is a desirable character trait.

    (E) A comment that was intended as praise can sometimes be interpreted as criticism by an individual, but most people wouldn't misinterpret the comment.

GO ON TO THE NEXT PAGE.

12. In order to promote off-season business, Mt. Dunmore Lodge made the following "Welcome Back" offer to their winter guests: guests who rent a room for at least a week during ski season can come back during the summer and get 25 percent off the standard summer price of any room they rent. After the summer passed, the owners of the lodge determined that the majority of their guests had taken advantage of the "Welcome Back" offer and paid the reduced rates. However, they were surprised to find they still managed to rent more rooms at full price than they did at the discount rate.

Which one of the following, if true, most helps to explain the apparent discrepancy in the passage?

(A) Most of the guests who stayed at Mt. Dunmore Lodge during the winter did not stay for a full week.

(B) Those guests taking advantage of the "Welcome Back" discount were more likely to bring their families with them than were those guests who were paying full price.

(C) Some of the guests who received the "Welcome Back" discount also received a 10 percent rate reduction through their auto club.

(D) In order to pay for the construction of a new gymnasium and a new pool, the owners of the lodge raised their summer prices considerably.

(E) On average, guests who took advantage of the "Welcome Back" discount spent more money at the hotel on additional goods and services than guests who paid full price for their rooms.

13. The weather this year was so poor, and last year's crop yield so unproductive, that many farmers in this county have had to take out loans just to make ends meet. To make matters worse, many farmers have had to sell some of their best farm equipment at auction, because many of the local lending institutions have regulations that allow loans only if a farmer's equipment is valued at less than a certain limit. Farmers whose equipment exceeded that value limit had to sell some of it in order to meet the lending requirements. Now, these farmers must harvest their crops without necessary equipment. The real problem, however, is that banks do not base their lending practices on how much farmers need, or even how much they produce, but on how much their tractors and combines are worth.

Which one of the following conclusions can most reasonably be drawn based on the information in the passage above?

(A) Local banks are paying less money for crops and more for farming machinery.

(B) Local farmers are being hurt by illegal banking practices.

(C) Local farmers are being forced to sell their assets in order to qualify for necessary loans.

(D) If they can endure present hardships, local farmers will eventually succeed.

(E) Unless the banks agree to subsidize local farmers, crop yields will be even lower this year than last.

GO ON TO THE NEXT PAGE.

14. When Euripides lived and wrote in ancient Athens, Greece was constantly in danger of civil war, and revolts among the slave class occasionally disrupted Greek society. The country of Erewhon is today in danger of civil war because of its unrelenting suppression of economically deprived classes, and guerrilla operations continually upset life in that country. It is surprising, therefore, that a dramatist of Euripides' stature has not appeared in Erewhon.

Which one of the following assumptions is most essential to the argument above?

(A) The behavior of guerrillas in Erewhon is very similar to that of the Greek slaves.
(B) Dramatists like Euripides can be expected to emerge during periods of civil war and social unrest.
(C) Greece was constantly plagued by civil wars as a result of its mistreatment of slaves.
(D) Ancient Greece and modern Erewhon have many similarities.
(E) The turmoil in Erewhon will produce a greater writer than Euripides.

15. Considering the current economy, the introduction of a new brand of cereal is unlikely to expand total sales of cereal, but rather will just cause some existing buyers of cereal to switch brands. So it makes no sense for the Coolidge Corporation to introduce another brand of cereal, since they will only hurt sales of the brands of cereal they already produce.

Which one of the following, if true, would most seriously weaken the argument above?

(A) Total sales of cereal will increase as the total population increases.
(B) Many new brands of cereal sell extremely well for the first year of their existence.
(C) Coolidge Corporation currently produces fewer brands of cereal than do its competitors.
(D) Some cereal buyers regularly switch from brand to brand, even when no new brands have been introduced.
(E) Research indicates that the new brand will attract more buyers of competitors' cereals than buyers of other Coolidge brands.

16. **Betty:** My opponent for the office of scout superintendent opposes a rule that would require all Wilderness Scout troop leaders to lead their scouts in the loyalty pledge before all meetings. How can my opponent claim she will represent the high moral standards of the Wilderness Scouts when she would forbid troop leaders from leading the pledge that proclaims our most important virtue?

Which one of the following points would be most useful to a person disputing the reasoning of the argument above?

(A) Some Wilderness Scouts also oppose the loyalty pledge rule.
(B) Loyalty is only one of many virtues espoused by the Wilderness Scouts.
(C) The opponent's position on the loyalty pledge rule may be atypical of her positions in general.
(D) Refusing to require an activity like the loyalty pledge is not the same thing as forbidding it.
(E) Opposing loyalty to an organization does not necessarily mean that one is disloyal to that organization.

17. No one can deny that, "This story is true," is a very different utterance from, "This story is long." A potential Bachelor of Philosophy does not, at the moment in which his degree is conferred, lose one attribute (potentiality) and gain a new one (actuality). Words like *true* and *potential* do not denote tangible, concrete qualities. Our minds cannot then learn them in the same way they learn words like *rectangular* or *blue*.

The author of the above passage is making which one of the following assumptions?

(A) Our minds can learn only tangible, concrete qualities.
(B) Attributes cannot be lost and gained.
(C) Abstract concepts are more difficult for the mind to grasp than are tangible qualities.
(D) Our minds are structured according to the types of words we learn.
(E) The process of learning words varies with the types of words learned.

GO ON TO THE NEXT PAGE.

Questions 18–19

Are we an active or a reactive society? Do we attempt to shape the world to our desires or do we merely respond by reflex to the harms that the world deals us? Most people would claim that we define ourselves as the former kind of society. Why, then, do many of these same people advocate capital punishment, a totally reactive response to crime? To execute violent criminals is to admit defeat, to assert that people cannot be changed or rehabilitated. Is it not better to be constructive rather than destructive, to regard criminals as flawed elements in our society that can be corrected, rather than irrevocable failures who must be written off?

18. Which one of the following best describes the point made by the author above?

    (A) The execution of criminals is not consistent with the idea of an active, constructive society.
    (B) Capital punishment does not deter other criminals from committing violent crime.
    (C) We should reconsider our conception of ourselves as an active society.
    (D) Our professed image of ourselves as a society is often at odds with our actions as a society.
    (E) We should outlaw capital punishment because it violates the spirit of our laws.

19. The author of the above argument would most likely agree with which one of the following principles?

    (A) Capital punishment makes a society as culpable as the criminals it executes.
    (B) Violent criminals are flawed human beings who cannot be held responsible for their actions.
    (C) A society that admits defeat in the matter of violent crime will not survive.
    (D) Destroying human life is inappropriate for a society in any situation.
    (E) Our society's treatment of criminals should be more rehabilitative and less punitive.

20. A recent survey found that all death row convicts in state penitentiaries who file petitions believe that there will be a substantial delay in the courts' processing of the paperwork attendant to their execution, and a more favorable outcome if the pardoning authority is made aware of the existence of the petition.

Which one of the following inferences can be most reliably drawn from the passage above?

    (A) Most death row convicts in state penitentiaries who believe that there will be a dilatory effect if they file petitions do file petitions.
    (B) All death row convicts in state penitentiaries who believe that there will be a dilatory effect if they file petitions do file petitions.
    (C) If any death row convicts in state penitentiaries believe that routine petitions will have little or no effect, these convicts have not been among those prisoners filing petitions.
    (D) Prisoners who file petitions have no sense of remorse for their actions.
    (E) Most death row convicts in state penitentiaries who do not file petitions believe that there will be no benefit attached to filing a petition.

GO ON TO THE NEXT PAGE.

21. **Jason:** I found money-saving coupons for half of the items on your food list for the party. I know that the coupons are for brands that you don't usually buy, but if we use them for our party shopping, we'll save money.

    Twyla: No, in order to buy everything we need for the party, we'll spend more money if we use your coupons than if we don't.

    Each of the following would help support Twyla's assertion that more money would be spent if the coupons were used than if they were not used EXCEPT:

    (A) The coupons can be redeemed only at a store that charges much higher prices overall than the store that Twyla was planning to patronize.
    (B) Each couponed brand has a much lower net weight than the brands on Twyla's original list, thus requiring that they purchase much more of each product.
    (C) Exactly half of the couponed items are specially priced so that the final price, including the savings, equals the price of the corresponding products on Twyla's original list.
    (D) The prices of the couponed brands are much more expensive than the original brands on Twyla's list, thereby outweighing the savings from the coupons.
    (E) Twyla included on her list only products she knew to be on sale.

22. Since the new board of directors was elected at the beginning of the last financial quarter, a higher percentage of our potential clients have decided to purchase our competitor's system. As a result, two out of ten of our engineers have been let go, and our company's financial future is at risk. New strategies are on the agenda for the next board meeting.

    If the statements in the above passage are true, which one of the following must also be true?

    (A) Current sales are at their lowest level since the company was founded.
    (B) The competition's product is better than the company's.
    (C) Since the beginning of the last quarter, more clients have purchased the competitor's system than have purchased the company's system.
    (D) Since the beginning of the last quarter, the company has been less competitive than it had been in the past.
    (E) Most purchasers of systems think the competitor's system is better than the company's system.

23. In friendship one sees one's friend as another "self." One cares about him or her in the same way that one cares about oneself. Since each of us desires to know that we exist and are in good circumstances, each of us also wishes to know that our friends are likewise alive and well. Thus, true friendship requires that one live with or near one's friends.

Which one of the following, if true, would most weaken the argument above?

(A) Most people care for themselves much more than they care for their friends.

(B) Technologies like the telephone allow us to confirm that our friends are alive and well even when we are separated from them by vast distances.

(C) It is possible to live near and even with a friend without knowing for certain that he or she is in good circumstances.

(D) Merely living near or with a friend will not necessarily ensure that the friend remains alive and in good circumstances.

(E) Often circumstances dictate that one friend must move far away, and for him instead to remain among his friends would be so inconvenient that it would place too much strain on the friendship.

Questions 24–25

Duane: Over half the homicides that took place in this country last year were committed by means of handguns. It's misguided to talk about the "right" to own a handgun; a more important right is the right to live in safety. It's difficult to see why anyone other than handgun manufacturers would continue to argue against strict handgun controls. Such strict controls will reduce the number of guns in criminals' possession, and a reduction of guns will bring down the murder rate. Anything else is simply ineffective.

Sylvia: Even if one accepts such a casual dismissal of our time-honored right to bear arms, there's still no evidence that laws against carrying handguns will reduce homicides. Criminals can't be expected to obey anti-handgun laws of their own free will, and the supply is so plentiful and cheap that it will always be easy for criminals to find guns, no matter how strict the law; only honest people will find themselves disarmed.

24. Which one of the following is the main point at issue between Duane and Sylvia?

(A) whether the strongest opposition to the passage of strict handgun control laws comes from the manufacturers of handguns

(B) whether a reduction of the number of handguns in the hands of criminals would actually bring about a reduction of the homicide rate

(C) the likelihood that stringent punishments for the possession of handguns will actually deter criminals from carrying handguns

(D) whether strict anti-handgun laws can significantly reduce the number of handguns in the hands of criminals

(E) whether handguns can be strictly controlled without an illegal violation of the right to bear arms

GO ON TO THE NEXT PAGE.

25. Sylvia adopts which one of the following strategies in criticizing Duane's position?

(A) She undermines his analysis of the cause of the problem he is trying to solve.

(B) She relies on sarcasm in order to make the proposed solution appear ridiculous.

(C) She suggests that the proposed solution may result in exacerbating the problem instead of contributing to its solution.

(D) She denies that the course of action proposed by Duane will bring about the situation that he has identified as being necessary to the solution of the problem.

(E) She suggests that Duane has exaggerated the seriousness of the problem, in order to dismiss possible legal concerns about his proposed solution.

STOP
**IF YOU FINISH BEFORE TIME IS CALLED, YOU MAY CHECK YOUR WORK ON THIS SECTION ONLY.
DO NOT WORK ON ANY OTHER SECTION IN THE TEST.**

PRACTICE TEST
ANSWERS AND
EXPLANATIONS

LSAT LOGIC GAMES

PRACTICE TEST ANSWER KEY

Section 1 Logical Reasoning	Section 2 Reading Comprehension	Section 3 Logic Games	Section 4 Logical Reasoning
1. C	1. C	1. D	1. E
2, D	2. A	2. D	2. E
3. B	3. E	3. B	3. D
4. C	4. D	4. D	4. C
5. B	5. B	5. C	5. E
6. A	6. A	6. E	6. C
7. C	7. D	7. B	7. D
8. B	8. D	8. A	8. B
9. C	9. D	9. C	9. A
10. B	10. B	10. E	10. C
11. C	11. D	11. D	11. B
12. B	12. E	12. B	12. B
13. C	13. D	13. C	13. C
14. E	14. C	14. C	14. B
15. A	15. C	15. A	15. E
16. E	16. A	16. D	16. D
17. B	17. D	17. E	17. E
18. C	18. C	18. B	18. A
19. A	19. E	19. D	19. E
20. E	20. C	20. E	20. C
21. C	21. B	21. A	21. C
22. B	22. B	22. C	22. D
23. E	23. C	23. C	23. B
24. A	24. E	24. E	24. D
25. D	25. E		25. D
	26. B		
	27. A		

CALCULATE YOUR SCORE

Step 1

Add together your total number correct for all four sections.
This is your raw score.

Section 1 _____
(# correct)

Section 2 _____
(# correct)

Section 3 _____
(# correct)

Section 4 _____
(# correct)

Total Correct _____
(raw score)

Step 2

Find your raw score on the table below and read across
to find your scaled score and your percentile.

Raw Score	Scaled Score	Percentile Rank	Raw Score	Scaled Score	Percentile Rank
0	120	0	19	129	1
1	120	0	20	130	2
2	120	0	21	130	2
3	120	0	22	130	2
4	120	0	23	131	2
5	120	0	24	132	3
6	120	0	25	133	3
7	120	0	26	133	3
8	121	0	27	133	3
9	122	0	28	134	4
10	122	0	29	135	5
11	123	0	30	136	6
12	124	0	31	136	6
13	124	0	32	137	8
14	125	0	33	137	8
15	126	1	34	138	9
16	126	1	35	138	9
17	127	1	36	139	10
18	128	1	37	140	13

Raw Score	Scaled Score	Percentile Rank	Raw Score	Scaled Score	Percentile Rank
38	140	13	70	157	74
39	140	13	71	158	77
40	141	15	72	158	77
41	142	17	73	159	80
42	142	17	74	159	80
43	143	20	75	160	83
44	144	23	76	160	83
45	144	23	77	161	86
46	144	23	78	162	88
47	145	26	79	162	88
48	146	29	80	162	88
49	146	29	81	163	90
50	147	33	82	164	92
51	147	33	83	164	92
52	148	37	84	165	93
53	148	37	85	166	95
54	149	41	86	166	95
55	150	45	87	167	96
56	150	45	88	167	96
57	150	45	89	168	97
58	151	50	90	169	97
59	151	50	91	170	98
60	152	54	92	170	98
61	153	58	93	171	98
62	153	58	94	172	99
63	153	58	95	173	99
64	154	62	96	174	99
65	155	66	97	175	99
66	155	66	98	176	99
67	156	70	99	177	99
68	156	70	100	179	99
69	156	70	101	180	99

PRACTICE TEST EXPLANATIONS

Section One: Logical Reasoning Explanations

1 (C) The author concludes that if civilians are to be kept out of harm's way, then any kind of armed conflict near populated areas is unacceptable. The missing link is the idea that armed conflict near populated areas will necessarily endanger civilian lives. If this weren't the case, then civilian safety could remain a priority while the warring forces in question romped around populated areas waging their armed conflict. In other words, if the conclusion is to stand, it must be assumed that there's no way to simultaneously engage in armed conflict near populated areas and maintain civilian safety.

(A) This is a scope error. The issue is armed conflict near populated areas, not armed conflict in general.

(B) The author tends to suggest the opposite: liberating the conquered islands will endanger the lives of civilians, which implies that conflict is inevitable.

(D) This one is tricky. If the author's only statement was, "We must refrain from liberating the conquered islands because the lives of some civilians would be endangered," then (D) would be a fair assumption. However, the author begins with the word *if*, suggesting that

holding off on liberation in favor of civilian safety isn't a foregone conclusion. The author may, in fact, favor liberation, civilians be damned—the antithesis of (D).

(E) The author may be leading to this conclusion (although we don't know for sure), but that doesn't mean that the argument depends on its being true.

Remember:

- An assumption bridges the gap between evidence and conclusion. It's a piece of information that the argument depends on for the conclusion to remain valid.
- The Denial Test can be used to check answers to assumption questions. Deny or negate your choice and see if the argument falls apart. If it does fall apart, the answer is correct. If the conclusion is unaffected, the choice is wrong.
- Read choices critically with meticulous attention to detail. Choices (A) and (C) are virtually identical but for the phrase *populated areas,* which alone is the difference between a point and a wrong answer.

2 **(D)** Translation of the first sentence: "*If* Marybeth is shopping, *then* she has her mother's permission." So (contrapositive here) if her mother doesn't give her permission, Marybeth can't go shopping. Next, deal with the "aloneness" issue. She can shop alone at the mall down the street, but downtown she has to go with Sue and Desiree. Thus *if* Marybeth is shopping at the downtown department stores, *then* both Sue and Desiree must be with her.

(A) This would be correct if it said, "the downtown department store." She can possibly shop alone at other department stores, just not the ones downtown.

(B), (C) Neither can be inferred, since we know that there are circumstances when Marybeth can shop alone.

(E) The three girls can be together in many places other than the downtown department stores.

Remember:

- The test makers test formal logic by burying formal statements in the context of a casual argument. Be on the lookout for sentences that you can boil down to hard and fast rules.
- For any if/then statement, the contrapositive can be formed by reversing and negating the terms. The general model is: Original statement, "If X, then Y." The contrapositive, and valid inference, "If not Y, then not X."

3 **(B)** The "unexpected result" is that a far greater percentage of "new and improved" bicycles came back for repair than did the original bicycles that prompted the recall in the first place. Only something that has a major impact on the

bicycle will effectively resolve this paradox, and (B) introduces the notion of the bicycle being used in a radically different way. If, in fact, the "Rough Rider" now appeals to people who are more likely to beat the heck out of it on "unusually rough terrain," then the rise in repairs would make much more sense.

(A) Irrelevant. Which service center is in operation doesn't affect the overall percentage of bicycles coming back for repairs.

(C) A better warranty may be incentive for a few extra people to bring their bikes back for repair, but a marked change in the way the bicycle is used (B) explains the dramatic increase in repairs much better.

(D) There's no reason to believe that not addressing this flaw would factor into the rise in repairs (it's part of both models), and considering the improvements in the metal and the rims, (D) doesn't come close to explaining the bizarre results.

(E) The rims were improved, and even if the improvements didn't have much of an effect, a factor consistent in both models can't account for the repair rate soaring from 20 to 50 percent.

Remember:

- A paradox is a seeming contradiction, an unexpected result contained in the argument. The correct answer will be the one that resolves this apparent contradiction.
- In paradox questions, the question stem may use the word *paradox* itself or can take the form of the stem of question 3.

4 (C) Ms. Maloney demands that Dr. Ortiz replace her daughter's current dosage of drug X with the same dosage of drug Y, because even though Y has side effects, it works faster. Dr. Ortiz argues to stay with drug X, because Y's side effects may prove harmful for children. Clearly the disagreement centers around the issue of the side effects. Is it worth taking a chance on Y when X is safely doing the job?

(A) Too broad. They're not arguing about whether Y should be taken off the market. The doctor's position is that Y simply hasn't been tested for use with children, which isn't the same as saying that it should be discontinued altogether.

(B) Neither person disagrees that X is effective in its current dosage, so whether that dosage is inappropriate for children is not an issue.

(D) Ms. Maloney wants the doctor to prescribe drug Y purely for her daughter's sake, and never brings up the issue of her daughter's viability as a test subject.

(E) This is a global issue that the two people ignore, focused as they are on the single, specific case of Ms. Maloney's daughter.

Remember:

• In LSAT dialogue format questions, try to boil down each argument to its simplest terms. That will help you avoid wrong answers that sound as if they relate to the argument but are extraneous in some way.

5 (B) Dr. Ortiz's position is based on the safety of the patient, so the "most closely conforming principle" has to highlight that issue, and (B)

hits the nail on the head: If two different yet equally effective treatments are available to choose between, safety should be the determining factor. That's essentially the basis of Ortiz's counterargument.

(A) The speaker's credentials aren't at issue here. This choice would be correct if Ortiz's only argument were, "Hey, who's the doctor here, you or me?"

(C) Dr. Ortiz doesn't refuse to prescribe drug Y because the patient is a child, but because drug Y hasn't been tested on children. Inferably, if an adult were in a similar situation and an alternative drug were available that hadn't yet been tested on adults, the doctor's treatment recommendation would be the same.

(D) This is tempting, but Dr. Ortiz refuses to switch from an effective treatment after judging the alternative as risky. (D) ignores the safety issue that's crucial to the doctor's position.

(E) The doctor's position focuses on a fear of the potential side effects of a drug, whereas (E) relates to the general working mechanisms of the two types of drugs in question.

Remember:

• Principle questions involve fitting a specific situation into a global generality (or, occasionally, vice versa). The answer is usually the choice that expresses the key concepts and contains the key terms that the other choices leave out.
• Try not to skip stimuli that come with two questions attached. Often the second question can be answered quickly after you've invested time in the first.

6 **(A)** The botanists conclude that the wild-flower in question died away due to auto emissions. Their evidence is that the wildflower flourished during colonial times, before cars, but doesn't grow now on modern roadsides built on the same land where other wildflower species continue to thrive. The idea that the argument presupposes, or assumes, is that no other factor was responsible for wiping out this particular species, and choice (A) plays off this. If disease caused the demise of the particular wildflower, the conclusion linking their disappearance to auto emissions falls apart.

(B) Since the argument is about wildflowers and auto emissions, the author needn't assume anything about pollution or botanical species in general.

(C) Areas sheltered from auto emissions are outside the scope of the botanists' argument, so this can't be a presupposition.

(D) and **(E)** are both irrelevant. If the growing toxicity of auto emissions were a factor, then why aren't the other species affected? And the behavior of "most" botanical species has no bearing whatsoever on the argument.

Remember:

• Be aware of the various ways that assumption questions are worded: "which is *assumed*," "the argument *presupposes* which of the following," "the conclusion *relies on* which of the following," etcetera.

7 **(C)** Two main pieces of evidence: 1) vegetables can provide all the nutrients necessary for life (followed by an example), and 2) a vegetarian meal can be as varied and interesting as a meat-based meal. Then the author kicks into overdrive: based on these two pieces of evidence, she advocates banning the raising and slaughtering of livestock in favor of wider cultivation of high-nutrition crops. This sudden jump from a few words on the merits of vegetables to the extreme conclusion in the last sentence should come as somewhat of a surprise to you, and lead you to (C). The author simply doesn't give enough support for the conclusion.

(A) No terms warrant additional explanation, and the author *does* define what she means by the proper combinations of vegetables.

(B) There's no analogy in the argument, inappropriate or otherwise.

(D) It's not the author's responsibility to demonstrate the feasibility of her plan. The argument is strictly about what we *should* do, not what we *can* do.

(E) There is no circular reasoning employed: the conclusion, unwarranted as it may be, is not a restatement of the evidence.

Remember:

• Reading the question stem before the stimulus is a good strategy for all Logical Reasoning questions, but is even more applicable to "flaw" and "weaken" questions—your job is easier when you know in advance that there's something wrong with the reasoning in the stimulus.
• Be alert when you read; try to put the text into a real-life context. Evaluate the reasoning as you go along, and trust your instincts. For example, after reading the last line, it should be natural for you to think, "Whoa, where

did that come from?" Then the answer becomes obvious.

- Use structural signals to help you sort out the key parts of the argument. The phrase *for instance* in the second sentence lets you know that what follows is not a new thought, but an example of the statement made in the previous sentence.

8 **(B)** The question, phrased another way, asks: "What's the point of the line, 'Daphne's litter was harder to pick up than Ewell's'?" By stating (or granting) this, the speaker concedes that Daphne's act had a worse result, knowing full well that this is the most obvious point the court could use to justify the difference in punishment. By arguing that the worse result of Daphne's offense was due to the wind, not a difference in the severity of their crimes, the speaker is acknowledging and countering a possible objection to his claim that the offenders deserve equal punishment.

(A) The statement, a concession that the speaker attempts to explain away, actually damages the author's claim when taken by itself, so it certainly couldn't be used as additional evidence to support the claim.

(C) The speaker attempts to discredit the judge's position later in the argument, and on other grounds. The line in question bears no relation to that effort at all.

(D) The speaker explicitly alleges that Daphne's wealth, and not the greater difficulty of picking up her litter, was the reason the judge imposed a harsher fine on her.

(E) The speaker actually uses the line in question to emphasize the opposite—that there is no differ-

ence between the seriousness of the two offenses, only between the seriousness of the two results.

Remember:

- When a question stem seems unwieldy, try to rephrase it in your own words. You'll never get the right answer if you're answering a question different from the one that's asked.
- When asked for the role a statement plays in an argument, make sure to relate the statement to the overall context. Stay away from choices that simply evaluate the statement unto itself.

9 **(C)** The principle that most justifies the speaker's position is the one that speaks to the most important elements of the speaker's argument—that the crimes were identical, and that mitigating circumstances (such as the wealth of the accused) shouldn't be factors in the judge's rulings.

(A) State versus public property is a nonissue. There's no such comparison to be made, since both offenders littered in a state park.

(B) Too vague. What "good" is the judge doing?

(D) Tempting, because it helps to counter the "worse result due to wind" issue. However, according to the speaker, Daphne's punishment didn't stem from this but from her wealth. (C) addresses the entire issue better.

(E) Deterrence of future crime plays no part in the argument, so a principle based on this wouldn't help the speaker's position at all.

Remember:

- In principle questions, look for a choice that most completely addresses the author's major concerns. Many choices seem to present principles that fit nicely around the specifics of the given argument, but the right answer is invariably the only one that fits perfectly, by ignoring irrelevancies and sticking to the author's main concepts.

10 (B) The argument is found right there in the first sentence: Delgado's hiring policy is unsound. Next comes the evidence: her policy of hiring recent business school grads for executive positions is dangerous. To the author, trying to make up for a lack of corporate experience with a solid grasp of theory is like trying to pilot a jumbo jet by simply reading flying manuals. No two ways about it—that's an analogy.

(A) The author's argument is not geared towards a general principle, but rather towards a very specific judgment.

(C) Delgado's motives are never brought into the picture. The author disagrees with Delgado's policy because he finds the policy unsound and its underlying thinking dangerous, not because its underlying motives are suspect.

(D) The author doesn't like the policy because it's fundamentally unsound; no conflict of interest is mentioned or inferred.

(E) The author does allude to another situation, flying a plane, but solely for the point of creating an analogy. No findings are included in the plane reference.

Remember:

- Read the stimulus differently when looking to identify an author's method of argument. Your focus should not necessarily be on *what* the point is, but rather on *how* the point is made.
- In a method-of-argument question, test a choice by trying to come up with an example of what the situation would sound like if the method in question were employed. For example, for (C) to be correct, the stimulus would have to include a motive on the part of Delgado—for example, a suggestion that she hired her friends over more qualified applicants. Since the argument doesn't include anything like this, (C) must be incorrect.

11 (C) The claim is that marsupials migrated from South America to Australia, inferably by way of the Antarctic link between the two. Any information casting doubt that the marsupials passed through Antarctica would serve to weaken this claim. If marsupials had to pass through Antarctica on their way from South America to Australia, it's hard to believe that the rich fossil fields could be searched extensively without yielding one marsupial bone. So (C) could be cited by a scientist wishing to dispute the author's claim.

(A) Present day Antarctic conditions are irrelevant, since the events of the stimulus obviously take place long in the past.

(B) The argument isn't contingent on the interchangeability of South American and Australian marsupials. Perhaps an Australian marsupial captured in the wild would even have trouble living in other parts of Australia.

(D) This is totally irrelevant. Who cares how old marsupials are, or that the oldest one is from North America?

(E) It's possible that the lack of resemblance between marsupial bones in the Antarctic and those from the other two continents is the result of time and (frigid) weather, so (E) doesn't necessarily attack the author's migration theory. The critters could still have traveled the suggested path. Note that merely by placing marsupials in all three continents, (E) could be seen to strengthen the theory, as opposed to (C), which breaks the link completely.

Remember:

• Get familiar with the most common Logical Reasoning question types, and recognize them even when the stem seems to go off into unfamiliar territory. If you cut away all the fancy wording, this one simply asks you to weaken the argument.

• To weaken an argument doesn't require positive evidence that blows the conclusion to kingdom come. Just as often, pointing out a lack of crucial evidence can make the author's point less believable.

12 (B) Since the school administrator assumes that Ms. Geschwitz communicates her views to her students, an evaluation of this position should center on whether this assumption is valid. If it's not, then the student has a good point and Ms. Geschwitz's views have nothing to do with her work as a guidance counselor.

(A) This circumvents the real issue at hand. We're asked to evaluate a very specific line of reasoning, and whether they can find a way to employ Ms. Geschwitz in another capacity has no bearing on the school administrator's position.

(C) Ms. Geschwitz's popularity and reputation are irrelevant to the charge of whether she is exerting "undue influence" on her pupils.

(D) The number of other "offenders" on the faculty is irrelevant to whether this particular teacher has been out of line.

(E) The administrator seems to assume that some parents, at least, don't share Ms. Geschwitz's views, but the argument doesn't hinge on that assumption, because the administrator's position could be logically sound even if a lot of the parents see eye to eye with her.

Remember:

• Once again, previewing the question stem is a winner. Here, it tells you to concentrate primarily on the second person in the dialogue.

• When asked to evaluate an author's position, pay careful attention to assumptions the author may be making. If there is a central assumption, the choice that questions it usually offers the best "relevant information."

13 (C) Even though the *Green Light Revue* was produced seven times, the director wishes to make an exception to the bylaws and include it because all seven productions were "short runs" in front of "small audiences." The exception, then, evidently is based on the fact that not many people saw the play, which means that the intention of the bylaws was inferably to ensure that the selected plays haven't been seen by many people.

(A) It seems that the opposite may be true; if they were looking for plays with proven appeal, the bylaws would probably encourage the inclusion of plays with more, not fewer previous productions.

(B) The director gives no consideration to the type of plays chosen, so it can't be inferred that the bylaws deal with this, either.

(D) That the play ran in tiny theaters is flanked by the phrases *short runs* and *small audiences*. From this context, it can be inferred that *tiny theaters* is intended to emphasize the small number of people who actually saw the play, not to suggest that an exception should be made for this revue based on its applicability to the small theater setting.

(E) There's no indication that simultaneous productions of the same play are a concern of the director or the bylaws. The bylaws deal strictly with the number of times a play has been produced, but where this number comes from—one company performing it five times, five companies performing it once simultaneously, etcetera—isn't specified.

Remember:

• Inference questions are one of the most popular types of Logical Reasoning questions. Be on the lookout for words and phrases in question stems that tell you that you're dealing with inference: *most probably, suggests, provides evidence for, implies.*
• A good inference always stays in line with the author's point of view and tone, as well as the passage's scope and main idea.

• Choices that contain ideas that are neither contradicted nor supported by the passage are usually irrelevant and therefore wrong.

14 (E) The advertisers wish us to conclude that using Treegro will result in taller oaks. As evidence, they cite that Treegro was used in East Hollow over the past ten years, and now the East Hollow oaks are 4 inches taller than the average New Jersey oak. The easiest way to weaken this argument is to show that the oaks in East Hollow are taller for a reason totally unrelated to Treegro. Maybe they were always taller; maybe East Hollow has the best soil in the state; maybe the trees in East Hollow are many years older than the trees in the rest of the state. The test makers went with the third reason, choice (E).

(A) This doesn't rule out a comparison to other New Jersey trees the same age, which could still demonstrate that the Treegro trees have the height advantage.

(B) Why the trees were planted is irrelevant. Also, we're not told which trees were planted under this program, so (B) does nothing to help us differentiate East Hollow trees from those in the rest of the state.

(C) Too vague. We're not told how long they've been using Treegro, so it's possible that Treegro is also helping the trees of non–East Hollow residents grow, but that the East Hollow trees are taller on average because they've been exposed to it for much longer.

(D) Too general. Fails to make a distinction between the oaks in East Hollow and the others in the state, so it does nothing to damage the validity of the claim.

Remember:

- Some stimuli are prime candidates for paraphrasing an answer. Try to react to this as if it were a real-life advertisement. Would it seem plausible? Would you rush out to buy Treegro, or recommend it to a friend (assuming either of you has a need for such a product)?
- The active test taker reads critically and questions the validity of reasoning, asking himself or herself such things as, "Does this make sense?" and "Am I convinced?"
- To weaken an argument, you can introduce another factor that could be responsible for the results in a passage. Such a statement undercuts the evidence and thus damages the conclusion.

15 (A) The argument, as it stands, is incomplete. The conclusion is, "Ban this chemical before it causes more harm to humans!" But the final sentence, presumably the evidence, concerns only the appearance of traces of the chemical in cow feed. In order to strengthen the conclusion, we need a connection—some additional information that identifies some extraordinary health-related problem in humans that could be reasonably linked to the biphenyls in cow feed. That's what (A) provides.

(B) This ignores the issue of harm to humans altogether.

(C) This is a general fact that provides no link between cancer rates and biphenyls or cows, so it's too broad in scope to help the argument.

(D) If anything, this would *weaken* the argument, as it provides support for the notion that the chemicals are, in fact, safe.

(E) This fails to make any connection between the cows' misfortunes and harm to humans.

Remember:

- One common way to strengthen an argument is to shore up a basic assumption. Here, the author's conclusion necessarily depends on an unstated yet implied connection, and the correct answer is the one that supplies it.
- Don't carelessly choose "opposite" answer choices, such as choice (D), a weakener. Glance over the question stem quickly before settling on your choice, to ensure that you're answering the question posed.

16 (E) Esmeralda's conclusion, that environment has little to do with the development of personality, appears in her last sentence. Her evidence is that identical twins reared in totally different environments nonetheless exhibit similar personality traits later in life. Lothar contests Esmeralda's concept of environment, stating that the significant aspect of environment is not socioeconomic and education levels, but the level of commitment to nurturing. This damages her argument by calling into question one of her key terms as ill defined, or imprecise.

(A), (B), (C) These hinge on the idea that Lothar's argument somehow supports Esmeralda's point, when in fact Lothar takes issue with it.

(D) Lothar's conception of the role of environment, and identical twins reared in totally different environments exhibiting similar personality traits, are not mutually exclusive events. In other words, Lothar's response and Esmeralda's evidence on the development of adopted identical twins can, in fact, both be true.

Remember:

- When dealing with one person's response to another's argument, take it one step at a time. First, make sure you have a good grasp of the argument in question. Only then can you clearly assess what relation the other's response has to it.
- Sometimes wrong choices fall into the same category; that is, they're wrong for the same overall reason, such as (A), (B), and (C) here. Choices like these that play on similar themes are easy to eliminate as a group.

17 (B) Esmeralda feels that her evidence fully supports her point, but Lothar disagrees with her concept of environment and therefore appears to be skeptical of her conclusion. Which aspects of environment are deemed as relevant to the issue will determine whether or not Esmeralda's evidence sufficiently proves her point. Therefore, the point at issue is whether Esmeralda's evidence adequately supports her thesis.

(A) They never get into the nature/nurture controversy per se. Lothar questions the validity of her evidence, but stops short of venturing an opinion.

(C) Outside the scope. Lothar argues that these aspects of environment are insignificant. The ability of different social classes to nurture their children is of no concern to him.

(D) Lothar questions Esmeralda's use of the concept of environment, but never hits on the issue of environment as a factor in overcoming genetic traits.

(E) Lothar believes that the most important aspect of environment related to personality development is the family's level of commitment to nurturing a child. Which children (adopted or biological) are better nurtured, however, falls outside the scope.

Remember:

- Zero in on what's actually said and weed out faulty interpretations. Lothar basically says one and only one thing to Esmeralda: "Your evidence stinks because you're neglecting the most important aspect of environment." That's it. Recognizing that this is negative rules out most of the choices in question 16. And for all of the choices in 17, you can ask yourself: "Does Lothar care about this?" A statement can't be a point at issue if one of the speakers is indifferent to it.

18 (C) This is not just a search for a similar argument, but also a search for an argument similarly flawed. Since the author is trying to assert that if Larry studied harder, he would have more confidence, the evidence should back this up by showing how studying leads to confidence. Instead, the evidence (Larry is feeling better about himself, is glad he decided to study more, and has a better outlook) is the effects caused by the increased confidence—which, of course, is the conclusion the author's trying to establish. In other words, the conclusion is being used to set the evidence in motion. This is called circular reasoning—when the evidence and conclusion are, for all intents and purposes, identical. Likewise, in (C), if TV were made more educational, more parents would approve, but the first piece of evidence (parents recommending programs for their kids) depends on parents approving of TV.

(A) Although this sales pitch may not work on everyone, the reasoning is certainly not circular. Also, the word *probably* in the last sentence makes the argument more qualified, whereas the conclusion in the original is stated in more absolute terms.

(B) The merits of tutoring seem plausible, and the conclusion seems justified based on the evidence. No flaw, no parallel.

(D) Perhaps there is a slight flaw here, in that the evidence doesn't fully support the conclusion, which is worded pretty strongly in the last sentence. But not just any goofy choice will do. The correct answer has to be goofy in the same way as the original, which in this case means it must be circular.

(E) Not circular. It begins by concluding that something needs to be done, and ends with a specific recommendation for how to go about it.

Remember:

- Parallel reasoning involves mimicking the structure of an argument. Try not to get caught up with specifics; it's the general framework of the original that you're looking to locate in one of the answer choices.
- Stay away from answer choices written about the same subject matter as the original. This is an old trick of the test makers, intended to catch those who are not aware that they are to mimic the structure, not the content, of the stimulus.
- Due to its sheer length, this is a good question to skip and return to later (if time permits; if not, guess).

19 (A) The conclusion is based on the opinions not of random people, but rather of people "who filled out our questionnaire." This presents the possibility that only those who have an interest in solar energy filled out the questionnaire, which would tend to skew the results. If people who oppose solar energy refuse to take part, then the conclusion holds even less water.

(B) So what if it is? The argument is based on the results of the questionnaire, and therefore needs to be challenged on those grounds.

(C) The knowledge level of the respondents in regard to their stated positions is irrelevant. The study concerns merely the number of people who support solar energy research, not their background in the subject matter.

(D) The Administration's intentions and honesty record don't affect the argument. The author and the Administration believe different things, but by simply stating that the Administration has never willfully mislead the public does not imply that the Administration in this case is right and the conclusion based on the questionnaire is wrong.

(E) Totally irrelevant, playing no part in breaking down the evidence or the path from the evidence to the conclusion.

Remember:

- The concept of the nonrepresentative sample comes up often in Logical Reasoning. Whenever a stimulus includes a poll, or a survey, check to see whether the people involved belong to a certain group or share a common belief. If so, the findings are probably suspect.

20 (E) Though the conclusion is found right in the first sentence, the question asks for another conclusion, one that's most strongly supported by the argument as a whole. One single bus crash and the town is virtually branded by the newspapers as a death trap, which in turn has negatively affected tourism and the citizen's perceived safety. This is an indictment of media misuse of data.

(A) The argument doesn't preclude in any way the occurrence of worse accidents in Dalyville; it simply focuses on the ramifications of this particular crash.

(B) A little harsh. The author presumably wishes that the newspapers would use more discretion and not blow accident-related statistics out of proportion to the point where it negatively affects the town. That's not to say that the author thinks the newspapers should check with the tourism people for any kind of statistic they wish to print.

(C) It's not the publication of statistics that is scaring the wits out of residents of Dalyville, but the hysterical headlines. In fact, the publication of the statistic quoted would probably serve to quiet down, rather than stir up, the town, by counterbalancing those headlines.

(D) There's nothing vague about the term *violent death,* especially since the bus crash is offered as an example. And the issue isn't the appropriate interpretation of statistics, but whether the statistic in question—one favorable to Dalyville—can be heard, given the noise of the shocking headlines.

Remember:

- Inferences tend to stick very close to the important phrases in the passage. Note that in correct choice (E), *misuse of statistics* refers to the bus crash and *poor reputation* is another way of saying that tourism and the citizens' confidence in their town are both sagging.
- Be wary of choices that use extreme words, such as *never, always, all,* and *none.* Such statements are by nature very strict and thus harder to infer. More often, correct choice are ones that are more qualified in tone.

21 (C) Barbara switches her advertising to a vehicle that offers two major advantages, yet her revenue from advertising plummets. Finding an unforeseen factor about *Paper Money* that negatively impacts on revenue would explain away this paradox, which is essentially what (C) does. *Paper Money* may reach more of her clients than *People and Places,* and is even cheaper, but if the former is a budget magazine and its readers spend much less than do the latter's readers, then the drop in ad revenue would make sense in spite of the positive factors.

(A) Since *Paper Money* should reach more of Barbara's potential clients, it's therefore irrelevant that *People and Places* has a higher overall readership or serves a more diverse population.

(B) Family trips? Phooey. We're talking business travel here.

(D) Irrelevant. Even if true, it does nothing to counter the current advantages of *Paper Money,* so it fails to explain the strange result.

(E) Meant to be tempting, because it hits on the weekly-versus-monthly issue. But even if the yearly rates came out exactly even, this still negates only one of *Paper Money*'s advantages. It's still a mystery how *Paper Money* is doing a worse job for Barbara even though it reaches many more of her potential clients.

Remember:

• Learn to recognize paradox questions even when they don't actually use the word *paradox* itself. If a stimulus ends with a strange, bizarre, seemingly contradictory result, and you're asked to explain how it's possible, then you know what kind of question you're up against.

22 (B) It seems that the moderately overweight category from the study overlaps with the average-weight category on the insurance charts. So even some average-weight people, according to the insurance charts, have an increased risk of heart disease, which is the essence of (B).

(A), (C), and (D) are fairly obvious outside-the-scope choices, easy to pick out because they deal with things that bear no relation to the passage: insurance premiums, heart disease versus smoking and alcohol, and overweight men.

(E) Outside of the scope, but subtle. There's no information about women in other age groups and their risk of heart disease, relative to the women in the study aged thirty to fifty-five.

Remember:

• In questions involving a study, look to quickly cross off choices that don't stay within the

confines of the study. A correct inference is always consistent with the tone and scope of the passage, and often sounds very similar to the author's key concept or main idea.

23 (E) The question seeks information that would be most useful for the doctors to consider before recommending that the overweight women in the study lose weight. It would help to know, of course, whether there are any advantages of being slightly overweight—advantages that, if sacrificed, would somewhat offset or negate the health benefits related to a decreased risk of heart disease.

(A), (B), (C) Another exercise in "Who cares?" With regard to this study, who cares about women aged fifty-five and older, or women between the ages of fifteen and thirty? And even within the correct age group, who cares about the overall percentage of women who are overweight? Certainly not the doctors. Their prime concern isn't women in other age groups, or the number of overweight women in an age group, so the information in these choices would be of little value to them.

(D) If even the moderately overweight run a high risk of heart disease, it's a safe bet that the very overweight are at risk as well. Still, this information has no bearing on the doctors' decision.

Remember:

• In a two-question stimulus, often the work you do in the first question can help you answer the second. In this case, many of the choices in the second question suffer the same weakness as the wrong choices in the first: they're outside the scope of the argument.

- It's very difficult to prephrase an answer to a relevant-information question, so your best line of attack is to move right to the choices and evaluate each until you find the one that has the greatest impact on the issue in question.

24 (A) Looks daunting on the page, but the structure that we're asked to mimic is quite straightforward. If we represent each statement with variables, the argument breaks down to this: if A, then B; if B, then C; if C, then D. Thus (here's the conclusion), if A, then D. Stated in words: "One thing leads to another, which leads to another, which leads to another, which leads to the conclusion that the first thing leads to the last." The correct answer must incorporate every facet, including a conclusion that ties the first statement to the last.

(B)'s structure is: if A, then a choice between B and C, followed by the results of B and C.

(C) is in this form: because A, then B; because B, then C. This is followed by a judgment about A. No good.

(D) is built like so: if A, then B; if B, then C; if C, then *not* A. Therefore, A is impossible. This one circles back on itself, creating somewhat of a paradoxical situation, something the original doesn't do.

(E) breaks down to: when A, then B; when B, then C. C, therefore, is incompatible with A. This isn't even close.

Remember:

- Some parallel reasoning stimuli lend themselves well to algebraic representation. If you can condense the structure to letters, do so, and then look for the choice with the same exact structural breakdown.

25 (D) The conclusion is right there in the question stem: fewer animals roam the streets of Fairvale during the warmer as opposed to the colder months. The evidence is that during the warm months, the city pound collected an average of twenty-five strays per month, but the average went down to seven when it got cold. For the conclusion to remain valid, the author has to account for other possible reasons for the drop in the number of strays, and one such alternative explanation (which would damage the argument), the possibility that there are fewer pound employees in the colder months, is taken care of in the last sentence. Another possible explanation for the drop is a conscious decision to impound fewer animals, and so the author must assume that no such decision was made. Had the drop been caused by a change in impoundment regulations, of course, it would no longer be valid to conclude that the drop was due to fewer animals on the streets.

(A) The specifics of the pound facilities don't matter. The argument holds up fine without this piece of information.

(B) The seasonal substitution of employees doesn't alter the total manpower available for catching animals, so this piece of information, which has no bearing on the argument, is not a necessary assumption on the part of the author.

(C) The relation between diseases and the number of animals on the streets is ambiguous at best, so this doesn't have enough of a bearing on the argument to serve as an assumption.

(E) Information on other pounds across the country is outside the scope. At best, this information could slightly strengthen the argument, if interpreted as support for the notion that fewer animals roam the streets in warmer weather. Still, this is quite a reach and the argument stands just fine without it.

Remember:

- The logic in some assumption questions bears a similarity to that in weaken-the-argument questions. If this question asked for a weakener, choice (D)—stated in the positive—would suffice. Therefore, another way to come up with an argument's necessary assumption is to recognize a possible weakener and negate it, thus shoring up the conclusion.
- Once again, we see why it's so useful to get into the habit of reading each question stem first. This one literally gives away the conclusion, and that means less work for you.

Section Two: Reading Comp Explanations

PASSAGE 1—Genetic Engineering

Topic and Scope
Genetic engineering; specifically, the potential impact of genetic engineering on society.

Purpose and Main Idea
Author wants to warn against the possible dangers (the "seeds of future problems," lines 14–15) of ever more sophisticated genetic techniques. The main idea is summed up in lines 26–27, and again in lines 48–52: The potential of using these new techniques to determine traits could lead to "a tragedy" (line 42)—the belief that genes determine personality and thus that we are not responsible for what we do.

Paragraph Structure
Paragraph 1 hinges on the signal "Largely overlooked" (line 6), which announces author's main interest. Paragraph 2: some ethical issues that future science will raise. Paragraph 3: the "more insidious problem" boils down to lines 31–33—the public's likely eagerness to embrace science's ability to determine traits. Paragraph 4: can't get more helpful clues than "What a tragedy this would be" (line 42) and "I find this a bitter prospect" (line 48).

The Big Picture

- When the structure and point of view are announced as clearly as they are here, then the passage is likely to earn you many quick points. You can tackle the passages in any order, so try to start off the Reading section on an up note, with a passage whose purpose and ideas are fairly evident.

- Pay attention to the author's wording choices; they often reveal his or her hand. The phrases "herein lies the seeds of future problems," "we face a more insidious problem," and especially "what a tragedy this would be" are strong indicators of the author's view.

The Questions

1 (C) This is the only choice that encompasses the clearly expressed topic, scope, and point of view.

(A) omits the topic (genetics) in favor of an unwarranted broadening to science in general. Also, the phrase *benefit or impair* makes it seem as if the author is ambivalent on the topic.

(B) implies that the topic is the effect of the environment on genes. Also, (B) takes a detail (lines 36–37) and blows it up to be the main idea.

(D) is too positive in tone, and pretty much echoes lines 9–11 only.

(E) is way off the topic, and far too positive in tone.

Remember:

- The answer to global questions has to cover the same topic and scope, and reflect the same tone, as the overall passage itself.

2 (A) Choice (A) recognizes that you have to read *forward* from line 34 to understand the context here, all the way to line 40: "Those overlooking" the fact that genetic predictability is limited "will . . . misjudge individual ability," a sentiment that (A) echoes.

(B) contains *illicit*, which probably refers to paragraph 2's hints about sinister abuses of power.
(C) hearkens back to lines 2–4.

(D): What genetic advances will "enlarge" is the magnitude of ethical issues (lines 19–20), not technical problems.

(E): No reference to scientists' "negligence" is made. On the contrary, the author assumes that scientists will be diligent in warning us of the limited power of genetic prediction (lines 33–36).

Remember:

• Learn to appreciate the way LSAT correct answers tend to paraphrase actual passage text, as (A) does here.

3 (E) This is a flat-out paraphrase of the final sentence: a lot of good is likely and a lot of bad is possible in this biological revolution.

(A) ignores the hypothetical nature of the whole discussion. These *could* be problems, says the author. The passage is a warning, not an apocalyptic prediction.

(B), (C), (D): The other choices are either too sunny (B) or coolly unconcerned (C), (D).

Remember:

• Any question dealing with the author's attitude requires you to take the passage's "temperature."

4 (D) *Political interests* is a synonym for the *ideological currents* (lines 27–28) that have dominated nature/nurture, the context for the author's fears about how the public may seize upon genetic advances to society's detriment.

(A) contradicts the sentiments that begin paragraph 3. Nature/nurture occurs after the author has shifted away from the use and misuse of data.

(B)'s *validity* is an impressively scientific buzzword that has no relevance to anything in the passage. The same can be said for the facts/assumptions distinction in (E).

(C) is tempting, since it suggests a plausible reason (moral failure) why the public might embrace genetic determinism, but a more likely reason is cited at line 32. In any case, nature/nurture is defined as a debate, not as a sign of moral weakness per se.

Remember:

• Dense choices containing a lot of jargon have to be read carefully, or else you can mistake vague buzzwords for relevant references.

5 (B) This choice is very similar to question 3's (E), reflecting the author's unease.

(A), (E): The key adjectives are plausible, but each choice veers off the mark. If anything, the author would support putting on some scientific brakes rather than worry about possible tech setbacks (A), and the "anxiety" (E) doesn't stem from the bio revolution's not getting enough press.

(C), (D): The key adjectives won't fly. *Encouraged* is too positive a word to describe the author's reaction to this revolution, and the author is far from "surprised" about anything, let alone the wide public support for the advances of science.

Remember:

- Sometimes two questions will test the very same idea, inference, or sentiment, like question 3 and question 5 here.

6 **(A)** Choice (A) recognizes the main cause of the problem as outlined in paragraph 4—the public's eagerness to accept the "nature" argument and see genetics as determinants of human traits. It follows that if the public weren't so willing to take that position, the risk of "tragedy" would be decreased.

(B): Contrary to (B), scientists are already plenty sensitive to the implications (lines 33–36), so more sensitivity would solve nothing. (This also points to why (D) is wrong. Far from being too dependent on public opinion, the scientists mentioned here take issue with the public's view.)

(C): What would improve prospects for the future would be more public skepticism, not less.

(E)'s implication that scientists are too arrogant is supported nowhere in the passage.

Remember:

- Answers to logic questions like this one must relate clearly to the topic and scope of the passage.

7 **(D)** Only (D) links up with the paragraph's sense that human complexity must be cherished and genes must not be seen as totally controlling behavior. After citing reasons why we ought to accept the "nurture" view (lines 42–46), the author cites the "bitter prospect" of wide acceptance of what is essentially a "nature" position. We must "craft" the proper "ethic" (line 50), one that echoes (D)'s sentiments.

(A)'s references to "common purpose" and "designing society" are wildly at odds with the author's embrace of individuality.

(B), (C): Not only are (B) and (C) both too detail oriented, but both cite positive effects of the genetic revolution when the purpose of the paragraph is to sum up the author's worries, notwithstanding the glancing reference to science's "enormous benefits" (lines 49–50).

(E), too, focuses on a detail. And anyway, the author is more worried that the public will misinterpret data than that biologists will do so.

Remember:

- Complete-the-thought questions are logic questions, and they require attention to structure. Don't look for a sentence that you can simply slap onto the paragraph, but one that flows from the overall discussion.

Passage 2—Gwendolyn Brooks

Topic and Scope
Gwendolyn Brooks's poetry; specifically, her "relationship to the Harlem Renaissance" (lines 3–6, question reframed lines 6–9).

Purpose and Main Idea
Using examples, the author wants to explore the Brooks/Harlem Renaissance relationship, specifically noting how she was in sync with the movement in some ways and took her own road in others.

Paragraph Structure
Paragraph 1 clearly frames the question. Paragraph 2 leaves Brooks behind to focus on the Harlem Renaissance, and sentence 2 is key in this regard: those poets were variously realistic and romantic.

Paragraph 3: Brooks's "unique contributions" (line 27) set her work apart. Note especially lines 29–31 (her 1945 collection uniquely demystified romance) and lines 39–42 (what for Brooks was a "predominant theme" was for others a "minor chord"). Paragraph 3 also offers summary; Brooks is described as carrying one Renaissance element (realism) forward and rejecting another (idealization). The last sentence briefly looks at Brooks relative to those who followed her.

The Big Picture

- Remember that everything in the passage is there to serve the overall purpose. By the time you got to line 40 or so, you may have left behind the key question framed in lines 6–9. Don't do this! Try to fit every new piece of information into the context of the passage.
- Make sure you don't let a last-minute side reference (like lines 50–55) distort your understanding of the passage as a whole.

The Questions

8 (D) This correctly cites the author's purpose, mentioning both the 1920s movement and Brooks, though properly emphasizing the latter.

(A) and (B) fail to mention the Harlem Renaissance, which cannot be separated from the author's discussion. Also, (A) goes in the wrong direction (forward in time rather than backward from Brooks), while (B) tends to deny Brooks's profound connection to the African American poets who preceded her.

(C) Scope error: passage is not about scholars (author uses *contemporaries* differently in line 4). Also, the passage is trying to make an interpretation, not correct one.

(E) is too strong a judgment for this passage, and cannot be correct because it leaves out the topic of Gwendolyn Brooks.

Remember:

- The answer to global questions has to cover the same topic and scope, and reflect the same tone, as the overall passage itself.

9 (D) The answer here requires a link between the two paragraphs in which the two works are described. The "realistic impulse" in McKay's work (lines 16–18) parallel the realism credited to Brooks at the end of paragraph 3.

(A) is explicitly untrue about *Harlem Shadows* (lines 18–20).

(B) Author makes no link between Harlem Shadows and the black arts movement of the '60s.

(C) implies that Brooks was wholly in sync with Harlem Renaissance romanticism, which we know was not so.

(E) The two works in question, as realistic representations of African American victimization, sound anything but optimistic. In any case, optimism is suggested to be more of a romantic than a realistic element in lines 47–50.

Remember:

• Don't overthink. Proceed to the relevant portion(s) of the text and take the clues you're given.

10 **(B)** This is a more general statement of lines 14–16.

(A) is a plausible idea but outside the scope of the passage, which encompasses not how the Harlem Renaissance began but Brooks's relationship to it, so we can't be sure the author would agree.

(C) and (E) fall outside the author's scope in that no reference is ever made to any critical assessment of the Harlem Renaissance.

(D) To recognize and laud Brooks's "technical accomplishments" is not to raise her above other poets, and the author does not fault this dimension of the Harlem Renaissance.

Remember:

• Sometimes there's no way to prephrase an answer. Just read through the choices and find one whose scope and "temperature" seem right.

11 **(D)** The key is line 34–35's *for example*. The Hughes poem is explicitly meant to illustrate how (as mentioned in lines 32–33)

Renaissance poets idealized African American women. This sets up the later contrast to Brooks's more "biting" approach.

(A) has no connection to the structure mandated by "for example." Moreover, no reference to a Hughes poem can in and of itself "prove" anything about Brooks, making this an example of the "true but nonresponsive" wrong answer choice.

(B) is a big time scope error—a lofty sentiment on general aesthetics that has no place in this tightly organized discussion of Brooks and the Harlem Renaissance.

(C) wrongly characterizes Hughes's romantic idealization of a streetwalker as "naive." Also, Brooks's work isn't painted as "ironic" in paragraph 3, just bitingly realistic.

(E) misses the sense that, far from being an influence, the Hughes poem is used to draw a contrast with Brooks.

Remember:

• This is a classic "purpose of a detail" question, reminding us to look at structure before content.

12 **(E)** A pretty direct paraphrase of lines 44–47.

(A) violates the whole spirit of the passage, in which Brooks's 1945 collection is repeatedly cited as "hardly imitative" (lines 43–44) of the Harlem Renaissance.

(B) is right in attributing optimism to Brooks's poetry but wrong in alleging that the author would call that a "marring" influence. Inferably, optimism is one of the offshoots of the ethnic pride that both the Renaissance and Brooks shared.

(C) goes too far in the other direction. To enlarge upon a tradition is far from "completely rejecting" it.

(D) is a conclusion whose scope goes beyond the passage. Any number of African American feminist writers could have preceded Brooks's appearance in 1945.

Remember:

• The answer to inference questions are often direct paraphrases of the ideas in the text. When faced with these, seek explicit passage support.

13 (D) This comes right out of the opening paragraph; critics didn't examine how Brooks's poems linked up with the Harlem Renaissance that preceded her.

(A) No such reaction on the part of critics is mentioned. Anyhow, (A) would be the judgment of sociologists, not literary critics.

(B) Even though Brooks did demystify romantic love (lines 30–31), there's no sense that critics failed to notice that.

(C) cites a comparison between Brown and Brooks that is nowhere made, let alone alluded to, by Brooks's contemporary critics.

(E) goes beyond the scope of the passage—Brooks's political agenda, whether in line with the New Negro poets or at odds with them, is never mentioned.

Remember:

• Yes, the location of right answers can be identified this easily, and yes, the right answer can be phrased this closely to the actual text.

14 (C) This choice works best because the last sentence is a conclusion for which no evidence is provided, and (C) provides that evidence. The author alleges "a vital link" (line 50) between Brooks and the black arts movement, and identifying the latter with Brooks's mix of the idealized and the realistic is just such a link.

(A) implies that paragraph 3's topic is how Brooks is remembered by readers, when in fact the paragraph exists to summarize Brooks's art and influence. Moreover, (A) focuses on technique, something we haven't really heard about since lines 1–3.

(B) makes the odd implication that Brooks (who first published in 1945) was influenced by a movement that came fifteen years later. Possible but unlikely; no evidence provided.

(D) is wrong in saying that "Brooks's relationship to the Harlem Renaissance" is "open to question," since the passage just got through assessing the same.

(E) wrongly implies that the topic has been how Brooks struggled for recognition, and wrongly attributes "anonymity" to her early work.

Remember:

- Complete-the-thought questions are logic questions, and require attention to structure. Don't look for a sentence that you can simply slap onto the paragraph, but one that flows from the overall discussion.

Passage 3—Risk Assessment

Topic and Scope
Environmental cleanup; specifically, the value of "risk assessment" as a way of gauging the threat posed by hazardous waste.

Purpose and Main Idea
The author wants to evaluate whether risk assessment is, as advertised, a "neutral policy tool," and answers in the negative. The author concludes that risk assessment is, in fact, an "ethical choice" and is thus to be used with caution and clarity.

Paragraph Structure
Paragraph 1 announces the topic and scope with the phrase *a relatively new element has . . . entered the controversy*. Paragraph 2 describes the earlier policy for assessing hazardous waste risks, and cites experts' approval of risk assessment as "factual and scientific," hence "neutral" and reliable.

Paragraph 3 begins with a rhetorical question, and answers it through a series of details about four elements of risk assessment that depend more on value judgments than on hard science. The inevitable conclusion in paragraph 4 is that we shouldn't forget the subjectivity inherent in the decisions that stem from the use of risk assessment, and therefore must treat those decisions with care.

The Big Picture

- Don't get bogged down on technical references; focus instead on the clear keyword signals and strongly expressed author viewpoints.
- Skim past lengthy details, noting their general purpose and location should you need to return to them later. For example, after introducing the concept of the four components of risk assessment, the author then belabors the point of each component individually, while the most important thing comes at the end of the sentence—that they all require the application of some judgment other than scientific proof. This ties in with the main point, and shouldn't be clouded by the definitions preceding it.

The Questions

15 (C) This elegantly sums up the author's skepticism at the claim that risk assessment is values-free.

(A) is the claim made by experts in paragraph 2, the very one questioned in the passage overall.

(B) is tempting only if you got the word *Nixon* stuck in your head early. In fact, the time line suggests that the Nixon presidency predates risk assessment by almost two decades.

(D) thinks the issue is the cost and practicality of using risk assessment, missing the ethical question altogether.

(E) is a judgment the author stops short of. And if he did sign on to it, it would be on the grounds of its ethical problems, not the success of earlier procedures (which sound even less reliable than risk assessment).

Remember:

• A "global" question has to cover the same topic and scope, and reflect the same tone, as the overall passage itself.

16 **(A)** Visual observation was the hallmark of the allegedly more subjective, less scientific approach to waste management that preceded risk assessment.

All "four components of risk assessment" (lines 29–37) appear explicitly in the four wrong choices.

Remember:

• Sometimes it's fastest in "all of the following EXCEPT" questions to toss out the four wrong choices and go with what's left.

17 **(D)** We benefit from the keywords *for example*. The context is the extent to which values judgments are inherent in risk assessment, and assigning a person's "confidence level" as a criterion for risk is manifestly more a matter of personal judgment than hard science.

(A) is something the author probably agrees with (if not vigorously), but the comparison between risk assessment and earlier efforts comes considerably before line 43.

(B), too, refers to the earlier efforts that involved visual observations, far removed from line 43.

(C) sounds sensible, but the call for greater clarity (the opposite of *ambiguities*) comes in the last paragraph, long after the detail in question has been left behind.

(E) takes us about as far back in the passage as you can get. The NEPA is a red herring, thrown in to confuse. It's in the passage solely to introduce the broad topic of environmental law and has no connection with either risk assessment or line 43.

Remember:

• When a question asks about a line reference, check out the context of the citation in question but be wary of moving too far away from the location.

18 **(C)** The environmental pros "consider risk assessment an improvement" (lines 14–15) over earlier cleanup methods, so (C) is easily inferable.

(A) goes too far. The earlier methods were faulted as too unscientific and arbitrary, but still may have been somewhat effective in identifying hazardous waste.

(B) drags in NEPA again. The passage doesn't make it clear that NEPA had anything whatsoever to do with methods for identifying hazards.

(D) is wrong because the earlier methods, which involved sheer visual assessment, were inferably much less precise. Surely they'd be easy, rather than difficult, to apply.

(E) hints at a potential amalgam of visual observations and risk assessment, but the author mentions no such scheme.

Remember:

- Before attacking an inference question, try to locate the likely source in the passage, and scan it quickly before moving to the choices.

19 (E) At the heart of this question, as so many others, is the main idea itself. Risk assessment is touted by environmental pros as scientific and free of values, a sentiment that the author spends most of the passage rebutting because he or she believes that such nonscientific elements as value judgments and ethical issues dominate, or "underlie," similar "scientifically derived policy choices" (lines 51–52).

(A) To the author, nonscientific elements complicate and muddy policy—far from being an "improvement."

(B) "Neutral" as used in the passage means scientific and (allegedly) values-free, quite the opposite of what the question is looking for.

(C) may tempt you if you decide that the author sees danger or "adversity" in the role of nonscientific criteria in hazard assessment. But as used in line 33, "adverse" refers to a health effect that is being assessed. You have to work too hard to justify (C) in this context, as opposed to the clear-cut echo of the main idea in (E).

(D) is too positive, like (A), and too far removed from the sense of the question, like (C).

Remember:

- When all five choices cite line numbers, prephrasing an answer may save time, instead of hunting down each reference.

20 (C) At line 16, the author is describing the background of risk assessment and the main reason why its supporters prefer it to the more subjective earlier approach. This feeds right into the claim that risk assessment leads to "sound technical judgments," which in turn leads to (C).

(A) mentions something the passage does not—namely government opposition to the risk assessment method.

(B) refers to a topic (the visual observation method) on which the passage's environmentalists are undivided. Also, it's the earlier method's imprecision, not its impracticality, that they're down on.

(D) The absence of an *a priori* scientific method in risk assessment—which to the author renders the policy less scientific—comes a paragraph too late for this question. It cannot describe the function of a detail twelve lines earlier.

(E) Good grief, NEPA again! It's dropped long before line 16 comes along.

Remember:

- Simply recognizing the location of a question can usually help you throw out several wrong answers, if not find the right answer directly.

21 (B) As a primary purpose answer, (B) may have surprised prephrasers looking for something like "assess (or criticize) risk assessment." But since the entire passage is proceeding to the call, in the last sentence, for government to acknowledge the values element of the (allegedly neutral) risk assessment policy, (B) is a satisfactory—and LSAT-like—paraphrase.

(A) was taken care of in paragraph 2, although the plural "other methods" is pushing it: only one other method is brought up.

(C) mistakes the issue at the heart of the passage as, "What policy will be effective?" In fact, it's, "Is a particular policy as objective as it's cracked up to be?"

(D) describes a passage with a chronological structure and an evolutionary scope. This ain't it.

(E) might be the basis of an interesting passage, but our author isn't seeking to modify or replace risk assessment, just to get the government to open its eyes to the policy's nature—which of course brings us back to (B).

Remember:

- The only real danger of prephrasing answers comes when you demand that the test makers choose just exactly what you've prephrased. Recognize that your quarry is the best answer of five, not the best of all possible ones, and keep an open mind.

Passage 4—Comparable Worth

Topic and Scope
Comparable worth; specifically, the arguments against the policy of paying men and women the same money for jobs in the same company that are comparable if not identical.

Purpose and Main Idea
The author asserts a desire to "examine" the anti–comparable worth arguments, but it becomes clear that the purpose is to shoot them down.

Paragraph Structure
Paragraph 1 announces the topic and scope but fails to identify where the author stands (and even fails to define *comparable worth* for those unfamiliar with the phrase, who have to be patient until lines 21–26). Each of the remaining paragraphs takes up one of the anti–comparable worth arguments mentioned in paragraph 1, and you have to hang in there until you see the author align herself against the "antis" through phrases like, "Each contention is misguided or flawed"; "This objection . . . goes too far"); and "Yet the argument sidesteps".

You should fix in your mind, preparatory to the questions, the topic of each paragraph: the allegation that gender discrimination isn't why women are paid less than men (paragraph 2), the impossibility of objectively comparing different jobs (paragraph 3), and the risk that comparable worth would cripple the free market (paragraph 4).

The Big Picture

- As soon as the passage raises a controversy or question, you must immediately seek to identify which position, if any, the author takes.
- If the author remains neutral, recognize that. In some cases, the author simply describes the different sides of the controversy, without actually weighing in with an opinion.
- When the author's viewpoint seems obscure, hang in there—if he or she intends to profess an opinion, that opinion will be made clear by the end of the passage. There's no point in reading deeper into the text, or answering questions, until the task of pinpointing the author's position is successfully completed.

The Questions

22 **(B)** strengthens the claim made in paragraph 2 (the wage gap paragraph) that the question of gender discrimination should come into play when differently paid men and women hold similar jobs in the same firm, like the programmers in (B). The disparity between the woman and the man, who is her junior, smacks of just that kind of discrimination.

(A) and (E) depart from the scope of the author's discussion in that they involve men and women working for different employers. The author frames the discussion of comparable worth around the necessary condition that the employees share the same employer.

(C) doesn't spell out that the pilots work for the same airline, but nonetheless is wrong because in this instance the woman has ten years less seniority, which would explain the disparity in pay. (B), rather than (C), is a much more likely case of discrimination as the author describes it.

(D) does not present two people working in "comparable" jobs, a necessary condition for comparable worth to be at issue.

Remember:

• Many test takers have trouble with analogy questions like this, let alone strengthen-the-argument questions. Skip 'em till last if they bug you. Why get all bent out of shape?

23 **(C)** This one refers to paragraph 3, whose topic is job evaluation and whose point is that one can fairly compare dissimilar jobs for the purpose of setting wages. The qualification is hinted at by the phrase *though partially valid* (line 32) and is then immediately spelled out: the comparison is never completely objective, synonymous with (C).

(A) comes from the wrong paragraph. The health of companies comes up in paragraph 4.

(B) is a plausible outcome of comparable worth, but the issue never comes up in the passage.

(D) and (E) are *au contraire* choices—choices that propose the opposite of what's stated. Job evaluation is "well established" (line 34), and objectivity is exactly what is "desirable" in comparable worth; it's just not 100 percent achievable.

Remember:

• It's inevitable that some questions will hinge on knowing which paragraph is at issue, especially when (as here) each building block has such a different topic. Know your paragraphs!

24 **(E)** The premise of the anti–comparable worth argument in paragraph 2 is that gender discrimination isn't the cause of the male/female wage gap—personal choice is the cause (lines 12–17). A bit later, advocates of the contention in paragraph 4 assert that "supply and demand curves create the wage disparity" (lines 41–42). (E) satisfactorily paraphrases both.

(A) goes way beyond the scope to cover "all social reform."

(B) On the evidence, those opposed to comparable worth find it economically crippling rather than helpful, and its social impact goes unmentioned (although opponents probably aren't too optimistic on that score, either).

(C) is a true statement made at lines 55–56, but it qualifies as a statement of fact, not as a conclusion drawn by opponents.

(D) is closer to the author's view. It hardly sums up the view of opponents, who basically deny sex-based wage discrimination altogether.

Remember:

• When more than one person's or group's viewpoints figure in a passage, read each question carefully to determine which person or group to focus on.

25 (E) The four wrong choices—the positions that are "rightly" called U.S.C.R.C. positions—can come from either paragraph (2 or 3) that mentions the agency by name. Happily (E) comes from paragraph 4, where no hint is made that the C.R.C. has signed on to a 100 percent hands-off attitude on the part of the courts with regard to market intervention.

(A) is the conclusion ascribed to the C.R.C. in lines 10–11.

(B) is cited in lines 29–31.

(C) is cited in lines 15–17.

(D) comes from lines 13–15.

Remember:

• Proper names stand out more than other words. When questions pick up on them, that may make it easier to decide where to focus your attention.

26 (B) The reference to "supply and demand" should direct your attention to market-centered paragraph 4. Then your search for something that sounds like "fails to take into account" should fix on "the argument sidesteps," and what it sidesteps is (B), the possible equivalence of jobs that are nevertheless paid differently.

(A) Paragraph 3 makes it clear that the author wouldn't subscribe to (A)'s idea that jobs "can only be measured subjectively."

(C) makes up the issue of political manipulation out of whole cloth.

(D) This choice, which refers to the judiciary, points to the proper paragraph. But the author turns to the topic of how judges have dealt with comparable worth only after concluding the assessment of whether supply and demand are at the heart of wage differentials. The last two sentences must be seen as parenthetical, a sidelong glance at another aspect of comparable worth but one essentially tangential to the passage's main thrust.

(E) A broad sociological issue unrelated to the author's topic and scope in general, let alone the paragraph in which supply and demand comes up.

Remember:

• When a question stem sends a strong hint about where in the passage the answer can be found, follow it. (You may want to target such questions to answer early on—often they are among the easiest.)

27

(A) There is no ambivalence at all in the author's opinion about the C.R.C.'s deeming discrimination to be unrelated to the male/female wage gap: "Each contention" supporting that position is "misguided or flawed" (line 17).

(B) is, of course, the exact opposite of the author's view.

(C) No hint of bewilderment, qualified or otherwise, can be seen in the author's text.

(D) The author's "opposition" is strongly argued, hardly quiet.

(E), like (B), is the opposite of the author's position—not that the author is impolite, just opposed.

Remember:

• A long or complex-sounding question stem needs to be read carefully, but the question need not be especially difficult once unpacked.

Section 3: Logic Games Explanations

Game 1—Basketball Teams

The Action

Choosing six out of eight people to play basketball, and breaking up the six players into two teams of three players each. The only unusual twist on this "grouping game of distribution" (meaning that it's a game in which you're putting the entities into subgroups), is that each player on a team plays opposite a specific player on the other team. Here are the key issues that you should anticipate the questions will be based on:

- Which players are chosen and which ones sit on the bench?
- Which players can or must play together?
- Which players cannot play together?
- Which players can and cannot play opposite each other?

The Initial Setup

If you were the coach for this situation in real life, how might you use pencil and paper to keep track of it all? Here's a simple, intuitive way:

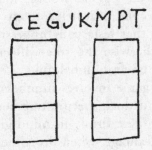

There's nothing concrete to fill in yet, so let's move on to the rules.

The Rules

1) Rule 1 simply breaks the players into two groups: C, E, K, and P are tall, and the others—G, J, M, and T—are short.

2) Thanks to rule 1, we can now get a little more specific about rule 2. C, E, K, and P, the tall players, can play opposite each other only. Let's analyze what this means in practical terms—terms that will help you answer the questions. Here are the implications of this rule that make the game much easier to handle.

- What would violate this rule? Answer: a tall player matched up with a short player. If that's unclear, form an example to test your understanding of the rule.
- If two of the tall players, Charles and Edna, for example, are chosen and placed on one team, then the other two, Katya and Paulina, have to be chosen and placed on the other team.
- There must be either two or four tall players chosen. There's no way to match them up with each other if an odd number is chosen. (This thought leads to a bigger deduction regarding the overall number breakdown, which you'll see below under "Key Deduction." Did you see it on your own?)
- A team cannot be made up of three tall players, because there would have to be three tall players for the other team, but there are only four tall players total.

- Likewise, a team cannot be made up of three short players. The tall player or players on the other team would have no tall players to oppose.

3) Rule 3 further clarifies the tall-people issue. If Paulina is chosen to play, then Charles is chosen and plays opposite her (inferably on the other team). This is straightforward enough. Just don't make the lethal mistake of inferring that the reverse is true, because it isn't. If Charles is chosen, Paulina can, but does not have to, play opposite him.

4) This one is similar to the previous one. If Terence is chosen, Charles is chosen but plays on the same team as Terence. Once again, the rule can't go backwards. Choosing Charles implies nothing about choosing Terence.

Key Deduction
The key deduction in this game involves the breakdown of tall and short players chosen. One of the implications of rule 2 is that there has to be either two or four tall players chosen. Taken one step further, this means that *the coach has to choose either all four tall players and two short players, or all four short players and two tall players.* One more deduction stems from this, but it's not as obvious, and therefore it's not a tragedy if you don't see it up front. In fact, it's tested for specifically in question 1, so we'll cover it there.

The Final Visualization
Here's everything we're armed with going into the questions.

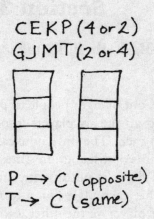

The Big Picture

- One way to latch onto the action of a game is to place the game in a real-life context. How would you handle this if you were the coach? Break down the mystique. If you approach the games as ordinary, everyday situations, they won't be as baffling and you'll be able to think through them more clearly.
- When the entities are broken down into two distinct groups, you may find it helpful to differentiate them by using capital and lowercase letters.
- A good way to grasp the meaning of a rule is to ask yourself, "What would violate this rule?" Take a second, if it helps, to try out a concrete example that tests your understanding of the rule. Otherwise the rule will continue to be abstract, unclear, unhelpful.
- When a game involves numbers, always see if you can deduce specific number breakdowns. Keeping these firmly in mind gives you a distinct advantage when it comes to working through the questions.

The Questions

1 **(D)** Given no new information, we're asked for the player who must be chosen. All the rules about Charles make him a likely suspect, and in fact, Charles is the one. You can get this by working off of the key deduction. If the coach chooses all four tall players and two short players, then obviously Charles, a tall player, must be chosen. If, on the other hand, the coach chooses all four short players and only two tall players, then short Terence must be chosen, and Charles as well, thanks to rule 4. The big deduction pays off—there are only two ways to combine tall and short players to get the required six, and Charles is chosen in both of them.

Edna, choice (A), and Katya, choice (C), can both be bench warmers if Charles and Paulina are chosen along with all four short players. However, Terence, choice (B), and Jerrod, choice (E), can sit out if Greg and Mort play along with all four tall players.

Remember:

- When a question offers no hypothetical information (no if-clause), it means that it must be possible to deduce the answer from the rules alone. Build the new piece of information (in this case, the fact that Charles must be chosen) into your global view of the game.

2 **(D)** We saw earlier from the implications of rule 2 that choice (C), three short players on one team, and choice (E), three tall players on one team, are both impossible. Both cases result in at least one tall player not being matched up against another tall player. (A) violates rule 3—Paulina and Charles can never be on the same team. Choice (B) is a little more subtle, but the key deduction comes in handy to help us see why tall Charles, short Jerrod, and short Mort cannot form a team. If they were a team, then the four-short-and-two-tall scenario would be in effect, placing Terence and Greg on the other team. But that contradicts rule 4, so it's no good. The players in the remaining choice, choice (D), form an acceptable team; the opposing team would have to include Charles, Jerrod, and Terence.

Remember:

- When facing an acceptability question, simply check the choices against each rule, eliminating the ones that violate the rules until you're left with only one choice. If you do your work carefully, there's no need to check the remaining choice; just circle it and move on.

3 **(B)** The shortcut that answers this question stems from our key deduction. There must be four tall players chosen, and two short to round out the roster, or four short players chosen with two tall to complete the teams. Therefore, the two bench players must be in the same category: If one were tall and the other short, then the 4-2 split would be impossible to achieve. Specifically, choice (B) is the only one that places one tall and one short player on the bench, leaving three tall and three short players for the game, which we've already deduced is an impossibility.

Remember:

- You can often find a shortcut by focusing on the categories that the entities fall into rather than the entities themselves. Notice that we quickly answered this question by finding a choice that includes one tall player and one short player, rather than working out possible lineups for each choice.

4 **(D)** Paulina can't play on the same team as Terence, because according to rule 4, Charles would have to be on that team—but that would violate rule 3, which states that Paulina must play opposite Charles. All of the players in the other choices make fine teammates for Paulina.

Remember:

- In questions like this, scan the list of choices for entities that jump out, ones that seem suspicious. Terence is a good bet because he has a whole rule dedicated to him, which by nature restricts him more than the players in the other choices.

5 **(C)** According to rule 2, if Katya and Charles, two tall players, are one team, Paulina and Edna must play on the other team. The third player on that team can't be Terence (rule 4), but could be any of the other three short players, giving us PEg, PEj, and PEm as possibilities. The correct answer is therefore 3, choice (C).

6 **(E)** is correct. This is the one that's impossible. If Terence is chosen, then Charles must play on his team, resulting in a team of Terence, Edna, and Charles. Thanks to rule 2, the other tall players, Paulina and Katya, must play on the other team to oppose Edna and Charles, so it's impossible for Katya to sit on the bench.

(A) Paulina-Greg-Jerrod versus Charles-Trent-Mort. Bench: Edna and Katya. Could be true—cross it off.

(B), (C) Paulina-Katya-Mort versus Charles-Edna-Terence. Bench: Greg and Jerrod. Could be true—cross them both off.

(D) Charles-Mort-Terence versus Katya-Greg-Jerrod. Bench: Paulina and Edna. Could be true—cross it off.

Remember:

- In questions that offer no hypothetical information, sometimes the only way to proceed is to work out each choice, which could be time consuming. A question like this is therefore a good candidate to skip and come back to later if time permits.
- You can eliminate an answer choice to a "cannot be true" question simply by coming up with one example in which the choice is true.

Game 2—Chimp Testing

The Action
Scheduling six chimps for language testing into ten time slots during a five-day week. The key issues for this sequencing game are:

- Which chimps are tested on which days, and in which time slot (morning or afternoon)?
- Which chimps are tested before and after which other chimps?
- Which chimps are tested on the same day?
- Which time slots are free?

The Initial Setup
In a sequence game with a calendar aspect, a days-of-the-week sketch like the one shown on the following page may come in handy, as it does in everyday life when we need to keep track of a week's events:

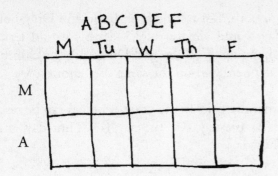

The Rules

1) Put an "A" in the Thursday morning slot.

3) Put an "X" (or whatever you feel will do the job) in the Monday morning slot to indicate that that time slot is free.

7) Jot down that Carlo is tested either Tuesday morning or afternoon.

(Note: See "The Big Picture" below to see why we recommend handling the rules in this order.)

2) You can jot down the info on the three late risers, but there's no way—yet—to narrow down their placement further.

4) This helps clarify Elmo's place in the ordering. Combined with the previous rule, we know that Elmo has to be tested in the afternoon of Wednesday, Thursday, or Friday.

5) Alonzo is tested on Thursday morning, which means that according to this rule, Wednesday afternoon must be free.

6) Dingo, Alonzo, and Frank must be tested in that order, from earliest to latest. Since Alonzo is tested on Thursday morning, Dingo must be tested

Monday, Tuesday, or Wednesday, and Frank must be tested on either Thursday or Friday afternoon (taking rule 2 into account). Jot that stuff down.

Key Deduction

Elmo has to be tested in the afternoon, but not on Monday or Tuesday, and we now know that Wednesday afternoon is off limits. So Elmo must be tested on either Thursday or Friday afternoon, the same as Frank, which we deduced by combining rules 1, 2, and 6. So: *Elmo and Frank must be tested on Thursday and Friday afternoon, in either order.* The other heavy sleeper, Bobo, therefore will be tested on Monday or Tuesday afternoon. No chimp is left for Friday morning, so this time slot must be free.

The Final Visualization

Putting all of this information into one sketch will allow us to dispose of the questions quickly.

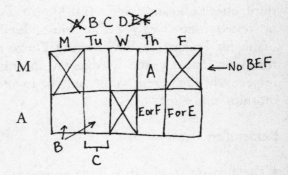

The Big Picture

- You don't have to take the rules in order. Seek out and incorporate the most concrete rules first, in order to build a solid foundation.
- Always turn negative information around to the positive. For example, in rule 4, it's easy to figure out (and more powerful to know) when

Elmo *can* be tested than when he can't be.

• Always search for the implications of rules. Don't recopy rule 5 on your page, but rather think it through and then build it into your visualization of the game.

• Don't be intimidated by games that contain many rules. The more the merrier. That's because, in general, the more information you're given to work with, the more structured the game is and the more restricted the entities are. This is good for you. Games with few rules tend to be the tough ones, as they involve much more ambiguity.

The Questions

7 **(B)** With Bobo, Carlo, and Dingo before Alonzo, and Elmo and Frank after, Alonzo must be fourth, so (B) is correct.

(A) Bobo could go on Tuesday. (C) Carlo could be third, after Bobo and Dingo. (D) Alonzo could be tested immediately before Elmo, leaving Frank for Friday. (E) If Carlo and Dingo are tested on Tuesday and Wednesday morning, respectively, then there would only be two free morning time slots.

Remember:

• The first question can solidify your conception of a game. Answering this one helps to reinforce, and show the value of, all the work we did up front.

8 **(A)** We deduced that Bobo must be tested on Tuesday or Wednesday afternoon, and Dingo must be tested Monday, Tuesday, or Wednesday. There's room for only one chimp on Monday and Wednesday, so Tuesday is the only common day

open to both. But testing both Bobo and Dingo on Tuesday would violate rule 7, as this would leave Carlo hanging. So Bobo and Dingo are the chimps that can't be tested on the same day, choice (A).

Days that the pairs in the wrong choices can be tested are (B) Tuesday, (C) Tuesday, (D) Thursday, and (E) Thursday.

Remember:

• Logic Game answers are objectively correct, so once you find an answer that works, even if it's (A) or (B), have the confidence to choose it and move on. This saves valuable time on a time-intensive section.

9 **(C)** If Dingo goes on Tuesday morning, then Carlo must go on Tuesday afternoon (rule 7), leaving unfortunate Bobo in the first open slot, Monday afternoon (remember, the key deduction limits Bobo's choices to Monday or Tuesday afternoon). Bobo on Monday is (C).

Elmo and Frank are unaffected, so as we deduced, either could be on Thursday or Friday, killing choices (A) and (B). With Bobo, Carlo, and Dingo placed, Wednesday morning must be free, resulting in three free time slots in the morning and only one in the afternoon, eliminating (D) and (E) as well.

Remember:

• When a question stem includes a hypothetical, you can sometimes save time by scanning the choices for the entities that are the most affected by the *if*-clause. In this case, Dingo's actions directly impinge upon the placement of Bobo and Carlo, and scanning the choices for either of these chimps brings us quickly to choice (C).

10 **(E)** The key deduction mandates that Frank's choice of days is limited to Thursday and Friday, while Bobo must take either Monday or Tuesday. The only way to satisfy the condition in the question stem is if Frank takes Thursday afternoon and Bobo demonstrates his language proficiency on Tuesday afternoon. There are two corollaries to this— Carlo must sneak in on Tuesday morning to satisfy rule 7, and Elmo gets the last slot, Friday afternoon.

The question stem seeks something that could be false. Dingo is the only chimp not precisely slotted in: she can be tested on Monday afternoon *or* Wednesday morning. Therefore, choice (E) could be true, but need not be; she could be tested Wednesday morning, which would place her third behind Carlo and Bobo. The other choices conform perfectly to the arrangement outlined above.

Remember:

- Play out the chain of deductions as far as you can before moving on to the question. The more info you're armed with, the greater the chance the answer will be a breeze to locate.
- In a "can be false" question, focus on the entities that are the least restricted. In this case, the exact time slot of every chimp but Dingo is determined, which virtually guarantees that Dingo will be part of the answer.

11 **(D)** If Dingo is tested in the afternoon, that must happen on either Monday or Tuesday afternoon. If Dingo's on Monday afternoon, Bobo must be Tuesday afternoon, and Carlo Tuesday morning. Elmo can be tested Thursday and Frank on Friday, or vice versa. So there are two schedules possible if Dingo goes on Monday. However, if Dingo is tested on Tuesday, then Bobo must be tested Monday afternoon, Carlo still goes on Tuesday morning, and Elmo and Frank can still float between Thursday and Friday. This adds another two possibilities to the mix, resulting in a grand total of four, choice (D).

Remember:

- When asked for the number of possible arrangements, start with a key entity—in this case, Dingo—and determine the number of possibilities for it. Then build as many arrangements around each of these possibilities as you can. This takes time and care. If you're going to take that time, don't rush and get sloppy.

12 **(B)** Start with the second piece of information. Elmo's time slots are limited to Thursday or Friday afternoon, so if Elmo is tested on the same day as another chimp, it must be on Thursday, the same day as Alonzo. This puts Frank in the Friday afternoon spot. Now for the other hypothetical: "At least one chimp is to be tested each day." The only chimp available for Wednesday morning is Dingo. Carlo can be tested only on Tuesday (in this case, morning or afternoon), leaving Bobo as the chimp to represent Monday (in the afternoon, of course). Breezing through the choices, (B) looks correct, with Elmo on Thursday and Dingo on Wednesday.

(A) need not be true. Carlo could be tested on Tuesday afternoon, in which case the time slot immediately preceding would be Tuesday morning, and we know Bobo's on Monday. However, Carlo could be tested Tuesday morning, in which case (C) bites the dust. (D) and (E) are both out-and-out false; Carlo on Tuesday comes between Bobo and Dingo, and two chimps, Dingo and Alonzo are tested between Carlo and Elmo.

Remember:

- When a question stem contains more than one hypothetical, focus on the one that seems to be more concrete first.

Game 3—Four Pictures

The Action
This game centers around matching four pictures with the color and medium in which each picture will be created. The key issues here are fairly straightforward:

- What color is used for each picture?
- What medium is used for each picture?

The Initial Setup
For matching games like this, a grid or a list that places the entities on one line and their properties underneath will generally be most helpful. A simple sketch, for starters, might look like the following table.

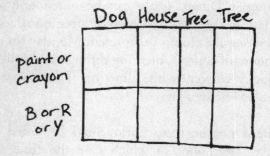

The Rules

1) By telling us that exactly one picture will be blue and one will be yellow, we know that the remaining two must be red. Next to the "color" line of the list, you may wish to write "B, Y, R, R" to represent this.

2) Here we learn that the two tree pictures share the same medium but have different colors. It might be helpful to note this directly on the sketch, perhaps by placing an equal sign between the two Ts on the medium line and a separation or unequal sign between them on the color line.

3) Basically, this says that if the blue picture is done in paint, the yellow picture must be done in crayon, and vice versa. This doesn't result in any great deduction at this level, but will be critical when we move on to the questions.

4) and 5) These are the most concrete rules, the kind that can go directly into your sketch. As in the previous game, you could have jumped to these two first to get off to a good, concrete start. Place a C in the "medium" line under *dog,* and an R in the "color" line under one of the trees.

Key Deduction
Combining rules 2 and 5, we now know that *the other tree picture must be either blue or yellow,* since one tree is red and the two trees can't be the same color.

The Final Visualization
After incorporating these rules into the sketch we developed earlier, here's what we can now use to attack the questions:

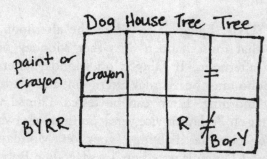

The Big Picture

- Sometimes a key deduction breaks open an entire game, while other times a deduction is somewhat helpful, but not a major factor. In this case, focus on the rules that don't play a big part in the setup (rule 3 and the second half of rule 2). Lacking major deductions, these are the kinds of rules that the questions will hinge on.

- As the name implies, matching games involve matching up various characteristics about a group of entities. Resolve right now to 1) learn how to recognize a "matching" game, and 2) decide which, if any, form of sketch (such as a grid or a list) you're most comfortable using to keep track of matching information.

The Questions

13 (C) This is a classic acceptability question. If your sketch is set up properly, it is just a matter of glancing at each choice and testing it against your sketch. (A) can be eliminated because both the blue and yellow pictures are drawn in the same medium (rule 3). In (B), the two tree pictures are in different media (rule 2). (D) also violates rule 2, which requires the tree pictures to be of different colors. Finally, (E) can be knocked out since the dog must be in crayon, not paint (rule 4).

Remember:

- In acceptability questions, try to focus on a rule, and then scan the choices to find the ones that don't conform. This saves time.

14 (C) We know that all four pictures can't be done in crayon because the blue and the yellow pictures must be in different media. What about three pictures in crayon? Sure, that's possible: the dog

is always crayon (rule 4), and since the two tree pictures must be in the same medium, let's make those two crayon as well. The house must therefore be done in paint. Does this new info correspond to any of the choices? No, so we must press on.

Let's now consider the color aspect. We already know that one tree will be red and that the other tree must be blue or yellow. Since the latter is in crayon, we know that the other picture done in blue or yellow must be painted (rule 3), which in this case is the house. Since the second red is all that is left, we can mark the dog as red and the answer as (C). The house and one of the trees will be the blue and yellow pictures, although we don't know which is which. The other four choices, therefore, could be true, but need not be.

Remember:

- Whenever you figure out any new piece of information, and the question asks, "What must be true," it's worth taking a few seconds to scan the choices looking for your deduction. Sometimes you're rewarded with a quick and easy point.

15 (A) If the dog is blue, the second tree will be yellow, according to our key deduction. This leaves red for the house. Now rule 3 comes into play: The blue dog and the yellow tree must be done in different media, and since the dog is always done in crayon, the yellow tree (and the red tree, for that matter, thanks to rule 2) must be done in paint. The only information we're missing is whether the red house is in paint or crayon.

The question asks us for what must be false, and (A) fits the bill. At best, the house is crayon and there's an equal number of paint and crayon pictures, but in this situation there can't be more crayon pictures than painted ones. (B), (C), and (D) all could be true, while (E) is a statement that must be true.

Remember:

- When testing whether a choice must be false, attempt to make it true. If you can make it true, in even one case, then cross it off. However, if you fail to find a way to make it true, then you've found the answer.

16 (D) By making the house yellow, our key deduction tells us that the second tree must be blue, which makes the dog red. So far, we know nothing about the media of the house or the trees. As with question 15, we're asked to find the choice that cannot be true or, in other words, that must be false. Once again, test to see if you can make each choice true. This time it's (D) that's impossible, as the red dog must be done in crayon. (A) and (B) could be true, as the trees could be done in paint or crayon. Likewise, (C) and (E) could be true if the house was done in crayon and the trees in paint.

17 (E) The first *if*-clause tells us, essentially, that the second tree will be blue. The second hypothetical is a roundabout way of telling us that there will be three pictures done in paint and one in crayon—and we know which one that is: the dog. So the trees and the house must be done in paint. The blue picture, in this case a painted tree, must be done in a different medium from the yellow picture, so the yellow picture must be the crayon dog, once again leaving the house as the second red picture. This supports correct choice (E).

(A) and (D) bite the dust because the dog is done in yellow crayon. The house, on the other hand, must be done in red paint, killing both (B) and (C).

Remember:

- Don't be intimidated by question stems that contain a lot of information. The more you get to work with, the more you can figure out. Here, everything's determined, which means there's not a question in the world you can't answer.
- When the question stem contains more than one *if*-clause, you don't have to take them in order; if one is more concrete than the other, begin with that one first.

18 (B) Although it is possible to try out each of the choices in turn, it is really best to try to think out which of the rules can be used to derive the answer. We are asked to figure out how to force the dog to be blue or yellow. We know from our key deduction that one of the trees must be blue or yellow. So the easiest way to force the dog to be blue or yellow would be to make the house red. However, we're not so lucky to find this easy solution in the choices.

So let's search the choices for the one that brings about the desired result. Exactly three crayon pictures? The house could still be the other blue/yellow picture, instead of the dog. What about three paint pictures? Since the dog is in crayon, this means that the house and both trees must be paint. Could the house still be the other blue/yellow picture? No; this would violate rule 3, because both blue and yellow pictures would be done in paint. So (B), in fact, does force the dog to be done in blue or yellow. (C), (D), and (E) all result in situations in which the house and one tree could make up the blue/yellow pictures.

Remember:

- Questions that ask you to employ backwards reasoning may be time consuming, because if the solution doesn't hit you intuitively, you're left trying out each choice. Such questions may therefore be prime candidates to skip and return to later if time permits.
- Logic Game answers are objectively correct. When you find the correct answer, have the confidence to move on without double-checking the remaining choices to "make sure."

Game 4—The Nine Chair Circle

The Action

Arranging seven people and two empty chairs in a circle. The key issues on which the questions will be based are:

- Who can sit next to whom?
- Who must sit next to whom?
- How far away are some entities from other entities?
- Where are the entities with respect to the empty chairs?

The Initial Setup

Before attacking the rules, it should be helpful to create a sketch representing the circle of nine chairs. Anytime you have an odd number of entities to place, you can't draw a standard circle sectioned off like pieces of a pie, because this will always come out even. So instead, try drawing nine dots spaced out in a circle, and number the seats 1 through 9, putting number 1 at the top and working clockwise for numbers 2–9, like so:

(Note: Assigning actual seat numbers is, in fact, a step beyond what you would normally do in this type of game—they're included solely as convenient reference points for the following explanations.)

Since this game specifies how people will be seated in terms of being to the left or right of one another, we must also take into account which way is left and right. In circle sequence games, people always sit facing the center of the circle; those sitting at the top of the circle, therefore, will have their left and right reversed from those on the bottom, who perceive left and right as you do. (Try to picture yourself sitting at the top of the circle, facing the center, and again at the bottom; you'll see how left and right reverse themselves.) Make a mental note that left always points clockwise and right always points counterclockwise.

The Rules

1) With any circle sequencing game, we start by picking one of the entities and placing him/her at some point on the circle. Since we see S mentioned in most of the rules, we will start by placing her in a seat, let's say number 1, with M to her immediate right in seat number 9 (remember, right is counterclockwise).

2) Since Sybil's already placed, rule 2 is a good one to incorporate next. Counting off three chairs to the right of Sybil (remember—counterclockwise) places R in chair number 7.

3) This means that seats number 2, number 6, and number 8 can't be empty, so indicate this in your sketch.

4) If L and O sit immediately next to each other, we need to locate a pair of adjacent chairs for them.

The possible candidates are: numbers 2–3, numbers 3–4, numbers 4–5 and numbers 5–6. Numbers 3–4 and numbers 4–5 won't work since each of those cases would necessitate placing an empty chair next to Randi or Sybil, which violates the previous rule. So, we know that the L-O pair will sit in either seats 2–3 or seats 5–6. Note that even if we determine which of those pairs L and O actually sit in, we still don't know which person will sit in which chair.

Key Deductions
If L and O sit in numbers 2–3, the two empty chairs must be number 4 and number 5. Similarly, if L and O are in numbers 5–6, the empties must be numbers 3–4. (Incidentally, this answers question 19.) In any event, *we can now ascertain that chair number 4 MUST be empty.* Also, in either case one of the two remaining people, *P or N, must sit in chair number 8.*

The Final Visualization
The placements of S, M, and R are determined; L and O are restricted to two pairs of chairs; the empty chairs are next to each other in one of two ways (numbers 3–4, or numbers 4–5); and N and P, the people not mentioned in any rules, are left to fill in the spaces as necessary. Here's what a sketch encompassing all of this info might look like:

The Big Picture

- In circle sequence games, always begin by placing the most prominent entity (the one connected to the most rules) into the circle first, and then build around it.
- It doesn't matter where in the sketch you place the first entity; the relationships between the entities is the crucial thing, which will remain consistent whether you begin by placing S in seat 1 or seat 6, for example.
- Check to see if the game cares about left and right. Some games will simply say "next to" and "across from." Others, like this one, care about direction.
- If left/right is an issue, make certain which way is left and which way is right from any chair. If the entities are facing inward, as is usually the case, right will be counterclockwise and left will be clockwise.

The Questions

19 (D) As mentioned earlier, a key deduction answers this one. We deduced that the two empty chairs must be either chairs 3 and 4, or chairs 4 and 5. Either way, the two empties are adjacent.

Neither (A) nor (B) needs to be true, as Pam and Naomi could sit in chair 2. Although L *could* sit next to an empty chair, L in number 6 and O in number 5 proves that L doesn't *have to*, so (C) is out. This also shows that (E) isn't necessarily so.

Remember:

- When the first question offers no hypothetical information, the answer will be something that will hold true for the entire game. So, if you hadn't already picked it out as part of the key deductions, build it into your visualization and treat it as a valid rule for the rest of the game.

20 (E) This would place O in seat 5, and L next to O in seat 6 (rule 4). The empties must therefore take seats 3 and 4. The only uncertainty remaining is that N and P are free to float between seats 2 and 8. The answer is derived from this fact. While Pam *could* sit in seat 2, next to Sybil, she could also sit in seat 8.

(A) must be true, since three seats away from R is empty seat 4. Furthermore, O, in seat 5, is next to empty chair 4, so (B) can't be false, either. We can rule out (C) since in this case L does sit next to R. Finally, (D) gets thrown out because regardless of which of N and P sits in number 2 and which sits in number 8, there must be exactly two people (S and M) between them.

Remember:

- When questions look for something that could be false, it's a good bet that the answer will involve one of the more ambiguous entities. In this case, Pam and Naomi were the only unplaced people, which quickly narrowed down the choices to (D) and (E).

21 (A) With no new hypothetical information to go on in this "cannot be true" question, we're left to test each choice by trying to make each one true. When we find the one that can't be made to work, then that's our winner. Luckily, the answer comes immediately in choice (A): if L and O take seats 2 and 3, Pam must sit in either number 6 or number 8, next to Randi. If the other scenario exists (L and O in number 5 and number 6), then Pam must sit in seat number 2, next to Sybil, or seat 8, next to Randi.

By placing O in seat number 3 or number 5, we can make (B) true. The fact that P can sit between R and M rules out (C). (D) and (E) are out as well, since seat 2 can be occupied by L or N.

Remember:

- If you can't decide where to begin in a question or to test out a choice, work with the entities that take up the most space—in this case, the L/O combo. When major entities are limited to two possibilities, simply try each and see what happens.

22 (C) Lisa can sit next to an empty chair if she sits in seat 3, with O in seat 2, or if she sits in seat 5, with O in seat 6. In the first case, P and N must sit in seats 6 and 8, in either order. So there are actually two possible arrangements attached to the first case. The same holds true for the second case, the scenario with L and O in seats 5 and 6, respectively. P and N could then float between seats 2 and 8. So, there are two general ways to place Lisa next to an empty seat, each containing its own two variations, resulting in four different possible arrangements overall.

Remember:

- When asked for the number of different possible arrangements, simply try each variation of the seating until you've exhausted all possibilities.

23 (C) In order to determine the exact locations of everyone, we need to resolve the ambiguities. What are the major ambiguities? Well, there's uncertainty as to where N and P sit, and there's the question of placing the L/O twosome.

The intuitive approach to this problem, therefore, is to look for a choice that mentions the people in each of these pairs. (A), (C), and (E) look like good candidates, so let's begin with those.

If Pam sits in seat 8, we can take care of (A) in two ways: L in seat 2 or L in seat 5. (E) can be discarded in the same way, by simply substituting O for L and N for P. (C), however, does the trick: the only way to get exactly one person between L and N is if N sits in number 8 and L sits in number 6. This forces O into number 5, P into number 2, with number 3 and number 4 left empty. As for (B) and (D), which we never had to check after all, neither one allows for a definitive placement of the two perpetual free agents, N and P.

Remember:

- When looking for a statement that will precisely determine the placement of every entity, scan the list of choices for ones that deals with the game's most ambiguous characters, and test those out first.

24 (E) The best approach here is to create a fresh sketch for this question (it doesn't take long at all), and reapply the rules. Continue to keep S in seat number 1. Now, instead of being in number 9, M will be in seat 3. Following original rule 2, R remains in seat 7. Reapplying rule 3 tells us that now seats 2, 6, 8, and 9 can't be empty, so the only remaining seats, 4 and 5, must be the empties. Finally, applying rule 4 tells us that L and O must share the only two remaining adjacent seats, 8 and 9 (in either order), while N and P are left to float between seats 2 and 6.

Armed with all of this information, it's easy to see that (A) through (D) can all be true (choice (A) in fact must be true), while choice (E) can't possibly be true. The chairs that are three chairs away from Sybil are number 4, which is empty, and number 7, which is Randi's.

Remember:

- If you're pressed for time, you may wish to skip a question that involves a change in the original rules, especially one that pretty much requires you to rethink the rules from scratch.

Section Four: Logical Reasoning Explanations

1 (E) The argument breaks down into two crisp components: the conclusion (that public education has deteriorated in the last fifty years) and a piece of supporting evidence (the inability of high school seniors to compose a business letter). (E) does the best job of strengthening the argument, as it adds meaning to the evidence. If 80 percent of seniors could write acceptable business letters fifty years ago, and only 50 percent of today's seniors can do so, then the conclusion is more believable.

(A) Contradictory. If the seemingly poor statistic was actually an improvement, then one might conclude that public education has succeeded, and not failed, in recent years.

(B) attempts to shift the blame for the poor performance of some students to something other than their education. However, nothing indicates whether the students who aren't native English-speakers are among the 50 percent who can write the letters or the 50 percent who cannot.

(C) No way to know whether this represents an increase or a decrease in math capabilities, so it has no bearing on the argument.

(D) simply clarifies the evidence by giving us a more precise statistic. We are still left with the question of whether this represents improvement or deterioration in the students' skills.

Remember:

• The choices that best support an argument will be those that add additional support for the conclusion or forge a stronger link between support and conclusion.

2 (E) By describing how the seemingly "crumbling infrastructure and hopeless traffic congestion" problem was rectified by a mayor who put the money into a solution, the writer draws a parallel with the current air pollution problem. A mayor who makes this current problem a priority and invests money in it, the writer implies, will be able to fix it, and those people who are currently settling for the status quo need not do so.

(A) The only link between the transportation problems and the pollution is the analogy. At no point are we told that there is any causal link between the two issues.

(B) On the contrary, the incumbent mayor has proven himself willing to spend money on programs he considers important, as evidenced by the transportation example.

(C) To an extent, the ability to correct the air pollution problem is implied, but there's no actual demonstration that the problem can be fixed, just that Schwartz will give it a shot.

(D) The argument does not suggest that voters should alter their priorities; it merely exhorts those who already share her concern about air pollution to vote for Schwartz.

Remember:

• When an argument relies on an analogy, be wary of choices that infer an unwarranted connection, or causal link, between the two analogous situations.

3 **(D)** The argument can be broken down algebraically (X, wisdom, needs Y, adversity; Constanza is wise, X, therefore she must have suffered adversity, Y) and checked against the choices. However, you can also take a less algebraic and more verbal approach, by recognizing that the argument boils down to, "Someone with a particular trait must have another specific trait, because the latter is a prerequisite for the former." By noting that Constanza is wise, the writer concludes that she shares an experience common to all wise folk. Similarly, by noting that Francois is "a brilliant musician," the writer of (D) concludes that he must, therefore, share an experience common to all excellent musicians.

(A) "Character requires training" follows the basic model, but then an extra leap to the source of the attribute is made. The required attribute is training in patience and fortitude, but the conclusion states that the training must have come from Leon's parents. It's this extra leap that ruins the parallel.

(B) Winning a gold medal requires the "very best training and preparation." While good coaching might fall within this realm, it is not necessarily so. As with (A), an extra logical jump is taken.

(C) This one's conclusion is a prediction. No good.

(E) This one's conclusion is a prediction. No good.

Remember:

• Parallel logic tip: Whenever possible, try to translate the argument into simple content-neutral words, or even algebraic letters. This will help you avoid the trap of letting the content of the answer choice become confused with the content of the original argument.

• Many times, the elements of an argument will be mirrored in an answer choice, although not in the same order. The order is unimportant, provided that the correct elements exist.

4 **(C)** The passage refers to the use of statistics to judge economic systems in two ways: with respect to operational effectiveness, and "as a whole." When judging operational effectiveness, the passage suggests that the statistics speak for themselves. However, when looking at the big picture, economists need to determine the significance—or "value"—of unquantifiable aspects. Choice (C) stays consistent with the passage's theme, recognizing that economists must use some subjectivity in analyzing systems as a whole.

(A) Contradictory to the first sentence of the passage, this is the area in which statistical analysis can be used with reliability.

(B) Statistics are mentioned in relation to specific tasks within a system. The issues here comprise the "unquantifiable aspects" of systems as a whole, so statistics aren't relevant.

(D) The passage strongly implies that productivity is a good way of comparing economic systems, so this one looks bad right from the start. It also refers to what "most economists would agree" upon, something that the author doesn't address in any way.

(E) calls for a consensus among economists, something that is not dealt with in the passage. In fact, the passage implies that economists may reach different conclusions without any one being "wrong."

Remember:

- In inference questions, the correct choice is often one that's closely related to the passage's main idea. Wrong choices often focus on points that are either tangential or wholly irrelevant to the passage.
- Read carefully to separate the viewpoint of the author from that of other people whom the author may mention.

5 (E) The difference between chronological age and physiological age is that the latter is a more complete descriptor, because it places the chronological age of a species into the context of the life span of that species. (E) sticks very closely to this theme and is reinforced by the illustration in the last sentence.

(A) Off the mark. The passage deals with the issue of how to assign meaning to a particular "age"; ascertaining that age is not discussed.

(B) Whether an animal is old or young is relative with respect to the life span of its species. The words *old* and *young* have meaning, but those meanings merely vary from one animal to another.

(C) Beyond the scope. At no point is anything said about an animal's physiological condition.

(D) raises a distinction the author never makes, between humans and "other animals." To the author, the two different types of ages are applicable to both.

Remember:

- The opposite of a good inference will make little or no sense in light of the main idea. The best inferences actually tend to be restatements of a passage's gist.
- As with Reading Comprehension passages, don't focus on specific details or examples when approaching an inference question.

6 (C) The author argues that giving grants to the lowest bidder results in substandard and dangerous construction, a point (C) attacks by attacking the assumption that a low bidder must necessarily demonstrate shoddy workmanship and materials. If (C) is true, then all bidders, high or low, demonstrate high standards to begin with.

(A) at best suggests that concerns other than inferiority and safety ought to be considered when evaluating the city council's policy, but since this falls outside the scope, the conclusion remains untouched.

(B) may tend to strengthen the argument, by implying that contractors lack one particular "oversight mechanism" for keeping standards high.

(D) suggests another factor (design flaws) that can result in dangerous buildings, but fails to speak to the critical issue, namely whether going to the lowest bidder will result in dangerous buildings. Implying that the city should keep an eye on the architects, too, doesn't take the onus off the builders.

(E)'s message is merely, "We can't afford to do better," which doesn't address the argument at all. As with (A), this is a justification, not an attempt to weaken the argument.

Remember:

• The most important step in weakening an argument is actually defining the argument itself. Break it down as simply as you can. The correct choice will directly challenge the premises or conclusion of the argument, whereas wrong choices will often dwell on tangential points.

7 **(D)** In the case of this particular war movie, the author argues that the visual message is the true one and that we shouldn't be distracted by the verbal themes. Thus the author must be assuming that a film's true message can, in fact, be conveyed by visual means only. If it can't, then the whole argument falls apart.

(A) may be true, but isn't a presupposition to the argument. In fact, the author admits that the verbal component of the film is a significant factor—insofar as he is fearful of the viewer's being distracted by the conversational elements.

(B) Although the author suggests that there's a risk of being misled by the verbal element of this particular film, what "moviegoers frequently do" isn't an essential part of this argument.

(C) The author isn't troubled because audiences "are prone to ignore the visual" as a habit, but because in the case of this particular film the verbal elements send a different signal from the visual ones.

(E) Whether this is true (and it's doubtful) is irrelevant. The visual message of the film doesn't hinge on this insight.

Remember:

• Be careful not to let the specifics of a stimulus cause you to stray from the argument itself. The main issue here is films, not World War II.
• Stay away from choices that talk about what most (or all) members of a group do or want, particularly when such tendencies are never identified in the passage.

8 **(B)** Two courses of action could be taken to achieve the same result, and one is more expensive than the other. Therefore, says the author, the cheaper one should be chosen. While some choices attempt to strengthen or weaken the argument, the only thing we are asked to do is find a possible explanation for the disparity in costs, and only (B) stays within that limited scope in that it provides a simple scenario whereby more costs would be incurred in building the Abaco site than the Bornos site.

(A) This choice is an added argument in favor of Bornos but makes no mention of the disparity in cost.

(C) merely offers a long-term benefit to building on Bornos, whereas we're looking to explain the difference in building costs.

(D) A good argument against Abaco, but it fails to address the cost issue at all, unless you work harder than you should to make the inference that protecting those endangered species would jack up the costs. We cannot be sure that even if (D) were true, a single dollar would be spent on species protection.

(E) We can infer that the issue of future expandability isn't factored into the cost estimates of the two plants, so again, we're given information that does nothing to explain the cost discrepancy.

Remember:

- Read the question, and don't embrace choices that don't address the question at hand. If you're asked for an explanation, look for choices that explain. If you're asked for a counter argument, look for one of those. Don't confuse the two.

9 (A) Since the question asks for a principle that would determine which is the right course of action, we must find a choice into which the specific facts of the stimulus will fit snugly. (A) states that if a patient is in a situation such as Mrs. Menendez's, the doctor's obligation is crystal clear. Under this principle, the doctor's argument against terminating life support would clearly fail.

(B), (D) The situation describes someone choosing to refuse life support, whereas these choices focus on any terminally ill patient, which is too broad. Interestingly, (B) also implies that such a patient may compel a doctor to act ("intervene") medically to kill her, which is pretty extreme for this situation.

(C) Two problems here. First, we are not told that Mrs. Menendez is in a vegetative state. Second, the choice addresses the issue of how to handle a disparity between family wishes and those of the patient, but in this case, those wishes are one and the same.

(E) This choice focuses on resolving a discrepancy which does not exist. Here, the patient, her living will, and her nearest relative are all in accordance with each other.

Remember:

- When asked to reconcile a dispute, always look for choices that most closely mirror the facts in the dispute. Most often the correct answer is a choice custom-tailored to the fact scenario.

10 (C) Since the doctor relies on the statement that he cannot "play God" to provide a moral ground for his position, Menendez can counter the doctor's position by showing that the doctor's actions in fact constitute "playing God" whether he realizes it or not.

(A) The issue of who can afford life-saving treatment goes beyond the scope of the passage.

(B) On the contrary, the distinction between the two is clear: the doctor simply argues that, despite patient wishes, his obligations do not permit him to honor those wishes.

(D) The doctor's argument is centered around his obligation to preserve life, which would still exist regardless of the possibility that the patient would change her mind. This possibility, therefore, would be of no help to Menedez in countering the doctor's position.

(E) The patient's mental capacity is way beyond the scope of the passage.

Remember:

- Read past the wordiness of complex question stems. This one simply asks how to weaken the doctor's argument.

11 **(B)** All this author is saying is that most statements can be interpreted both subjectively and objectively. (B) echoes this theme by pointing out both the varying "looks" of a tie (subjective) and the "definite individual traits" that aren't subject to interpretation (objective).

(A) fails to address the subjective. Fact: many compete to be the best. Fact: only one can wear the crown. There is no room for interpretation on either of these issues.

(C) focuses only on the reactions (subjective) people will have to artwork. It doesn't make mention of some concrete, indisputable quality that would cover the objective realm.

(D) The only interpretation discussed here is the subjective opinion of "most people" of a particular character trait (consistency).

(E) The objective, concrete thing here is that a comment was intended as praise, and is followed by the possibility (but not likelihood) of a subjective misinterpretation of it. This differs from the structure of the original, where the objective aspect itself isn't subject to interpretation.

Remember:

- When looking for a parallel principle or situation, make certain that the full point is covered in the choice; going halfway isn't enough.

12 **(B)** The discrepancy we are asked to resolve is how most winter guests availed themselves of discounted pricing but the lodge nevertheless rented more rooms at full price. And if the discounted folks were comprised mainly of families, packing in more guests per room, while the full-price guests tended to come solo with fewer guests per room, then it's easier to explain how there could be many discounted guests in the hotel but more rooms rented at full price.

(A) These guests aren't even eligible for the summer discount, so they play no part in the argument or the confusing result.

(C) That some people got an added discount doesn't serve to explain the paradox. If anything, it makes even more mysterious the increase in full-price rooms.

(D) The argument centers on a full versus discounted rate. What that rate is is irrelevant; it does nothing to explain why more rooms were rented at full rate in light of the evidence.

(E) goes beyond the scope of the passage. Other charges above and beyond room rates are never discussed and are therefore not an issue.

Remember:

- When resolving a paradox, look for elements in the evidence and conclusion that appear to be similar, but are in fact totally different things (in this case, number of guests versus number of rooms). Usually, this will be at the heart of the seeming contradiction.
- As in Logic Games, feel free to work out an example to clarify your understanding of a concept. Imagine, for instance, that the hotel

has ten rooms, and rents three at a discount and seven at full price. Now suppose that the discounted rooms contain five people per room, while the full-price rooms each contain one person. Voilà! More full-priced rooms than discounted, but more discounted guests than full-priced ones.

13 (C) The passage describes a cycle whereby farmers have a poor crop, need additional money, apply for loans, sell off expensive, quality equipment in order to qualify for loans, and are then left with fewer resources with which to harvest their crops, since their good equipment is now gone. Correct choice (C) follows this pattern, and indeed can be derived directly from the passage's second sentence.

(A) The passage doesn't address the issue of banks paying for crops or equipment; it simply cites the value of equipment as a factor in the bank's decision to approve a loan.

(B) While the passage implies that the farmers are hurting as a result of the banking practices, nothing suggests that these practices are illegal.

(D) Whether the farmers will succeed in the future is beyond the scope of this passage. Many other factors may very well come into play.

(E) The passage doesn't argue for banks to subsidize farmers. The author merely points out that the regulations surrounding lending are causing problems for farmers.

Remember:

• Don't confuse questions that ask you to find the author's conclusion (implying that it's some-

where in the passage) with questions that ask which conclusion "can most reasonably be drawn." The latter is usually looking for the next logical step of the statements in the passage.

• Sometimes the answer to this type of conclusion question is nothing more than an inference staring you in the face.

14 (B) Drawing a parallel between the turbulent times in Athens and Erewhon, and noting a causal link between the emergence of Euripides and the civil war in Athens, the author generalizes that a comparable dramatist should emerge in Erewhon. The argument lacks evidence—that is, information to back up this generalization—but (B) forges the link between what happened in Athens to what the author expects to happen in Erewhon.

(A) So what? This may increase the chances of civil war, but we still know nothing about why we should expect another Euripides.

(C) So what? Where's the link to Erewhon? What about the emergence of a dramatist?

(D) is too broad in scope. We know some of the specific similarities, just not the one on which the argument depends.

(E) merely says that a greater writer than Euripides will emerge, but we're still missing the vital link, the essential assumption that explains why it is we should expect a fine dramatist to appear at all.

Remember:

• In an assumption question, the author will have taken a "logical leap" in formulating the conclusion. Your job will be to find where that leap occurs and then find the choice that bridges the gap.

- To test a choice in an assumption question, ask yourself, "If this is true, is the conclusion made more believable? Without this, does the argument fall apart?" If you can answer "yes" to both, you have a winner.
- Unlike inferences, assumptions don't come directly from the passage, nor will they be mere expansions of statements made in the argument. Remember that an assumption refers to that which is not explicitly stated.

15 (E) Coolidge, it's argued, won't benefit from introducing a new cereal since doing so will merely "steal" its own customers away from other Coolidge brands. Anything that demonstrates that Coolidge may actually benefit from introducing a new brand will weaken this argument, and (E) does exactly that. If introducing a new brand will attract buyers of competitors' cereals, Coolidge will have succeeded in increasing its overall customer base without cannibalizing its own product.

(A) The argument is centered around the effect of introducing a new brand, so the relation between cereal sales and population increase is irrelevant.

(B) While the first year may produce great sales for Coolidge's new brand, that might still be at the expense of its older brands, in which case the argument still stands.

(C) has no bearing on the argument, as it does nothing to suggest who will actually switch to Coolidge's new product.

(D) Be this as it may, this still fails to address the fundamental issue in the argument: the effect of Coolidge introducing a new brand of cereal to the market.

Remember:

- An LSAT argument about the predicted success or failure of a sales plan is no less speculative than it would be in real-life business. Use your common sense about real-life customer behavior to help you zero in on a plan's weak points.

16 (D) Betty opens by saying that her opponent opposes a rule requiring the leading of the loyalty pledge. Later, however, she attacks the opponent for trying to forbid the pledge. Yet, if Betty's first statement were correct, the unnamed opponent may see the pledge as merely optional, so it's unfair to jump from that to the claim that her opponent will forbid the pledge.

(A) While this might be a good campaign point to argue on the opponent's behalf, others' opposition to the rule doesn't address the flaw in Betty's reasoning.

(B) Betty describes loyalty as the scouts' "most important virtue." The mere fact that there are other virtues doesn't undermine any part of her argument.

(C) Like (A), potentially a good campaign point in favor of Betty's opponent, but whether her position is out of character doesn't deal with the substance of Betty's reasoning.

(E) implies that Betty is accusing her opponent of disloyalty to the Wilderness scouts, but Betty doesn't go that far, so the distinction that (E) draws doesn't counter Betty's reasoning.

Remember:

- When reading a question stimulus, circle words that jump out as being inconsistent with each other. Often, the question will center around that discrepancy.

17 (E) The substance of the argument is found in the last two sentences. We're told that some words don't refer to concrete qualities and, consequently, they're learned differently from words that do represent the tangible. The assumption that learning varies with the type of word is, therefore, crucial to the argument.

(A) contradicts the passage, as we're told that the intangible can be learned, albeit differently.

(B) Beyond the scope of the argument. The issue of gaining and losing attributes is only mentioned with respect to the given example. The point of that example was simply to show the difference between two words.

(C) At no point is it suggested that it's more difficult to learn the abstract than the tangible. All we're told is that the two are learned differently.

(D) The structure of our minds has no bearing on the argument.

Remember:

- Don't let the language in somewhat philosophical examples throw you off track. It's still just one main point supported by evidence.

- If an argument is loaded down with examples up front, it may make sense to skim down to the end and locate the conclusion that the examples are leading to. Then you can return to the evidence with a firmer grasp of the author's purpose.

18 (A) Vigorously, if somewhat obliquely, the author wants to point out an apparent hypocrisy, and to call on society to reconcile this hypocrisy in accordance with the author's beliefs. We say we're an "active" society, but going by the author's definitions, advocating capital punishment is more a part of a "reactive" society.

(B) The author doesn't deal with the idea of punishment as a means to deterrence. Instead, he or she argues against capital punishment by saying that we should work to reform criminals rather than execute them.

(C) On the contrary, the author would rather we retain the concept of being "active," and change our view of capital punishment to fit that mold.

(D) Certainly suggested by the argument's subtext, but this is too broad to be the author's main point, which, of course, is the issue of capital punishment.

(E) To this author, capital punishment doesn't violate the spirit of our laws. Rather, it's the laws permitting capital punishment that violate our image of our society.

Remember:

- When an argument deals with a political issue or a high-profile debate or controversy, be careful not to let your own personal views influence your thinking.

- Rhetorical questions are those whose answers are meant to be self-evident. It's easier when the author says flat-out what he means, so rhetorical questions can be difficult under LSAT time pressure. Consider saving arguments that employ rhetorical questions until later in the section.

19 (E) The author's last sentence and choice (E) say essentially the same thing: an active society, for which the author argues, would work to "correct the flawed elements in society" or, in other words, rehabilitate criminals rather than simply react and punish them.

(A) A little too extreme. The author simply argues that there are better, more productive routes to take than capital punishment.

(B) While the author describes criminals as "flawed," he never discusses whether they should be held responsible for their actions.

(C) Too extreme. The author does believe that the use of capital punishment is an admission of defeat, but that doesn't mean he'd agree that a society with this mindset won't survive.

(D) Too vague. War, for example, involves the destruction of human lives, which the author may feel is okay in some situations. The answer has to have some connection to criminals and capital punishment.

Remember:

- "Agreement with principles" questions follow the same general rules as inferences. However, note that a correct choice may relate to a point much more narrow than the overall passage.
- Learn to recognize extreme-sounding choices like "will not survive" and "inappropriate in any situation." Unless the author's tone is extreme, these choices are often wrong.

20 (C) This is essentially a formal logic statement disguised as a casual one. Translation: *if* a death row convict in a state pen filed a petition, *then* that convict believes there will be a delay, and a more favorable outcome if the pardoning authority knows about the petition. The contrapositive is stated in choice (C): if an inmate were to be pessimistic about the effect of filing a petition, we can safely conclude that that inmate did not actually file one.

(A), (B) These choices have it backward. The original states, "If you file, then you believe, etcetera." The structure of (A) and (B) is, "If most or all believe, then they file."

(D) The issue of remorse is way outside the scope. Also, since the argument is tailored around a very specific type of prisoner (the death row inmate in state pens) we would not be able to deduce anything about petition-filing convicts in general.

(E) The scope of the passage is limited to those who have filed petitions. Those who didn't file are irrelevant.

Remember:

- For any true if/then statement, its contrapositive must also be true, and it's formed by reversing and negating the terms. The general model is: Original statement—if X, then Y. The contrapositive, and valid inference—if not Y, then not X. This is very important for LSAT Logical Reasoning.

21 (C) Although Jason believes that coupons will save money, Twyla counters that more will be saved if they don't use the coupons. The "odd man out" statement is (C), because while half of the products would cost the same, the other half could very well be cheaper if Jason's coupons are used.

(A) furthers her argument by explaining why, even after using coupons, the money spent would be greater than what Twyla would otherwise have paid.

(B) If using the couponed brands requires buying more of each product, then the net result would likely be a higher bottom line.

(D) That the higher prices of the couponed brands outweigh the savings from the coupons clearly strengthens Twyla's argument.

(E) If Twyla has already taken the trouble to find bargains, then it's reasonable to believe that less money could be spent on her sale items than on Jason's couponed items.

Remember:

- As in Logic Games, read the question stem carefully, and always take note of the word *except*.

- When you're asked, "Which choice does *not* support the argument?" understand that the right answer will either weaken the argument or have no effect on it.

22 (D) Within the last quarter, the company lost customers to a competitor, which rather readily leads to the conclusion that the company simply isn't as competitive as it once was.

(A) At no point are sales figures discussed, particularly with respect to the company's history. All we know is that some problems have occurred in the past quarter.

(B), (E) Not necessarily true. Perhaps customers left because the treatment they received from the company wasn't as good as that which they could receive elsewhere.

(C) A greater percentage of potential clients are buying the competitor's system, but that doesn't mean that more clients have purchased the competitor's system than have purchased the company's. Suppose last year there were 100 clients; eighty bought the company's product and twenty bought the competitor's. Further suppose that this year, out of 100 potential clients, sixty buy from the company and forty from the competitor. A greater percentage of potential clients are purchasing the competitor's system this year, but more clients are still purchasing from the company than from the competitor.

Remember:

- Learn to recognize the difference between percentages and actual numbers. The test makers love to play on this distinction, in wrong choices and in questions demonstrating faulty logic.

- Use real, simple numbers to help clarify numerical relationships for yourself.

23 **(B)** The author argues that physical proximity is necessary for friendship, because friendships are based on us knowing that our friends are alive and well. Anything alleging the possibility of keeping abreast of friends' well-being at a distance would seriously weaken the argument. (B) presents a way in which friends can live apart from one another and still keep in contact.

(A) seems to attack the second sentence of the argument. It doesn't really, because "the same way" is different from "the same amount," but even if it did it wouldn't injure the claim that friendship means physical proximity.

(C), (D) The argument doesn't say that proximity guarantees knowing that everything is okay. It merely implies that without proximity, such knowledge is impossible. (Note that that is pretty much the contrapositive of the author's argument.) As for (D), the author doesn't claim that living near or with a friend will guarantee the friend's well-being, so this doesn't damage the argument either.

(E) brings up a new and unrelated situation, and fails to address the key points raised in the argument. It therefore can't be a weakener.

Remember:

- Recognize and cross off choices that sound damaging, but, in fact, damage an argument other than the one the author is making.

24 **(D)** The point common to both Duane and Sylvia's arguments is the effect gun control will have on the number of guns possessed by criminals. Duane argues that strict measures will reduce that number, while Sylvia argues that gun control will not alter that number but may in fact make it difficult for the honest person to get a gun. (D) is the only choice that stays within the scope and isolates this issue that's critical to both arguments.

(A) Only Duane mentions the opposition by handgun manufacturers. Furthermore, identifying the most effective opponent is part of neither person's presentation.

(B) Duane seems to support this notion, and Sylvia doesn't disagree. She merely bases her counter-argument on other grounds—whether gun control laws will be effective in actually reducing the number of handguns in the possession of criminals.

(C) In neither argument is the effect of strict punishments explored.

(E) Neither suggests that gun control is a constitutional violation. Only Sylvia hints at it, and even so she puts that issue aside for the purpose of making her main argument.

Remember:

- When reconciling two arguments, limit yourself to choices that center around facts or points mentioned in both arguments.
- Don't get sidetracked by tangents.

25

(D) Duane presents a course of action (gun control) that will lead to a situation (fewer guns in the hands of criminals) that will in turn bring about a desired result (decrease in the murder rate). Sylvia attacks the middle piece: she asserts that the "fewer guns for criminals" scenario will not result from the proposed course of action, namely gun control.

(A) At no point does Sylvia argue against Duane's claim that guns are a cause of the homicide problem.

(B) There is no use of sarcasm by either person.

(C) This one's tempting; Sylvia does suggest that even with gun control laws, the bad situation will continue, and that honest people may find themselves disarmed. That, however, is not enough by itself to suggest that she believes the homicide problem will get worse, which is what "exacerbating the problem" implies.

(E) Way outside the scope. Sylvia never suggests that Duane engages in exaggeration to make his point, and besides, legal concerns are not raised by either person.

Remember:

• When choices employ abstractions (*course of action, the situation, the problem*), try to be conscientious in relating back to the specifics of the stimulus. You can't evaluate such choices until you understand the general framework in the context of the passage.

GETTING INTO LAW SCHOOL

BY PAT HARRIS

CHAPTER 7

INTRODUCTION TO LAW SCHOOL ADMISSIONS

I can still remember the day I received my LSAT score report in the mail. I was jubilant about my score, which put me in the top two percent of all test takers. This kind of LSAT performance, I thought—combined with my high college GPA—would surely get me into any law school I desired; all I had to do was decide which one I would deign to attend. I proceeded to apply to ten top law schools, fully confident that I would be accepted by all ten.

Well, it didn't turn out quite that way. By the following April, I had received a meager two acceptance letters, one wait-list letter, and an appalling seven rejection letters, including ones from Harvard and Stanford. As the rejection letters rolled in, one after the other, my original hubris slowly and painfully gave way to humility.

Two weeks after the last rejection, still reeling from the shock, I had the good fortune to bump into an admissions officer from a local law school at a party. I cornered her and began peppering her with questions about what could possibly have gone wrong. She mentioned several potential problems and suggested that I call a friend of hers at one of the law schools I had applied to and ask her to critique my application. What I found out was eye-opening: my application could not have been more inept. In fact, just about everything I'd done had contributed to preventing my admission to law school, including carelessly misspelling my name on the application (fortunately, the University of Michigan Law School saw fit to let me attend despite these blunders).

GREAT CANDIDATES, MEDIOCRE APPLICATIONS

Being a strong, well-quali-fied candidate isn't enough to ensure admission to the law school of your choice. You have to *show* the admissions officers how strong and well-qualified you are—by conducting an effective, meticulously organized campaign for admission.

Today, after years of conversations with other lawyers, law students, and members of my Kaplan LSAT classes, I realize that my experience was hardly unique. An astonishing number of people apply to law school without a clue about the admissions process. That's why I've made something of a career out of ensuring that others don't make the same mistakes I did. In the last several years, I've spoken to admissions officers at more than sixty-five schools in all regions of the country, gleaning as much information from them as I could. And I've gathered together their combined wisdom in this book.

One cautionary note—admission officers are human beings; they don't all think alike. Attitudes and priorities vary from law school to law school. However, the suggestions that follow are the ones I've heard over and over again, straight from the most important source—the admissions officers themselves. Stick closely to these suggestions and you'll increase your chances of getting in the law school you want to attend.

CHAPTER 8

WHERE TO APPLY

The question of where you should apply is usually a two-part question. What schools should you consider, regardless of your chances, and which of these schools can you actually get into? Let's begin with the first question.

What Schools Should You Consider?

In a recent article about law school education, I came across a remarkable statistic. Upon graduation, according to one study, 58 percent of all law students end up living and working within a one-hour drive of where they went to law school. That's nearly six out of every ten students!

There are many reasons for this surprising statistic. Obviously, a lot of people attend the local law school in the town where they have always lived and want to continue living. Also, since employers tend to interview and hire from nearby law schools, many recent grads stay put. Some students find that they just like the area and don't want to leave. Still others meet and marry a local person during their three years. Whatever the explanation, a majority of all law students end up spending more than just the required three years in the city or region where they attend law school.

Despite the importance of law school selection, however, it's frightening how lightly many applicants treat the whole process, even students who spend a great deal of time studying for the LSAT or working on their applications. Horror stories abound—of distant relatives convincing a cousin to attend State University Law School just because they themselves did forty years ago, or of a student who decides not to apply to a school because his girlfriend's cousin heard that the social life was not so hot.

I cannot emphasize this point enough. *Choosing a law school is a major decision in your life and should be treated as such.* There are several factors to consider when choosing where to apply, including reputation, location, and cost.

DON'T TAKE IT LIGHTLY

Deciding which law schools to apply to is an important decision. Treat it with the appropriate seriousness, which doesn't mean that you can't have a fun time researching schools.

Reputation

How much does a law school's reputation matter? The short answer is that it matters very much in your first few years out of law school, when you're looking for your first job or two. Most employers evaluating you at this time will have little else to go on, and so will tend to place a lot of weight on school reputation. After a few years, when you've established a reputation and a record of your own, the importance of your alma mater's rep will diminish.

The long answer to the question of academic reputation, however, is a little more complex. Each applicant must look at his or her situation and ask several questions:

- **Am I looking to work for a law firm or to do public-service work?**
  Law firms tend to put more emphasis on the reputation of the school.
- **Do I want to stay in the area or have more mobility nationwide?**
  Some schools enjoy strong local reputations as well as strong alumni bases, whereas other schools have a nationwide appeal.
- **How competitive do I want my law school experience to be?**
  Although there are exceptions, as a general rule the schools with better reputations tend to be very competitive.
- **Do I want to consider teaching as an option?**
  Virtually all law school professors come from a handful of top-notch law schools. The same also applies for the most prestigious judicial clerkships.
- **To what extent am I willing to go into debt?**
  The schools with the big reputations also tend to have the biggest price tags.

How to Research Reputation

What's the best way to research reputation? Many publications rank law schools. How accurate these rankings are is anybody's guess, but they tend to become self-fulfilling. Once published, they're discussed over and over by students, lawyers, and faculty until they become fact. Although the methodology behind these rankings is often suspect, the results are frequently heeded by employers. Studies rank the top fifty schools, the top fifteen schools, or categorize all schools into four or five levels. (Most of these books can be found in the reference section of your local bookstore.) Many law firms rely heavily on such rankings in making their hiring decisions.

But there are other methods to determine a school's reputation. Speak to friends who are lawyers or law students. Lawyers have a habit of noting who their most formidable opponents are and where they went to law school. Look through law school catalogs and see what schools the professors attended. Finally, ask the placement offices how many firms interview on campus each year, and compare the numbers. Their answers can give you a strong indication of what the law-firm community thinks of a school.

Location

Location is of prime importance because of the distinct possibility that you'll end up spending a significant part of your life near your law school—three years at the very least. Even under the best of conditions, law school will be a difficult period in your life. You owe it to yourself to find a place where you'll be comfortable. Pick cities or areas you already know you like or would like to live. Pay particular attention to climate problems. Think about rural areas as opposed to urban centers.

How to Research Location

Visit as many law schools as possible, your top two or three choices at the very least. You may be surprised at what you find. For example, a recent student was telling me that his dream was to get into the law school of one particular university because he'd visited its campus several years ago and loved it. I quickly had to crush his dream by explaining that the university's law school is not on the campus, but rather thirty minutes away in an area closer to downtown. Spend some time researching location by visiting *when school is in session*, which is when you'll get the most accurate picture. You should also:

- Buy a local newspaper and scan the real estate ads for prices near campus; check out campus housing to determine whether it's livable.
- Check out transportation options at the law school.
- Take the school's tour so you can hear about the area's good points.
- Look at bulletin boards for evidence of activities.

Finally, don't be afraid to wander into the student lounge and just ask several law students what they think. Most are more than willing to provide an honest appraisal, but be sure to get more than one opinion.

LOCATION, LOCATION, LOCATION

Statistics show that you'll probably end up spending at least part of your working life in the area where you went to law school. So be sure to pick one in a location you can live with (and in).

THE COSTS OF EXPENSIVE SCHOOLS AREN'T ALWAYS FINANCIAL

Cost should be a factor in your choice of law school, even if you're convinced that you can get enough loans to cover tuition. Loans have to be paid back, after all, and a high burden of debt might ultimately force you to make a less-than-desirable career choice.

Costs

Cost ranks at the bottom of many law students' list of criteria to consider, because law school financial aid works in much the same manner as a credit card—you get it now and pay for it later. Each year a number of students enter law school with the goal of doing some type of public-service work, but then are forced to take higher-paying firm jobs in order to meet their loan payments. This is certainly understandable when you realize that many law students rack up debts of $50,000 to $100,000 over the course of three years.

Among the cost issues to consider are:

- **Low-Cost State Schools**
  State schools tend to have lower tuition, particularly for in-state residents.
- **Urban versus Rural Living Costs**
  Schools in large urban areas will almost invariably have higher living costs than those in rural areas (although the larger cities also tend to have more part-time jobs for second- and third-year students, which can offset the extra cost).
- **Special Loan Programs**
  Many schools now offer special loan repayment or loan forgiveness programs for students who take low-paying public service jobs.
- **Special Scholarship Programs**
  Many law schools offer special scholarship programs that range from small grants to full three-year rides.

How to Research Cost
The law school application will tell you what the annual tuition was for the previous year. Many applications will even give you an estimate of living expenses. If you want to dig deeper, call the financial aid office and ask them to send you the breakdown of living expenses of the average law student. Also ask them to send information about any loan forgiveness programs and about scholarships offered by the law school.

Job Placement

With the legal job market shrinking, the proficiency of a law school's placement office is now a major factor to be considered. If my interviews with law students can be believed, the competency of placement officers varies widely. Some see their job as simply setting up on-campus interviews and making sure they run smoothly. Others call and write letters on behalf of students and are constantly selling the school to employers. Some schools direct almost all of their efforts into placing students into private law firms. Other schools provide information on an entire range of opportunities. At some schools students are lucky if the placement office even provides them with a list of alumni in cities in which they'd like to live. At other schools the office calls alumni to hunt for leads.

How to Research the Job Placement Office
Ask the placement office for the percentage of graduates in the most recent class who had jobs upon graduation. Don't be fooled by statistics that show 98 percent of all graduates employed. Almost all law students are eventually employed, even if they drive taxis. The key is to determine how many are placed in law jobs *before* they leave law school.

Second, stop by the placement office on your visit and look around. Ask to see the placement library and check whether it's well organized and up-to-date. Note whether it carries materials on public-interest or teaching jobs and how large this section is. Also ask whether a newsletter is published to keep alumni informed of any recent job openings.

Again, talk with law students. Most have very strong opinions about the performance of their placement office. Most students recognize and appreciate when the placement office is making an extra effort.

Course Selection

One of the nicest things about law schools in the 1990s is their growing number of course selections and the new areas of law that are opening up. International trade, employment discrimination, sports and entertainment, and environmental law are all areas in which schools are providing more offerings. Many law students nowadays are becoming specialists, because of both personal preference and better marketability. If you're one of the many students who enter law school without a clue about what kind of law they want to practice, look for schools that offer a lot of different areas of study.

How to Research Course Selection
As a rule, schools with larger student populations offer not only more classes but also a greater variety. They need more professors to handle the standard course load, and most professors also like to teach and explore new areas of law as well.

Schools list the courses most recently taught in their recruiting brochure, which they will gladly send you. One note of caution: just because a class has been taught in the past and is listed in the brochure doesn't mean that it's taught every year or will be taught in the future. If

DON'T PUT YOUR CAREER IN THE HANDS OF SLACKERS

Some placement offices are far better than others. It's a good idea to find out how effective the offices are at the schools you're considering.

CAN'T LIVE WITHOUT THAT COURSE ON MEDIEVAL TORTS?

Some courses, particularly unusual ones, may not be taught regularly. If a particular course offering is important enough to you to affect your school selection, just make sure that the course will indeed be available should you go to that school.

you're interested in a particular class, call the registrar's department and find out how often the class has been taught in the past and whether it will be offered again in the future. Ask to speak with the professor who has taught the course in the past.

Social Life

Although it's an important part of the law school experience, social life should rank near the bottom of the list of factors to consider when choosing a law school. Why? Because your social life at any law school is what you make of it. Almost all law schools have monthly parties or weekly Thursday night get-togethers at local bars. And if you choose to expand that schedule, you can always find a willing accomplice. Furthermore, most schools now have a comparably full range of social organizations that cover race, religion, political affiliation, and gender.

How to Research Social Life

Examine the area surrounding the law school. During your first year, locale probably won't matter much. But as you get into your second and third years, you'll likely find that you do have some free time, particularly on weekends. Think about whether you want a quiet rural area where canoeing or skiing are readily available, or whether you'd prefer a larger city with a vibrant restaurant and nightlife scene.

Additional Considerations

There are a few other factors that you may want to toss into the equation when deciding which law school is right for you.

Class Size

This factor is not as important as it is when choosing a college because, despite what you may read in a catalogue, virtually all first-year classes will be large. Nevertheless, there are some differences between a school such as Georgetown, with more than 2,000 students, and a school such as Stanford, with fewer than 800. In the second and third years, the larger schools tend to have more course offerings, whereas the smaller schools focus on smaller class size and more contact between professors and students. Smaller schools also tend to encourage a greater sense of camaraderie and less competition. Larger schools, on the other hand, produce more alumni and thus more contacts when it comes time for your job search.

Attrition Rates

Law schools generally try to keep their attrition rate below 10 percent. There are exceptions, however, and if the school you're interested in has an attrition rate above 10 percent, you should ask an admissions officer why. There may be a reasonable explanation, but you should probably approach the school with some caution.

Joint-Degree Programs

Joint-degree programs are designed to help students pursue two degrees jointly in less time than it would take to earn them separately. The most common examples are the Master of Public Policy (MPP) or the Master of Business Administration (MBA) combined with the law degree. These programs generally take four to five years to complete. Most schools are becoming more daring in this field—indeed, some are now encouraging students to create their own joint-degree program in any area that they choose, as long as it meets both departments' approval. It's not uncommon now to see joint degrees in law and foreign languages, music, or sociology. Check with the schools to see what joint-degree programs are routinely offered, but don't be limited by them. If you have a specialized program in mind, call the registrar's office and see how flexible they are.

Clinical Programs

Every law school in the country now offers one or more clinical programs. A clinic is a unique, hands-on opportunity that allows law students to see how the legal system works by handling actual civil cases for people who can't afford an attorney (and getting credit for it at the same time). Not only are these clinics a tremendous learning tool, but they are also the highlight of many law students' three years of study.

Usually the workload is heavy on landlord/tenant disputes or other debt-collection cases. However, many schools are branching out and offering specialized clinics in such areas as child abuse, domestic violence, and immigration. One word of caution: clinics tend to be popular with students. In many cases, it's very difficult to get a spot in the class, and admission usually depends on the luck of the draw. As a general rule, the schools in large cities have bigger and more clinics because they tend to have more clients.

Internships

Like clinical programs, internships are becoming more popular and varied. Internship programs vary widely from school to school, and may include

WHAT COLOR IS YOUR PARACHUTE?

At many colleges, you can create your own joint-degree program, combining a law degree with just about anything imaginable. If that kind of flexibility is important to you, make sure you choose schools that are willing to accommodate you.

CLINIC AVAILABILITY

If clinical work is important to you, find out now how many clinics are offered by the schools you're considering—and how hard it is to get into these clinics.

anything from working for an international trade organization in Europe for an entire year to getting three hours credit for part-time work at the local prosecutor's office. Internships are often overlooked by students who are afraid to veer from the traditional path. Yet they can be a welcome break from regular law studies and may also help in the later job search.

Computer Facilities and Law Library

Legal research is a big part of your three years in law school. Nothing will frustrate you more than to have a brief due the next day only to find that your library lacks essential volumes on the subject, or that the few computers they have are either occupied or not working. If you make a visit to the law schools, check out their facilities. Again, don't be afraid to ask students for their opinions.

Where Can You Get In?

Let's turn to the second major question in the selection process: "Where do you have a chance of being accepted?"

Anyone who tells you that he can predict where you'll be accepted is fooling himself and, worse, fooling you. Stories of students accepted by a Harvard, Stanford, or Michigan only to be turned down by schools with far less glamorous reputations are common. Yet what is often overlooked is how well the process does work, considering the volume of applications and the amount of discretion exercised by admissions officers.

One reason the admissions process runs smoothly is that all law schools use the combined LSAT score and GPA as the most important determinant in making the decision. This provides a degree of consistency to the admissions process and gives the applicants some direction in deciding where to apply.

Those Legendary Law School Grids

Each year, Law Services publishes the *Official Guide to U.S. Law Schools* (the LSAT application booklet tells you how to order it). This guide includes a wealth of information on all the accredited law schools in the United States. The schools themselves provide most of the information for the book, including the LSAT scores and GPAs of the most recently admitted class. These are generally presented in grid form and are the single most valuable tool in determining your chances of being accepted at any particular law school. The grid shown here is a hypothetical grid, similar to the ones found in the *Guide*.

NOBODY'S A SHOO-IN

Clearly, the numbers (GPA and LSAT) are the most important factors in the admissions decision. But, even a candidate with stellar numbers can be rejected if he or she makes a major tactical blunder on the application.

STATE UNIVERSITY LAW SCHOOL

LSAT Percentile Rank

GPA	< 40%	41–50%	51–60%	61–70%	71–80%	81–90%	91–99%
4–3.75	11/1	21/3	29/5	41/12	62/33	68/55	48/47
3.74–3.5	16/0	14/0	8/2	38/16	84/38	115/64	102/81
3.49–3.25	18/0	9/1	12/0	24/8	73/28	96/38	76/48
3.24–3.0	13/0	13/0	22/2	25/6	55/15	71/28	53/27
2.99–2.75	3/0	5/0	8/0	19/2	38/6	49/10	31/9
2.74–2.5	1/0	0/0	3/1	18/3	41/2	32/4	11/5
<2.5	1/0	1/0	3/0	9/1	9/0	6/2	3/1

Take a close look at the hypothetical grid above. Note that GPAs are divided into categories that drop .25 every line. Also note that LSAT scores are listed by percentile rank rather than by score. This is done because the scoring system for the LSAT was changed in 1991, and law schools still receive applications from students with scores under the old system. In order to use the grid, first find the line where your GPA fits in. Then read across until you find the percentage category of your existing or anticipated LSAT score. There you'll find two numbers, divided by a slash. The first number indicates the number of people in that range of LSAT scores and GPAs who applied to that school. The second number is the number accepted.

Most students apply to too few schools. According to Law Services, the average applicant applies to only about five schools. Admittedly, the cost of applications is rising, and sending out ten or more applications can result in an outlay of $500 or more. But keep in mind that if the cost of application presents a real hardship, most schools will waive the application fee—provided you give them a good, credible reason.

DON'T CHEAT YOURSELF

Don't skimp on the number of applications you make. Yes, it's expensive, but this is one of the most important decisions you're likely to make in life. It pays to give yourself as much of a choice as possible.

Assembling a List of Schools

Using the grid numbers as a guide for determining your chances of acceptance, you should create a list of schools to apply to, dividing the list into three categories: preferred schools, competitive, and safe schools.

Preferred Schools

These are schools you'd *love* to attend, but your numbers indicate a less than 40 percent chance of admission. Apply to two or three schools in this group. Long-shots rarely pay off, but daydreaming about them is always nice.

Competitive Schools

Competitive (or "good fit") schools are those where your grid numbers are in the ballpark and where, depending on the rest of your application, you have a decent chance of getting admitted. These are schools where your numbers give you a 40–80 percent chance of admission. These are the schools on which you should focus most of your attention. Applying to four to seven schools in this group is reasonable, and increases your odds of getting into at least one school where you are competitive.

"Safe" Schools

These schools are not high on your preference list, but your odds of admission are excellent there. Look at the grids and determine two or three schools where your chances of getting in appear to be 80 percent or better. One suggestion for this list would be to pick schools in locations that you particularly like.

Note: students with low numbers may need to be a little more flexible and work a little harder. Be willing to travel a little farther to go to school. Also, look at schools in areas that aren't quite as popular or that tend to draw mostly local students. Sometimes the more expensive schools are applied to by fewer applicants and can be easier to get into.

Drawbacks to Using the Law School Grids

Although the grid system is very helpful, it does have its problems. Remember that the law schools provide the grids. Some schools take the opportunity to enhance their reputation by making their numbers seem higher than they really are. This is not done by lying, but rather by the schools' selectively using pertinent information to artificially enhance the numbers. If a school's numbers don't jibe with its reputation, be skeptical.

Second, because each category in a grid covers a fairly wide range of numbers (i.e., 10 LSAT percentile points or .25 GPA points), don't be fooled into thinking that your 3.51 and 71 percent put you on the same level as the student with the 3.74 and 79 percent, even though you fall in the same place on the grids. There are wide gaps in every category.

Third, many law schools—including some of the very best—do not provide Law Services with grids. However, these schools generally will tell you the average GPA and LSAT score for the previous year's entering class. If you want to get a picture of your chances at these schools, try determining which schools are similar in reputation. You can do so using the published ranking lists discussed earlier. Then determine which one of these schools comes closest in number of applications and size of the entering class to the school in question and use that grid.

Use the application list on the following page to plot out your law school application campaign.

APPLICATION LIST

Note: you should apply to at least eight schools.

Preferred Schools
Chances of admission 40 percent or less. Choose two or three.

1. _____
2. _____
3. _____

Competitive Schools
Chances of admission 40–80 percent. Choose four to seven.

1. _____
2. _____
3. _____
4. _____
5. _____
6. _____
7. _____

"Safe" Schools
Chances of admission 80 percent or greater. Choose two or three.

1. _____
2. _____
3. _____

CHAPTER 9

WHEN TO APPLY

With the explosion in the number of law school applications in the 1980s, law schools have had to make a number of adjustments. Foremost among them has been the lengthening of the application season and the move toward rolling admissions. Now let's see how these changes affect you.

Admission Schedules

Prior to the 1980s, the typical law school application season began in October or November with the mailing of the brochures and application forms. The schools would begin accepting applications in December or January and set a deadline for all applications to be completed by around March. Once all applications were received, the schools would begin the decision-making process, usually sending out acceptances or rejections in April, May, or June.

Today, the scenario is quite different. Schools send out application forms in August and September, begin accepting applications in October, and start sending out acceptance letters by November. (As proof that they have a heart, most law schools will not begin sending out rejection letters until after the holiday season.) Application deadlines may still be in February or March, but because the schools have begun filling their classes in the fall, it is not unusual for more than 75 percent of the anticipated acceptance letters to have been sent by the spring deadline date. This is what's known as rolling admissions, which creates the scenario of unaware applicants who proudly deliver their applications on the deadline date only to find that they have put themselves at a distinct disadvantage.

GET THE WORM

Does it really pay to go to a lot of trouble to apply early? Yes, particularly in this era of rolling admissions. Start your campaign eighteen months before you intend to step into your first law class.

LSAT REGISTRATION AT A GLANCE

- Law Services, Box 2000, 661 Penn St., Newton, PA 18940-0998; phone: (215) 968-1001; Web site: http://www.lsac.org).
- Register early to secure a particular testing site. Many sites are very popular and have limited seating.
- Cost (at press time): $86 to take LSAT and receive one score report, $9 for each additional report.
- Fee waivers: Apply through the law schools you're applying to, not LSDAS. Once a school has approved a fee waiver, you mail notification to Law Services in lieu of payment.
- Phone registration (using credit card payment) is only available during the late registration period.
- Walk-in (day-of-test) registration is not permitted.
- You may only register for 3 LSATs in two years. Be aware that even cancellations count towards this limit.

The Advantages of Early Application

Does applying early really provide you with an advantage? The answer is a definitive yes! Here are the major reasons why.

Rising Index Numbers

The first reason has to do with index numbers. Your index number is based on the combination of your LSAT score and your GPA. At the beginning of the application process, most schools set an automatic admittance index number. Applicants whose index numbers surpass that figure are admitted quickly with only a cursory look at their application to confirm that they are not serial killers. At the beginning of the process, law schools are always afraid that they'll have too few applicants accepting their offers, which would mean less tuition money and almost certainly some complaints from the school's administrative office. Thus, they usually begin the application process by setting the automatic admittance index number on the low side. Then they gradually increase it as the admission season wears on and they discover that, their fears are unfounded.

Fewer Available Places

Because schools have a tendency to be a little more lenient early in the process, they begin reaching their admission goals fairly quickly. By February, the school may well have sent out more than 75 percent or more of all the acceptance letters it plans to send. Yet, at this point, all of the earlier applicants haven't been rejected. Instead many people are left hanging, just in case better applicants don't start coming through the system. This means that if you apply in March, you're now shooting for fewer possible positions, yet you're still competing against a fairly substantial pool of applicants.

The "Jading" Effect

If they are candid, admissions officers will admit that by the time they get to the two thousandth essay on "Why I want to go to law school," they're burned out, and more than a little jaded. Essays or applications that might have seemed noteworthy in the beginning now strike the reader as routine.

The Nay-Sayers

A handful of prelaw advisors and admissions officers dispute the importance of early applications, and at a few schools, there may indeed be no special advantage. Law schools are almost always open to exceptional applicants, and will sometimes admit someone well after the deadline if the student can give a good reason for the late application. Furthermore, a few schools routinely accept applications up until a week or two before classes start.

But these are exceptions. I became convinced of the importance of early applications while working with a student a few years ago. She hadn't taken the LSAT until December and was running late on her applications, barely making the deadline at the eight law schools to which she applied. Eventually she was rejected by seven of the schools and accepted by one. She decided to sit out a year and try again. The next time, she applied in November to the same eight schools, changed almost nothing on her application, and was accepted at five of the schools and wait-listed at two others. The only logical explanation was the timing of the application.

How Early Is Early?

For the most part, a pre-Halloween application is overdoing it. When schools are just gearing up, you run the risk of documents being misplaced. Pre-Thanksgiving is the preferable choice and assures that you'll be among the early entries. Shortly before Christmas is not as desirable, but should still hold you in good stead. After Christmas and the holidays, however, you're on the downside and may well find yourself among the last 30 percent of all applications received. And if you go with a post-Valentine's Day application—well, you'd better have strong numbers.

Remember that this discussion applies to the date on which your application is *complete*, not just the date on which the school receives your application forms. Applications are not considered complete until the LSAT score, LSDAS (Law School Data Assembly Service) reports, transcripts, and all recommendations have been received. Even though other people are sending these pieces, it's your responsibility to see that they arrive at the law school promptly. This does *not* mean calling the law school three times a week to see if they've arrived. It means prodding your recommenders or your college to send in the necessary documentation. Explain to them the importance of early applications.

When to Start

If you want to have a complete application at the law schools by, say, late November, you can't start planning just a few weeks in advance. Your

LSDAS AT A GLANCE

LSDAS organizes, analyzes, and summarizes biographical and academic information about school applicants, to provide a single, standard format for schools to compare candidates directly to one another. LSDAS provides member law schools with a single standard report with LSAT scores (including average), a normalized GPA, copies of college transcripts, and LSAT writing sample. The LSDAS service is mandatory.

- Cost (at press time): $91 for a twelve-month subscription to LSDAS.
- You sign up for LSDAS at the same time that you register for the LSAT. You will need to have your college transcripts forwarded to LSDAS.
- LSDAS sends your application, scores, transcripts, and writing sample to each school you apply to. You do not have to specify the number of schools you will be applying to when you sign up for the LSDAS, but if you do you will save some money.
- Check your college transcripts and your LSDAS files for accuracy.
- LSDAS sends you monthly updates on which schools have received your records.

Make a Master Schedule

Use the application schedule/checklist we give you at the end of this chapter to keep yourself on track. Check it often to make sure you're not letting an important deadline pass.

campaign for admission should begin five or six months before that deadline—i.e., eighteen months before your first day as a law student. We've included, at the end of this section, a schedule that you can use to organize your campaign. As you'll see, you should plan to devote plenty of time to your applications the summer before they're due.

Here are some of the important things to do each season. For convenience, let's assume that you want to go to law school the fall after you graduate from college.

Spring of Junior Year

Your first step should be to register for the June LSAT. You won't need your LSAT score for a while yet, but if you take the June test and bomb out, you'll be able to retake the test in October. Get a copy of the LSAT/LSDAS Registration and Information Book at any local college or law school admissions office or at any Kaplan Center. The registration booklet will tell you not only about the LSAT but also about the LSDAS. The LSDAS is the organization that will be sending your LSAT scores and transcripts to the law schools you apply to. You'll want LSDAS to open a file on you as early as possible. The book will explain exactly how to do this and how much it will cost (yes, they charge for their mandatory services).

It's a good idea to buy the *Official Guide to U.S. Law Schools*, which contains those grids we talked about, as well as other information about American law schools. If you can't find it in your local bookstore, you can order it from LSDAS.

The Summer Before Senior Year

Start thinking about a "theme" for your application, which can serve as a way to stand out from the crowd and as an organizing principle for personal statements, recommendations, and everything else in your file. Think about how you'd like to be identified. As the environmentalist who plays oboe recitals for the local recycling center? Of course, you don't *have* to have a theme, but any kind of "high concept" will help your application stick in the minds of admissions officers. You should also be assembling your list of schools at this point. Visit as many of them as you can. Send for their catalogues and applications.

Early Fall of Senior Year

This is when the action really starts. Applications will start arriving. (In filling them out, follow the procedures outlined in the How to Apply section.) Line up your recommenders. Make sure they have everything they need to write you a great letter. (I'll talk about how to do so in the How to Apply section.) Take the October LSAT, if you've decided to do so. Revise your personal statement. Revise it again. And again.

Late Fall of Senior Year
Complete and submit your applications. Mail your matching forms to LSDAS, so that they know where to send your scores and transcripts. Prod recommenders so that your applications are complete before Thanksgiving.

Applying to law school is a time-consuming process that tests your organizational skills and your attention to detail. Students who believe that they can simply plot out four hours on a weekend to complete this ordeal are kidding themselves. Plan to set aside some big blocks of time well in advance to work intensively on this important step in achieving your admission goals.

An Ideal Law School Application Schedule

Your campaign for law school admission should start up to eighteen months before you step into your first law classroom. Here's a schedule of what you should be doing when:

Spring of Junior Year
❏ Get the *Official Guide to U.S. Law Schools*.
❏ Register for the June LSAT (you can retake it in October if you blow it).
❏ Prepare for the LSAT.
❏ Subscribe to LSDAS (they take care of sending your transcript and LSAT scores to each school you apply to).

Summer Before Senior Year
❏ Take the June LSAT.
❏ Start drafting your personal statement.
❏ Think about whom you'll be asking for recommendations.
❏ Make a list of schools you'll be applying to, using the grids from the *Official Guide* as an aid.
❏ Send away for applications, and start visiting as many schools as you can.
❏ Register for the October LSAT if you're not satisfied with your June score.

TEST EARLY

Register for the June LSAT. Yes, it's early—you won't need your score until late fall—but taking the June test gives you the opportunity to take the test again in October if you're not satisfied with your score.

Early Fall of Senior Year

☐ Familiarize yourself with the applications as they roll in.
☐ Make a checklist and schedule for each application, and photocopy all forms.
☐ Send transcript request forms to all undergraduate and graduate schools you've attended.
☐ Line up your recommendation writers. Give them the specific info they need to write an outstanding recommendation of you.
☐ Revise your personal statement. Tailor it to specific essay topics, if any, on individual applications.

Midfall of Senior Year

☐ Finalize your personal statements.
☐ Transfer application information from the photocopies to the actual application forms.
☐ Make sure your recommendation writers are on board.
☐ Take the October LSAT (if necessary).
☐ Send in your applications. (Make sure you don't mix up the mailings!)

Late Fall of Senior Year

☐ Remind your recommendation writers to send in recommendations ASAP.
☐ Get Master Law School Report from LSDAS, summarizing transcripts, etcetera.

Winter and Spring/Summer After Senior Year

☐ Receive monthly updates from LSDAS, telling you which schools your records have been sent to.
☐ Cross your fingers while you wait for the acceptances to roll in.
☐ Decide which offer to accept.
☐ Send in acceptance.
☐ Apply for financial aid.

Fall After Graduation

☐ Start your first semester at the law school of your choice.

LSDAS CHECKLIST

❑ Get the *LSAT/LSDAS Registration and Information Book.*
You've already done this to register for the LSAT.

❑ Subscribe to LSDAS by completing the registration form in the Information and
Registration Booklet.
Parts A, C, and D apply to LSDAS.
You can subscribe to LSDAS on the same form you use to register for the LSAT.
Again, don't forget to sign the form and send payment!

❑ Use transcript request forms (they're in the Information Book) to request transcripts from
all undergraduate and graduate institutions you've attended.
They will send transcripts directly to LSDAS.

❑ Receive LSDAS Subscription Confirmation.

❑ Receive Master Law School Report—summarizing your academic information.
They get sent shortly after LSDAS receives your transcripts.
Check it carefully; report any inaccuracies to Law Services.

❑ Include an Application Matching Form (they're also in the Information Book)
with each law school application you make.

❑ If you've decided to apply to more schools than you originally planned to, order
extra reports from LSDAS and pay an additional fee.

❑ Receive monthly reports from LSDAS.
Check them for accuracy or discrepancies.

❑ If necessary, renew your LSDAS subscription after twelve months.

CHAPTER 10

HOW TO APPLY

After you've made the decision to apply to law school and have decided where and when to apply, you need to order the application forms from the various schools you've chosen. This can be done by mail, but the quickest way is just to call the admissions offices around July and get put on their mailing lists. Once the applications begin arriving (usually around Labor Day) you'll notice one thing quickly: *no two applications are exactly alike*. Some require one recommendation, others two or three. Some ask you to write one essay or personal statement, while others may ask for two or even three. Some have very detailed forms requiring extensive background information; others are satisfied with your name and address and very little else.

Despite these differences, most applications follow a general pattern with variations on the same kinds of questions. So although not all of this section is relevant to all parts of every application, these guidelines will be valuable for just about any law school application you'll encounter.

LIKE SNOWFLAKES

No two law school applications are exactly alike, but most ask for the same kind of information and look for the same qualities in the applicant. You won't be writing ten different applications so much as ten variations on a single application.

The Application as Marketing Tool

The most important thing to keep in mind about your law school application is that it is, above all else, a sales pitch. The application is your single best opportunity to sell yourself. Remember, every person who applies will have strengths and weaknesses. It's how you *present* those strengths and weaknesses that counts. *You* are in control of what that admissions committee sees on your application and how they see it.

So what's the best way to sell yourself? We all know that some people are natural-born sellers in person, but the application process is written, not spoken. The key here is not natural talent but rather organization—carefully planning a coherent presentation from beginning to end and paying attention to every detail in between. But be careful not to focus

DEVELOP A THEME

Start thinking early about what theme you want your application to convey. Decide what your real purpose is in applying to law school, and make sure that this sense of purpose comes through in all aspects of your application.

For instance, is it your goal to pursue environmental law? If so, give your entire application an environmental theme. Do some volunteer work for a local recycling organization (and make sure to list that activity on your application form); ask the head of the same organization to write a recommendation for you; use the personal statement to discuss your involvement in the organization's various causes. All of these efforts will give your application coherence and a sense of purpose—and help it stick in the minds of the admissions officers.

TAKE CONTROL

You control how you are perceived by the admissions committee—through your application. You can't afford to miss a single opportunity in the application process to make yourself seem desirable as a law student. And the first step is *getting organized*.

so much on the overall theme that you neglect the details. That can be disastrous.

Getting Organized

You must first put together a checklist of the forms that each of your chosen schools requires, double-checking to make sure you don't overlook anything. Some schools may require you to fill out residency forms or financial aid forms in addition to the regular application forms. Don't ignore these and put them off until last. Schools may require proof of residency or income verifications that you might not have readily available.

Next, make photocopies of all forms before you complete them. Changes and corrections will have to be made no matter how careful you are. These changes should not be made on the original form, which will go to the school. Almost every admissions officer I have spoken with explicitly prizes neatness. The feeling is that if the application is sloppily prepared, the student is not very serious about attending that law school. Work on your photocopied rough draft until you are sure you are ready to transfer to the original application.

The Application Form

For the most part, filling out the application form requires simply putting down factual information. But even in something so apparently mindless, you can still make sure you present yourself as a thorough, organized person who can follow directions.

The key to filling out the application form can be summed up in a single sentence: *don't make the admissions officers do more work than they have to.* Make sure that they have all of the information they need at their fingertips. If they have to hunt up your statistics, if your application is full of unexplained blanks, if they can't read what you've written—all of these things will just serve to annoy the very people you want to impress.

One key to not annoying the admissions people is to make sure you answer *all* of the questions asked on the application form. If some questions don't seem to apply to you, type in "not applicable"; leave nothing blank. If the admissions officers see blank spaces, they don't know whether you found the question not applicable, just didn't want to answer it, or overlooked it. Many schools will return the application if even a single question is left blank. This can be a real problem, because it may be a month or more before the application is looked at and returned and then filled in and looked at again. That kind of delay can easily turn an early application into a late one.

Along these same lines, don't answer questions by saying *see above* or *see line 22*. Most applications will ask you for things like your address or phone number more than once. Go ahead and fill them in again. Remember that law schools are flooded with documentation and may separate parts of the application. They don't appreciate having to find what you wrote back on line 22 if they've asked you for that information again on line 55.

As long as we're talking about practices that annoy the decision makers, another is the failure to follow directions on the forms. If the form says, "Don't write below this line," then don't write below the line. You are not an exception to this rule. If they ask for an explanation in 150 words or less, then don't give them 300 words. One admissions officer told me that the comment, "He couldn't even follow directions," is heard several times a year in committee meetings.

Addendums

An important part of the application form will not be in the package sent from the law school. These are your addendums. Addendums (or *addenda*, if you want to be fancy) are the additional page or pages that you staple onto the forms when the space they give you to answer a question is too small.

This is where an addendum comes in. Simply write "continued on addendum" on the application form after you've used their space up, and then clearly mark what you are listing at the top of the addendum. Staple this addendum at the back, and you've solved a tricky problem. Law schools appreciate addendums because they're much neater than attempts to cram things into a limited space—*and* they show careful organization. But don't overdo it. One or two addendums should be sufficient for any application.

Addendums can be used to preserve neatness when the application blanks are of insufficient length. But they can also be helpful if an answer requires further explanation. For example, if you won the Grant R. Humphrey Science award, it's not enough just to list it. You need to explain what it is, what it's given for, and possibly how many others were competing for it or how prestigious it is.

Honesty

One final topic about the application form that needs to be discussed is honesty. If you think you can get by with a lie or two on your applica-

NEATNESS COUNTS

A sloppy application says more about you than you may think. Law schools want people who display organization and care in *all* of their endeavors. So put in the extra time to make sure your application is neat and free of typos.

DON'T BE ANNOYING

Admissions officers are human beings. They're overworked. They've got piles of applications on their desks. Many of them will be looking for any little excuse to reject yours and get on to the next one. Don't give them that excuse. Make sure that nothing about your application is annoying to them.

The Truth, the Whole Truth, and Nothing but the Truth

There are plenty of practical reasons for being honest on your applications (e.g., you might get caught in a lie if you're not). But there's a more important reason. The temptations to cheat only get worse when you actually become a lawyer. Why start off in a state of moral compromise?

tion—well, you may be right. Law schools as a rule don't have the resources to verify all aspects of every application. But before you go overboard and decide to put down that you were once the Prince of Wales, you should realize that you're taking a big chance.

First of all, many schools are beginning to devote more time to checking up on applicants' claims. Last year I spoke to the president of an undergraduate prelaw society who told me that she regularly gets calls from law schools verifying membership of applicants. Secondly, there's always the chance that, if you lie, some other part of your application will contradict the lie and get you booted.

Finally, even if you fool the law school, get in, and graduate with honors, you'll find that any state in which you apply to take the bar exam will do a much more extensive background check than that done by the law school. This check very well might include looking for contradictions in your law school application. Lying on your law school application, in fact, is considered grounds for refusing admittance to a state bar.

Additional Points

Here are a few more things to take note of when filling out the application form:

Be sure to type the application from start to finish. A surprising number of applicants still hand-write the application—something that, according to admissions officers, costs you dearly.

Don't use application forms from previous years. Most applications change from year to year, often substantially. Also, don't use other school's forms because you lost the form of the school you're applying to (yes, people have done that, believe it or not).

Staple extra sheets to the forms. Don't use paper clips unless told to do so. Paper clips—and the pages they attach—tend to get lost.

Always double- and triple-check your application for spelling errors. You lose a certain amount of credibility if you write that you were a "Roads Scholar."

Check for accidental contradictions. Make sure that your application doesn't say you worked for a law firm in 1990 when your financial aid forms say you were driving a cab that year.

Prioritize all lists. When a question asks you to list your honors or awards, don't begin with fraternity social chairman and end with Phi Beta Kappa. Let the admissions committee know that you realize what's important—that is, always list significant scholastic accomplishments first.

Craft your list of extracurricular activities. Don't list every event or every activity you ever participated in. Select the most significant and, if necessary, explain them.

Don't mention high school activities or honors. Unless there's something very unusual or spectacular about your high school background, don't mention it, even if it means you don't take note of the fact that you were senior class president.

Clear up any ambiguities. On questions concerning employment, for instance, make sure to specify whether you held a job during the school year or only during the summer. Many applications ask about this, and it may be an important point to the admissions officer.

The Personal Statement

There are about as many theories on what constitutes a winning personal statement as there are theories on the Kennedy assassination—and, unfortunately, many of them have about the same validity. To begin with, how can you tell 85,000 annual applicants with 85,000 different personalities and backgrounds that there is one correct way to write a personal statement? Furthermore, if even a small percentage of those applicants read and come to believe that a certain way is the correct way, it automatically becomes incorrect, because law schools despise getting personal statements that are familiar—that are, in other words, *im*personal.

For that reason, I've broken down the section on personal statements into two parts. First, we'll look at the procedure of putting together a personal statement. Then we'll look at a list of DOs and DON'Ts that admission officers most frequently mention.

Putting Together an Outstanding Personal Statement

Next to your LSAT score and GPA, the personal statement is probably the most important part of your application. If your numbers are excellent or very poor, the essay may get only a cursory glance. But if your

BE COMPULSIVE

When juggling several applications at once, it's easy to make careless mistakes. Double-check yourself at every step.

YES, THE PERSONAL STATEMENT IS IMPORTANT

Next to your numbers, your personal statement is probably the most important part of your application, particularly at the top schools (where so many applicants have great numbers).

numbers place you on the borderline at a school, then it may very well make the difference between acceptance and rejection.

What Kind of Essay to Write

The personal statement is exactly what its name implies—a statement by you that is meant to show something about your personality and character. But that doesn't mean you are to create a lengthy essay detailing every aspect of your life since birth. Nor is the personal statement intended to be a psychological profile describing all of your character attributes and flaws. Several admissions officers have told me that the best essays are often only remotely related to the applicant. The point is that you need not write an in-depth personality profile baring your innermost soul. Admissions officers are adept at learning what they want to know about you from your essay, even if it doesn't contain the words *me, myself,* and *I* in every sentence.

One exception, however, should be noted. Although most schools still provide wide latitude in their directions about what the personal statement should be about, some schools are becoming more specific. The problem with specific requirements like these is that you may well have to write a separate essay for that school alone. Be sure to check the instructions carefully and follow them closely. If a law school asks for a specific type of essay and you provide them with a more general one, they'll likely feel that you're not very interested in attending that particular school.

But take heart. Most schools provide few restrictions on what you can write about, so unless you're very unlucky, you should be able to limit the number of essays you must write to two or three.

How Long an Essay to Write

How long should the personal statement be? Some schools place a word-limit on the essay; others specify one or two typed pages. Always follow the specific directions, but you should be in good shape with virtually all schools if your essay is one and a half to two pages in length.

Writing the Essay

The personal statement shouldn't be done overnight. A strong personal statement may take shape over the course of months and require several different drafts. One practice that many have found particularly effective is to write a draft and then let it sit for four to six weeks. If you leave it alone for a significant period of time, you may find that your first instincts were good ones. On the other hand, you may shudder at how you could

DON'T DRONE ON

Your reader might not find your life quite as fascinating as you do, so be careful not to go on at length. A boring personal statement is a good excuse to toss an application onto the "No" pile.

TIME LENDS PERSPECTIVE

Start drafting your personal statement now, so that you'll be able to put it aside for a few weeks or even months. You'll be amazed at how different it will look when you go back to it.

ever have considered submitting such a piece of garbage. Either way, time lends a valuable perspective.

Try to start the essay sometime during the summer before you apply. Allow at least three months to write it, and don't be afraid to take it through numerous drafts or overhaul it completely if you're not satisfied. Get several different perspectives. Ask close friends or relatives to scrutinize it to see if it really captures what you want to convey. Be sure to ask them about their initial reaction as well as their feelings after studying it more carefully. Once you've achieved a draft that you feel comfortable with, try to have it read by some people who barely know you or who don't know you at all. If certain criticisms are consistently made, then they're probably legitimate. But don't be carried away by every suggestion every reader makes. Stick to your basic instincts because, after all, this is *your* personal statement, no one else's.

Proofreading is of critical importance. Again, don't be afraid to enlist the aid of others. If possible, let an English teacher review the essay solely for spelling and grammar mistakes.

Essay Content

We now move to the content of the personal statement. As stated earlier, there's no one correct way to write an essay, but admissions officers do provide some helpful tips about what they like and don't like to see in a personal statement. Let's begin with a list of the things that officers most often mentioned they disliked seeing.

Personal Statement DON'Ts

Don't turn your personal statement into a résumé. This is the personal statement that begins at birth and simply recites every major (and sometimes minor) event of the person's life. Most of this information is repetitive since it's included on other parts of the application. But worse than that, it's just a boring format.

Avoid the "why I want to go to law school" essay. Although this can be a *part* of any law school essay, too many people make it the entire focus of their statement. The problem is that there are not many new variations on this theme, and the admissions officers have likely heard them all before, probably many times.

LINE UP YOUR READERS

Try to let as many people as possible read and comment on your personal statement. But don't be swayed by everything that every person says. Listen to all comments, but only take them to heart if you really think they're valid.

OH NO, NOT ANOTHER ALBERT SCHWEITZER!

Admissions officers read about a lot of noble intentions in personal statements. Naturally, they're skeptical of such claims, especially if the rest of your application demonstrates no such selfless impulse. So be careful with protestations of high ideals. If you can't back them up with hard evidence, they're bound to come off sounding empty and insincere.

Don't try to impress your
reader with many difficult
words. It won't work. Take
our word for it.

NO AMBULANCE-
CHASER JOKES,
PLEASE

You may think it'll come
across as refreshing when
you put down lawyers and
the law profession in your
personal statement. It
won't. Your reader won't
be amused.

Avoid talking about your negatives. The personal statement is not the place to call attention to your flaws. Don't forget that you're selling yourself, and the personal statement is your most prominent sales tool.

Don't be too personal. Stories of abuse or trauma are often very moving and can be particularly effective if tied into a person's reason for wanting to practice law. Several admissions officers, however, have noted a trend toward describing such problems in graphic detail in personal statements. This kind of confessional essay can easily cross the line and become too personal.

Don't discuss legal concepts. Along those same lines, don't try to impress the reader with much you already know about the law. The school assumes that they can teach you what you need to know, regardless of the level at which you start. By discussing a legal concept, you also run the risk of showing a certain amount of ignorance about the subject, while at the same time appearing arrogant enough to have tried to discuss it.

Don't put down lawyers or the legal profession. Although it may seem that spewing cynicism about the legal profession is a clever device, trust me when I tell you that it isn't. Once you become a member of the legal profession, you can make as many lawyer jokes as you want. Until then, watch your step.

Don't try to cover too many subjects. Focus on one or two areas you really want to talk about. One of the worst mistakes applicants make is writing essays that ramble from one subject to another and back again. Fight the desire to talk about every highlight of your life.

Now that you've got a sense of what not to do in your personal statement, let's turn to a list of suggestions for things that you *should* do.

Personal Statement DOs

Tell stories. Readers respond much better to a concrete story or illustrative anecdote than to an abstract list of your attributes. Instead of just writing how determined you are, for instance, tell a story that demonstrates it. Stories stick in people's memories. The same holds true when you're trying to make sure the admissions officers remember you.

Be funny—if you can pull it off. Humor, particularly self-deprecating humor, is a very effective device. Admissions officers appreciate occasional flashes of irony. However, be careful in your use of humor. Don't overdo it—a couple of funny lines or a funny story can be great, but include too many jokes and you start to sound flippant. Finally, think about using *self-deprecating* humor. Law schools often complain about the lack of humility among students and appreciate those who show some.

Be unique. The term *unique* has been overused. Even some applications now ask you to describe what is unique about you. Applicants rack their brains trying to figure out how they're different from the other 5,000 people applying to that law school. Or worse, some interpret *unique* to mean disadvantaged, and rack their brains trying to think how they have suffered more than others. But what the admissions officers want to know is what qualities or experiences in your life would make you a particularly valuable member of a law school class.

Start strongly. In private moments, admissions officers will often admit that they don't read every essay carefully. They may just glance at an essay to get a general impression. That's why it's important to grab them from the beginning. Tell the ending of a story first and make them want to read on, to see how it all started, for example.

The above points, I feel, are as much general advice as one can responsibly give about the personal statement in a book such as this. I hope that they'll provide you with some ideas or keep you from making some costly mistakes. In the end, however, it *is* a personal statement, and it must come from you.

Recommendations

During the last ten years, as law school applications have increased dramatically and the odds against being accepted at any particular school have risen, applicants have taken various approaches to stand out from the crowd. Too often overlooked in this mad pursuit, however, is one of the very best ways for an applicant to stand out—that is, by getting terrific, vividly written recommendations.

Because so many recommendations tend to be blasé, an outstanding recommendation that goes beyond the standard language can really make

SHE'S SO UNUSUAL

Admissions officers try to assemble a law school class that includes a rich variety of perspectives. Let them know what you could contribute to the diverse intellectual atmosphere they're trying to achieve.

THE IMPORTANCE OF RECOMMENDATIONS

To be honest, your recommendations probably won't matter all that much in the admissions decision—unless, of course, your recommendations are outstanding.

I CAN WHOLEHEARTEDLY RECOMMEND . . . UH, WHAT WAS YOUR NAME AGAIN?

Beware the impersonal recommendation. It's a definite red flag to the admissions officer. Better to have a recommendation written by a lab assistant who knows you well rather than the Nobel-winning professor who doesn't remember your name.

an applicant stand out. Not only does such a recommendation serve the purpose of pointing out an applicant's strengths, it also shows that the recommender thought enough of the person to put time and effort into carefully writing it.

What Makes a Recommendation Outstanding?

Outstanding recommendations can vary in format, but there are several qualities they all tend to have in common.

An Outstanding Recommendation Must Be Personal

By far the most common mistake made by applicants is believing that the prestige or position of the recommender is more important than what that person writes. Admissions officers tend to treat recommendations from senators, governors, and chief executive officers of major corporations with a great deal of skepticism, because very few applicants have a truly personal relationship with such people. To make matters worse, these officials tend to respond with very standard recommendations that rarely offer any real insight into the applicant's character; in a worst-case scenario, they may even be computer-generated.

Find people who truly know you and are able to make an honest assessment of your capabilities. This means that it may be better to have the teaching assistant with whom you had daily contact write the recommendation, rather than the prestigious professor you spoke to once during the year.

An Outstanding Recommendation Compares You to Others

When an admissions officer reads a recommendation, he or she often has to put into perspective the meaning of overused phrases—such as *hardworking* and *quick mind*—as they relate to the applicant. A much better format, and one that admissions officers appreciate, is the comparison recommendation, one that compares the applicant to other people that the recommendation writer previously knew in the same position, or (in a best-case scenario) to people he or she has known who are alumnae of that particular law school.

An Outstanding Recommendation Tells Stories

A concrete and specific recommendation stands out. Rather than merely listing attributes, a good recommendation engages the reader by telling an insightful story about the applicant. Recently, a professor of political science chose not to submit the standard phrase about what a quick study a student was. Instead, he related a story about the student in class. It seems the professor introduced a new and difficult concept in class that the student discussed intelligently and actually took further than the professor was prepared to do. That kind of story sticks in a reader's mind.

An Outstanding Recommendation Focuses on Scholastic Abilities

Although recommendations often cover a lot of ground, from the applicant's attitudes about school to his or her personality traits, admissions officers focus on comments about a person's scholastic ability. Obviously, this means that a strong recommendation from a professor carries a great deal of weight. However, a lot of people are in a position to observe a person's intellectual aptitude. Employers, friends, clergy, and workers at volunteer agencies are all usually able to discuss an applicant's scholastic abilities—and should.

An Outstanding Recommendation Will Contain Some Negative Comments

In many ways, this is the trickiest area of writing a recommendation, yet it can also prove to be a vital component. A recommendation that is only laudatory, failing to mention a single negative thing about an applicant, may lose credibility. By pointing out a small character flaw or a potential weakness, the recommender gains credibility with the admissions officers and tends to make them less skeptical about the preceding positive comments.

One word of caution, though: Admissions officers universally hate "fake" negatives—for example, "If Suzy has one fault, it is that she works just too darn hard." Much more appreciated are such comments as, "Joe can afford to improve his attention to detail." Combined with effusive praise for the applicant's strong points, this sort of comment impresses admissions officers as being straightforward and helpful.

How to Ensure You Receive Outstanding Recommendations

Now that you know what makes for an outstanding recommendation, all you have to do is ensure that each of your recommenders produces one. While you can't actually write the recommendations yourself, you *can* have a great deal of influence over how accurate and persuasive they are.

Choose the Right People to Recommend You

What are the qualities of a good recommender? Obviously, you should choose someone who likes you, and who thinks you're good at what you do. This doesn't mean that you have to be intimate pals, but sworn enemies don't often write good recommendations. It helps if the person is a

HE SAID, SHE SAID

Discrepancies between your personal statement and a recommendation can undermine the credibility of your entire application. Make sure your recommendation writers know who you are and what you're about.

JUST SAY NO

When asked whether you want to see what your recommendation writers have written about you, *say no!* If admissions officers know that you'll be seeing your recommendations, they'll discount much of what is said in them.

LET'S DO LUNCH

Try to set up an appointment with each of your recommenders—to make sure they're up to speed on who you are and what you're all about.

DON'T BE (OBVIOUSLY) MANIPULATIVE

Be diplomatic. Make sure you let your recommendation writers know what *kind* of things you'd love their recommendations to contain. But be careful not to create the impression that you're manipulating them. It could easily backfire.

good writer, so that he or she can clearly express an opinion about you.

Most, if not all, of your recommendations for academic programs should come from professors or other academic faculty. If you've been out of school for a few years and haven't kept in touch with your professors, call or write the admissions offices of the schools to which you're applying. Don't assume that it's okay to send fewer letters than required or to substitute other kinds of information for recommendation letters. Most likely, schools will allow you to submit recommendations from employers or from other nonacademic people with knowledge about your background, skills, and goals.

Balance Your List of Recommendation Writers

Three professors from your undergrad major department probably will have similar things to say about you, so why not include someone from another field who can speak to your thinking and writing skills?

Be Considerate of Your Recommendation Writers

As soon as you decide to go to law school you should start sizing up potential recommenders and letting them know that you may ask them for a letter. This will give each plenty of time to get to know you better, and to think about what to say in the letter. Once they've agreed, let them know about deadlines with plenty of lead time to avoid potential scheduling conflicts. The more time they have, the better the job they'll do recommending you.

Make Sure Your Recommendation Writers Know What They Need to Know

Once someone has agreed to consider writing a letter for you, you should arrange an appointment to discuss your background and goals for your future. If you live thousands of miles away from your recommender, arrange a telephone appointment.

Bring to the appointment copies of appropriate documentation such as your transcript, papers you've written, your résumé or curriculum vitae, your personal statement, and a sheet of bullet points that you plan to feature in your application and essay. Supply the appropriate form or forms, as well as stamped, addressed envelopes and a copy of your home address and phone number.

Keep the appointment relatively brief—you're already taking up enough of their time. Give your recommenders a good idea of why you want to go to law school. Play up your good points, of course, but be reasonably humble. If you have a very specific "marketing" image that you're trying to project, let your recommenders in on it—they may want to focus on some of the same points you're trying to stress. But don't tell your recommenders what to write! Don't even give them the impression that you're doing so! Recommenders tend to resent any attempts at manipulation, and may, as a consequence, refuse to write your letter. What recommenders *do* appreciate, however, is some direction as to what you'd like to see.

Keep Your Recommendation Writers on Schedule
Finally, make sure your recommenders know how important it is to complete the letters as early as possible. If they procrastinate, gently remind them that their deadline is approaching and be sure to remind them of the importance of early applications.

Common Questions About Recommendations
Here are other points about recommendations that should be considered.

How Long Should a Recommendation Be?
Like the personal statement, the recommendation should be short and concise. A one-page recommendation is usually sufficient. In any case, it should be no longer than two to two and one-half pages.

Should I Request to Look at the Recommendation?
Easy answer—NO! Almost all schools have a box you check to indicate whether or not you would like to be able to see the recommendation once it's provided to the school. Just say no! If the school believes that the recommender cannot be completely honest for fear of offending the applicant, the school will heavily discount what is written, no matter how laudatory.

Can I Send More Recommendations Than the School Requests?
Be careful. Law schools may request anywhere from one to four recommendations from an applicant (the recent trend is toward fewer recommendations). Invariably, the situation arises in which a student has three good recommendations, but the school only asks for two. Some schools are very specific in their instructions that they will not accept more than the exact number requested. If the application doesn't spell out how the school handles it, call the school and ask to make sure.

Should I Use the Letter of Recommendation Service?
The Letter of Recommendation Service is set up by Law Services as a convenience. Basically, the service allows your recommenders to send letters to LSAC, who then forwards them to the law schools. Note that the same

YOU OUGHTN'T TO BE IN PICTURES

Don't send videos or pictures of yourself with the application (unless you're specifically asked to). The admissions officers usually aren't terribly interested in what you look and sound like.

letter is sent to each school, and so school-specific letters should not be sent through this service. For more information, check out the latest LSAT/LSDAS Information book, or contact your target schools to see if they prefer that you use the service.

A Final Check

After you've completed everything and are getting ready to place it in a manila envelope and mail it, make sure you go through one more time and check each document. Law schools frequently receive documents that were intended to go to another law school. With all of this paperwork, it's easy to see how that can happen, and the law schools expect a certain amount of it. However, it can be embarrassing if you've written in your personal statement that ABC Law School is the one and only place for you—and then you accidentally send it to XYZ Law School instead.

APPLICATION CHECKLIST

The three major parts of your law school application:

    1. the application form
    2. the personal statement
    3. recommendations

The Application Form
- ❏ Working photocopies of applications made
- ❏ Information/addresses/other data gathered
- ❏ Addendums (if any) written
- ❏ Information transferred to actual application
- ❏ Application proofread
- ❏ Final check done

The Personal Statement
- ❏ Theme finalized
- ❏ Readers selected and notified
- ❏ First draft written
- ❏ Self-evaluation made
- ❏ Second draft written
- ❏ Comments from readers received
- ❏ Final draft written
- ❏ Final statement proofread

Recommendations
- ❏ Recommendation writers chosen
- ❏ Recommendation writers on board
- ❏ Informational meeting with recommendation writers conducted
- ❏ Reminders to all recommendation writers sent

❏ Notice of complete application received

NOTES

NOTES

Want more information about our services, products, or the nearest Kaplan center?

Call our nationwide toll-free numbers:

1-800-KAP-TEST for information on our live courses, private tutoring and admissions consulting
1-800-KAP-ITEM for information on our products
1-888-KAP-LOAN* for information on student loans

(outside the U.S.A., call **1-212-262-4980**)

Connect with us in cyberspace:

On AOL, keyword:"Kaplan"
On the World Wide Web, go to: **http://www.kaplan.com**
Via e-mail: info@kaplan.com

Write to:

Kaplan Educational Centers
888 Seventh Avenue
New York, NY 10106

Educational Centers

Kaplan Educational Centers is one of the nation's premier education companies, providing individuals with a full range of resources to achieve their educational and career goals. Kaplan, celebrating its 60th anniversary, is a wholly owned subsidiary of the Washington Post Company.

TEST PREPARATION AND ADMISSIONS CONSULTING

Kaplan's nationally recognized test prep courses cover more than 20 standardized tests, including secondary school, college, and graduate school entrance exams and foreign language and professional licensing exams. In addition, Kaplan offers private tutoring and comprehensive one-to-one admissions and application advice for students applying to law and business school.

SCORE! EDUCATIONAL CENTERS

SCORE! after-school learning centers help K-8 students build confidence, academic and goal-setting skills in a motivating, sports-oriented environment. Our cutting-edge interactive curriculum continually assesses and adapts to each child's academic needs and learning style. Enthusiastic Academic Coaches serve as positive role models creating a high-energy atmosphere where learning is exciting and fun.

KAPLAN LEARNING SERVICES

Kaplan Learning Services provides customized assessment, education, and training programs to elementary and high schools, universities and businesses to help students and employees reach their academic and career goals.

KAPLAN PROGRAMS FOR INTERNATIONAL STUDENTS AND PROFESSIONALS

Kaplan services international students and professionals in the U.S. through *Access America*, a series of intensive English language programs. These programs are offered at Kaplan City Centers and four new campus-based centers in California, Washington and New York via Kaplan/LCP International Institute. Kaplan and Kaplan/LCP offer specialized services to sponsors including placement at top American universities, fellowship management, academic monitoring and reporting, and financial administration.

KAPLAN PUBLISHING

Kaplan Books, a joint imprint with Simon & Schuster, publishes titles in test preparation, admissions, education, career development and life skills; Kaplan and *Newsweek* jointly publish the popular guides, **How to Get Into College** and **How to Choose a Career & Graduate School**. *SCORE!* and *Newsweek* have teamed up to publish **How to Help Your Child Succeed in School**.

KAPLOAN

Students may obtain information and advice about educational loans for college and graduate school through **KapLoan** (Kaplan Student Loan Information Program). Through an affiliation with one of the nation's largest student loan providers, **KapLoan** helps direct students and their families through the often bewildering financial aid process.

KAPLAN INTERACTIVE

Kaplan InterActive delivers award-winning educational products and services including Kaplan's best-selling **Higher Score** test-prep software and sites on the internet (http://www.kaplan.com) and America Online. Kaplan and Cendant Software jointly offer educational software for the K-12 retail and school markets.

KAPLAN CAREER SERVICES

Kaplan helps students and graduates find jobs through Kaplan Career Services, the leading provider of career fairs in North America. The division includes **Crimson & Brown Associates**, the nation's leading diversity recruitment and publishing firm, and **The Lendman Group and Career Expo,** both of which help clients identify highly sought-after technical personnel, and sales and marketing professionals.

COMMUNITY OUTREACH

Kaplan provides educational resources to thousands of financially disadvantaged students annually working closely with educational institutions, not-for-profit groups, government agencies and other grass roots organizations on a variety of national and local support programs. Kaplan enriches local communities by employing high school, college, and graduate students, creating valuable work experiences for vast numbers of young people each year.

Paying for graduate school just got easier...

KapLoan*, the Kaplan Student Loan Information Program, is a free service designed to guide you through the financial aid process.

KapLoan will send you a FREE booklet with valuable financial aid information and connect you with one of the nation's largest student loan providers. With KapLoan, you'll receive personalized guidance through the financial aid process and access to some of the least expensive educational loans available.

- **The Federal Stafford Loan**—Eligible students may borrow up to $18,500 each year toward the total cost of education.
- **Private Loan**—If the federal Stafford Loan does not fully meet educational financing needs, eligible students may borrow from $2,000-20,000 at a reduced rate.

Make the most of your financial aid opportunities.

The Kaplan Student Loan Information Program

Contact KapLoan today!

1-888-KAP-LOAN

www.kaploan.com

Plan Ahead!

By returning this form to Kaplan, you will receive a personalized Stafford Loan application from a superior educational loan provider. You may not need a loan yet, so we'll send the application based on the earliest start date indicated below. This request does not obligate you to take a student loan (just in case you get that full scholarship!); it simply gets the ball rolling on your student loan options.

It's Easy!

Yes! Please send me a personalized Stafford Loan Application plus information on this loan.

_____
Last Name   First Name

_____
Permanent Address (where your application will be mailed)

_____
City   State   Zip

_____
Phone (Daytime)   Phone (Evening)   E-mail Address

_____
Current School Address (if applicable)

_____
City   State   Zip   Undergraduate GPA

_____
Top School Choice(s)

_____   _____
                                                    Earliest Start Date
                                                    (month/year)

Please return this form to Kaplan at:

Kaplan Educational Centers
Attn: KapLoan—22nd Floor
888 Seventh Avenue
New York, NY 10106

You may also return it by faxing toll free at any time to 1-800-844-7458.

The Kaplan Student Loan Information Program